Pelican Books
*Geography and Environmental Studies*
*Editor: Peter Hall*

Nan Fairbrother was born in Coventry. She attended the University of
London and graduated with honours in English. She then took up
physiotherapy and worked in various hospitals, finally settling in London.
In 1939 she married William McKenzie, a London doctor. An adventure in
country-living with her two young sons on a farm in Buckinghamshire
while her husband was serving in the R.A.F. was the subject of her first
book, *Children in the House*. After the war they returned to London where
she wrote *Men and Gardens*, *The Cheerful Day*, an account of London
living, and *The House*. When her children left home Nan Fairbrother took
up landscape architecture and became a member of the Institute of
Landscape Architects. She lectured and wrote articles and book reviews on
landscape and land use. Nan Fairbrother died in 1971.

# New Lives, New Landscapes

Nan Fairbrother

Penguin Books

Penguin Books Ltd, Harmondsworth,
Middlesex, England
Penguin Books Australia Ltd, Ringwood,
Victoria, Australia

First published by The Architectural Press 1970
Published in Penguin Books 1972
Copyright © Nan Fairbrother, 1970

Filmset in Photon Times by
Richard Clay (The Chaucer Press) Ltd, Bungay, Suffolk
and printed in Great Britain by
Fletcher & Son Ltd, Norwich

To Kaj Dessau

We can be of little service to
our fellows until we become disillusioned
without being embittered.

F. FRASER DARLING

# Contents

# Contents

*Illustrations appear throughout the book,*
*and are indexed under their respective subjects*

# Part One: A New Society in an Old Setting

# 1. Introduction

'Purely untutored humanity interferes comparatively little with the arrangements of Nature; the destructive agency of man becomes more and more energetic as he advances in civilization.'

So said G. P. Marsh in 1864, and by his ironic standards we are now quite wonderfully civilized, energetically interfering with Nature's arrangements in a highly advanced fashion all over the world. From the first hunter wrapping himself in skins against the cold to the present world disaster of the population explosion the effect of civilization has been to free man increasingly from the inbuilt controls of the environment. We have escaped the natural laws which have governed our development from amoeba to *homo sapiens*, and it is as if we had climbed to the top of a ladder whose support is now disappearing.

Evolution, said Julian Huxley, is in three different sectors. The first is inorganic – the cosmic processes of matter. The second is biological – the evolution of plants and animals. The third is psychological and is the development of man's cultures. It is this third stage which is now critical, and if we are to survive as a species it can only be by replacing nature's controls by our own, not only birth control but control of our use of the whole environment.

With his increasingly organized societies man is the first creature to change the habitat he lives in, and in Britain the process is already advanced. All our landscapes are man-made, countryside as well as towns, for though few fallacies are easier to accept than 'God made the country, man made the town', yet it is nonetheless a fallacy. 'No spot on this island can be said to be in a state of Nature. There is not a tree, perhaps not a bush, now standing upon the face of the country which owes its identical state to Nature alone. Wherever cultivation has set its foot Nature has become extinct.' So said William Marshall

11

in the eighteenth century, and he goes on acidly, 'Those who wish for Nature in a state of total neglect must take up their residence in the woods of America.'

In the two centuries since Marshall's day a great deal has happened even to the woods of America, and Nature in a state of total neglect is now rare the world over. Certainly if the only true country is God-made with no help from man, then very few people anywhere in Europe have ever set eyes on the country, and certainly no one in England. Our countryside was created by farmers as gardens are created by gardeners. 'A masterpiece of produced beauty', so Henry James called it – 'The perfection of the rural picturesque', and it can fairly be considered as one of our national artistic achievements.

'Nature knows nothing of what we call landscape' (it is Marshall again) for Nature's scenery is the natural habitat, while our landscape is the habitat manipulated by man for his own uses. Landscape therefore is not a static background which we inhabit, but the interaction of a society and the habitat it lives in, and if either man or the habitat changes then so inevitably must the resulting landscape.

$$\text{Landscape} = \text{habitat} + \text{man}$$

the natural environment changed by a creature who is himself constantly changing. It is thus the result of an equation which can never be stable, and if it has seemed so in the past it is because the pace of landscape change has been slow compared with our brief human generations.

The first inhabitants of Britain were hunters and food-gatherers, and through the quarter million or so years of their occupation their effect on the natural forest environment was negligible. But as man progressed to farming the changes were increasingly thorough, and habitat + farmer produced a very different landscape from habitat + hunter; an open landscape of crops and grassland which continued with variations through nearly five thousand years of our agricultural economy.

But modern man is no longer a farmer. In Britain agriculture is now one industry among many and employs less than one in twenty-five. We have changed in fact, and at violent speed, from agricultural man to industrial man, and are living through a new human transformation as profound as the ancient change from hunting to farming, and inevitably habitat plus industrial man must produce a new landscape.

In the United States of America much of the West has never known an extensive agricultural society and therefore shows modern man taking over the natural landscape. To a visitor from long-lived-in Europe this is a strange new experience, and explains our bewildered sense of the dissociation of population and land. People do not belong to the country they live in: they travel through it and settle in it, but the chief contact is amenity and recreation, and farming itself is an industrial process. In Britain we have roots at least in an agricultural past, but the American West shows the direct impact of an industrial society on the natural habitat with no transition of man-made agricultural landscape.

To many of us in Britain our countryside is the most beautiful landscape in the world: farms and villages and local towns; fields, woods, leafy lanes, changing coasts and open hills – all evolved as a varied and harmonious whole by a long living-together of man and nature in a gentle climate. But the modern world is now destroying this countryside inherited from the past; exploding the towns, swamping the villages, tearing up the farmland and spattering the old harmonious landscape with alien intrusions. Loving the country now means loving the pre-industrial country, and it is bitter to realize that most of the landscape we still enjoy unreservedly is where the twentieth century has not reached. With a few heartening exceptions this is true everywhere from crowded city-centres to lonely uplands and it is profoundly depressing. But in another generation it will be disastrous, for by then the changes will have spread to every mile of our highly-populated island. No wonder we try to preserve the past, and at every level from private cottage-owners to national societies. Even official planning policy in treasured areas is chiefly protection of the existing scene by resisting unsuitable new uses. ·

But though preservation is an understandable attitude it is seldom a workable policy. The new world cannot be halted, nor is the countryside an inert composition like a painted picture, but a living entity which cannot survive as a museum piece. Our old rural landscape is the physical expression of the way of life of a small population of farm-labourers working the land by animal muscle-power and mostly existing at poverty level. And though we admire their scenery we have abandoned the life which created it; we are a highly-industrialized, rapidly-increasing, urban population with high living-standards and motor-cars; and if we imagine that in order to keep the old countryside we would also keep the old way of life, then since the expectation of life was thirty-four years how many of us would still be alive to make such heroic choices?

A negative policy of not disturbing the old cannot therefore for long succeed. We *must* disturb it to survive – on a vast scale and everywhere. The old agricultural landscape quite simply cannot accommodate our new industrial society, and the longer we take to accept this the more thoroughly we shall destroy what we have in the interval. In the period since our landscape was created the changes have been more sweeping than in thousands of years before, yet the translation of social change into changed environment has still barely started, and so far is chiefly the destruction of the old order which we resist where we can. Our industrial status is still very recent, and we are only now beginning the conscious adaptation of our habitat to new conditions by controlled land-use planning.

An agricultural society depends on land, and since it uses it inefficiently, it needs land in large amounts. But land is not the raw material of industry, and unlike agricultural man industrial man has plenty of land. Even with the population explosion a simple sum shows that the whole population of the world (3,000 million) could be housed in Britain (60 million acres) (24 million ha) at the medium density of fifty people per acre (125 per ha), and even the doubled numbers threatened for the end of the century could still be housed in France.

But though we have ample land as such we waste it extravagantly. We are squandering our habitat in entirely new ways for which we have no proper land-use pattern, and like all our resources we exploit and misuse our landscape. For essentially it is not resources we lack nor even knowledge, but the vision to use them constructively. This is now the perilous limitation of all human progress – that our understanding is inadequate for our knowledge. It is a potentially disastrous imbalance which Shelley recognized a century and a half

*Cotham Landscape Marble. Because the hedgerow elms of old farmland are our norm for the country scene we immediately see this section of marble as a landscape. We may be the last generation to do so.*

ago: 'We have more moral, political and historical wisdom than we know how to reduce into practice, we have more scientific and economical knowledge that can be accommodated to the just distribution of the produce which it multiplies . . . . There is no want of knowledge . . . . but we want the creative faculty to imagine what we know: we want the generous impulse to act that which we imagine: we want the poetry of life. Our calculations have outrun conception: we have eaten more than we can digest.'

Yet our only hope is exactly that – to *imagine* what we know and to plan creatively for the future. Industrial man must live in an environment organized for industrial uses, and this he must consciously create. 'The real want is want of a plan,' as William Robinson said of nineteenth-century London, for just as blind preservation of the past will not work, neither will blind trust in a future where new land-uses work out their own salvation without benefit of planning. The new landscapes for our new lives must now be consciously achieved by positive and clear-sighted adaptation of the habitat to our new industrial condition.

The old farming landscape evolved. Through generations of our farming ancestors the rural countryside developed by a long process of trial and error to suit the slowly-developing business of agriculture. Our field-pattern is a centuries-long creation, our lanes are older than the cottages which border them, our villages were here in Domesday Book, and long generations of workers developed the traditional ways of ploughing and hedging and planting trees – all the farming operations which created and maintained the old countryside. And this landscape which is the product of centuries of controlled evolution developed its present beauties slowly. Crude and primitive farming merely exploits the habitat, causing erosion and dust-bowls: it is mature agricultural landscapes which are beautiful, and if our crude and primitive industrial land-uses are ugly, so equally our mature industrial landscapes could develop their own beauties.

It is possible in fact that given enough time good industrial landscape would also evolve of itself to suit our new land-uses. But there is no longer enough time. Swiftly-changing conditions are part of our impatient new world, and have not only swept away old traditions but leave no chance for new ones to develop. Before any new method is perfected it is replaced by a newer and that by the newest. The proverb is now reversed, and though the mills of God may grind small they also grind exceeding slow, and we no longer wait for the grinding. Our landscapes no longer evolve but are crudely manufactured by destruction of the old.

New ways therefore no longer produce their own aesthetic solution – it is a new and depressing truth of the industrial age which is only too evident everywhere. And the conscious control which must now replace unconscious evolution to achieve good design must do so in the whole of our environment from small-scale to large – cups and chairs and rooms and houses and streets and towns. And also landscape. This realization began with the small and has gradually climbed the scale as far as towns. 'A city is not a tree,' said W. H.

Auden, and no one now imagines that left to grow like a tree an industrial city will achieve spontaneous beauty – or if they do there are plenty of examples all over the world to disabuse them. It is in fact the disastrous results of uncontrolled industrial growth which have convinced a reluctant public that control is essential.

What we have not yet accepted, however, is that the design process must now also include landscape; that the days of spontaneous rightness are over here as everywhere else in our environment, and that to achieve good landscapes for our new ways of living we must deliberately design new settings to suit our new land-uses. And the past cannot help us. There are no traditions for industrial landscape, nor for mechanized farming, nor pylons in the countryside, nor urban housing in rural areas, nor mass motorized leisure, nor for any of our other new land-uses.

The choice then is not between old and new but between good landscape and bad. But it *is* choice, and even though it is sad that the old must go (as it always has been), the true tragedy is not that the old must go but that the new should be bad.

Nor need the old beauties go with the old pattern, for though we cannot preserve them in the old landscapes we can re-create them in new ones. We want our leafy lanes and bosky hedge-bottoms, the country flowers and birds and casual wild places; above all we want the trees whose loss is reducing much of our countryside to large-scale allotments. We also want much more besides; cities which are a pleasure to live in and roads to travel on, properly-planned areas to play in and attractive places to work in. We want in fact new landscapes for our new lives, and if they are to be valid and therefore viable they must be created in terms not of the past but of our new industrial condition.

And we *could* create them. The powers are already there, so are the resources if we choose to use them, so too, and increasingly, is the essential goodwill. Already there is a vast though uncoordinated concern about our environment, and the number of well-wishers grows daily – some inarticulate, others angry or disillusioned, but thousands already organized into societies to fight for what they want. If all this energy and goodwill were drawn together and fused into positive action it could move astonishing mountains. But *positive* action. *Dos* as well as *Don'ts*. Preservation can only succeed if it is part of a new creative plan; if the past in fact has a living part in the future.

'What matters,' says a recent Government White Paper, 'is whether the physical environment as a whole is being properly shaped to meet evolving social and economic needs.' But the proper shaping will depend on first understanding the operation of cause and effect in producing the physical environment. The first section of this book is therefore an attempt to analyse social and economic changes in terms of their effect on the landscape, since unless we understand their action we cannot use their energy – as we must – to create a new pattern.

The next chapter is a brief account of the history of our landscape, for without the past the present is merely an incomprehensible point in time, not part of a continuous process. But though the past may explain the present it is not a mirror of the way ahead, and many of the mistakes we blunder into (in landscape as everywhere else) are because we use it as such a mirror – we are looking backward while moving forward. The only relevance of the past to the future is to show us the direction of the path we are travelling.

# 2. The History of Our Landscape

Britain is a group of islands on the western edge of the Continental Shelf, and consists of the land which is at present high enough to rise above the shallow seas which separate us from the rest of Europe. At different periods in the geological past both sea and land levels have varied, and the history of the area has been a long alternation of drownings and risings from the sea in changing patterns of land and water.

The Continental Shelf which underlies Britain is composed of ancient rocks, and in the seas which have intermittently drowned the land these have been covered by layers of newer sediments. In the alternating periods when the land has risen above sea-level the sediments have been worn away to a greater or lesser extent by weathering. Britain therefore consists of two different elements: the ancient underlying rocks exposed at the surface in the uplands of the North and West, and the newer sedimentary rocks of the lowlands. The uplands are in six main areas: the Highlands and the Southern Uplands of Scotland, the Pennines, the Lake District, Wales, and the South-West Peninsula. The lowlands are the triangular half of Britain lying east and south of the upland areas, with an extension into Cheshire.

The differences between these two regions are thus basically determined by geology and are very definite. 'This great tract of country', says a nineteenth-century guide-book to the Highlands of Scotland, 'is of a mountainous character of unmingled wildness and grandeur. Here the admirer of Nature finds profusion and diversity of all that is beautiful and sublime; the deep solitude of an ancient forest, or the dark craggy fastnesses of an alpine ravine, the open heathy mountainside whence "alps o'er alps arise" whose summits are often shrouded with mists and almost perennial snows, and their overhanging precipices furrowed by deep torrents and foaming cataracts. The extreme steepness, ruggedness and sterility of many of the mountain chains impart to them as magnificent and imposing character as are to be seen in the much higher and more inaccessible elevations of Switzerland.'

There are various things we must allow for in this description, such as the fashionable taste for mountains (it was written in 1842) and also for keeping up with the Joneses (the Joneses in mountains being Switzerland), but even so we can recognize a fundamental difference between the Highlands and the Home Counties.

This geological difference is accentuated by climate, for our weather comes chiefly from the south-west on moist Atlantic winds which rise over the hills and give a rainfall far higher to the west (where the record is 257 inches (650 cm) in Cumberland) than the east, where the lowest British average of 18·4 inches (47 cm) is in the Thames Estuary. The high rainfall further impoverishes the upland soils, which in any case are thin and poor on the ancient rocks compared with the fertile lowlands, and the inherent differences have been intensified by the recent Ice Age. The ice-sheets moved over the land like a huge rasp stripping the uplands of soil, and when the ice melted it released vast quantities of water which further eroded the land unprotected by vegetation. The surface features of our mountain landscape are everywhere witness to this recent destructive force of the ice.

In the lowlands on the other hand the effects were reversed, for the eroded material was deposited by the melting ice, and many areas between the uplands and the southern extent of the ice-sheets are covered by glacial drift – rock material of all sizes from boulders to the finely-powdered dust of glacial clays.

The uplands and lowlands of Britain are thus very different, in solid geology, climate, soils and therefore in the kind of life they support. As good farming country the lowlands can provide for a comfortable population, but the uplands support only a penurious life, and their chief export is people. People in fact, like geological deposits, have moved down from the uplands and settled in the lowlands; eroded like the land by the same harsh upland environment, and deposited as secondary layers in the milder lowland conditions. People might even be considered as an unusually mobile type of geological strata.

In the period since the ice the climate of Britain has varied considerably, producing different types of vegetation which botanists have established by examining pollen-grains preserved in peat. The present world climate occurs in broad bands between the equator and the poles, and this gives corresponding bands of soil and vegetation. Tundra lies furthest north, then conifer forest, deciduous forest, steppe or evergreen woods, desert, savanna and tropical rain-forest.

*The odd trees growing high up the slope show that the area is below the tree-line and the open hillsides are a man-made landscape.*

Britain lies in the world belt of deciduous forest, overlapping the conifer zone in the north of Scotland. The natural type of woodland varies in different areas, is dense in the fertile lowlands, sparse in the poor conditions of the uplands, but except in the bleakest and wettest areas the potential vegetation of land in Britain below 2,000 feet (610 m) is probably some sort of woodland, although at present this is a potential drastically limited by man.

Man seems first to have reached Britain during one of the temporary retreats of the ice, moving south when the cold increased and north again when the climate improved. It was not, however, until the third millennium B.C. that farming reached Britain from the Middle East and the weeds of cultivation appear commonly in the pollen analysis − dandelion, chickweed, creeping buttercup, and plantain which the North American Indians called the white man's footprint. These are plants of open ground which had been common on the land left bare by the ice but rare in subsequent forest conditions, and their reappearance is a vital stage in our landscape history, since they mean that man had begun the long process of changing his environment to serve his needs.

The pollen also shows an increase of trees like birch and hazel which colonize open ground, suggesting that early farmers cleared and worked an area for a time then moved to another, and this primitive agriculture, combined with grazing, prevented the natural development of forest (as in historical times in the Mediterranean goats have stripped large areas of vegetation and lowered the tree-line by 1,000 feet (305 m) in 400 years). This changed vegetation is reflected in our soils, for under early Bronze Age barrows in the New Forest for instance there is forest soil with remains of oak-trees, but under later ones infertile podsols with heather. There is similar evidence from barrows on the Yorkshire moors, and from pollen in Breckland and East Anglia.

'Our old Fathers can tell us how Woods are decayed, and People in the room of Trees multiplied.' Here in a sentence is the history of our landscape, for however far back the seventeenth-century writer had traced his fathers their tale would still have been the same − the long-continuing change from a land of trees to a land of people. It was farming which made large settled communities possible, and farming consists essentially of altering the natural vegetation to produce more food for human beings. Until the Industrial Revolution, in fact, man had little effect on the landscape except through his agriculture; the rest was too small to count, for though he built barrows and earthworks and later on villages and towns, these were scattered incidents in a wide countryside, and if the original forest had still engulfed them they would scarcely have shown in the sea of green.

Neolithic farming increased the population density of the rare animal man to two per square mile, and this rose steadily to ten per square mile (4 per km$^2$) in the Iron Age and fifty in the Middle Ages (though such figures are guesswork compared with the fact that our present population of England and Wales averages 825 a square mile − 318 per km$^2$). The history of Britain is of successive waves of invasion which are the final spread of wide movements across Europe; there are swirls and eddies (especially the seaborne invasions of our west coasts) but the general flow is of new people and ideas coming in from the east and the old retreating westwards before their advance. Thus any new farming methods are most evident in the lowlands, which in any case are the land most suited to farming and settlement.

The early farmers with their primitive tools settled in the areas where the forest was thinnest and the soil was easiest to work, on the light dry soils of the limestone hills in the east and south, especially the chalk. Here they cleared the trees and planted crops, while their grazing animals destroyed the young trees in the surrounding forests and gradually changed whole areas to grassland. For in the English climate grazing alone will create grassland without direct interference by man, simply by preventing the growth of trees and shrubs and creating conditions where grasses flourish.

This early farming steadily developed with the use of metal for tools, but the pattern stayed much the same through Celtic and Roman times: the limestone hills and some of the lighter lowland soils were cultivated, but the heavy clays were still covered by impenetrable woodland. In any case the population was too small to have any serious effect on the landscape, and it is estimated that only two to three per cent of the potential farmland was cultivated. Most of Britain was still undisturbed by man.

23

The Anglo-Saxon invasions which followed the Roman retreat introduced a new landscape pattern. This new type of farmer preferred the low ground and river valleys to the hills, and with his heavier ploughs could work the richer, more profitable soils. This led to clearance of forest and settlements on the lower land, and the evidence is crystallized in our place-names which are chiefly Anglo-Saxon. There are hundreds of names with some word for wood as one of their elements, not only -wood or -grove or -forest, but less-known forms like -hurst, -holt, -shaw, -hanger, -firth (Scandinavian) and all the -wold, -wald, -weald variants. Equally names in -lea, -ley, -dene (and -thwaite in the Scandinavian North) are of places which were clearings in woodland.

But despite this widespread forest clearance there were still plenty of trees. The damp oakwood of the Midland and Wealden clays was still barely touched, and the old hill-farms, not cultivated by the Anglo-Saxons, reverted to forest. The Domesday Survey shows the distribution of the new farmlands and also the natural reafforestation of the hills. There were still probably little more than a million people in Britain.

The open-field system of Anglo-Saxon farming is well known, with its nucleated villages surrounded by several large arable fields which were planted in rotation and divided between the villagers, who each owned one or more separate strips in the different fields. The method of ploughing in furlongs produced ridges and furrows between the strips, and the turning of the ox-teams gave these the shape of a long 2 which is still preserved under grass in the Midlands and very obvious in light snow. Beyond the fields was the common pasture where the villagers each grazed their allotted number of animals and also cut wood for fuel. William Marshall, an 'improver' of the eighteenth century, describes this as 'a system of husbandry which, howsoever improper it is become in these more enlightened days, was well adapted to the state of ignorance and vassalage of feudal times'.

The uplands knew nothing of this improper system, and in the harsh mountain habitat life remained poor and primitive, with little change in farming methods through the centuries: a few small fields on the better soils of the valleys, reaching higher or lower up the hillsides as farming prospered or declined, and the rest of the land rough grazing. The changes in the mountain regions have been less in farming methods than in farming spread, which was combined with the destruction of the forests for timber and fuel. This was a steady process which stripped the hills of trees, first in more accessible regions, then further afield, until by the eighteenth century even the great Caledonian Forest of the Scottish Highlands was ruthlessly destroyed. The hills once deforested were used for grazing, increasingly for sheep and in Scotland for deer, both of which prevent the natural regrowth of trees.

The mountain areas were not in any case suitable for arable farming and the open-field system, but even in the lowlands it did not develop everywhere. The South-West with its heavy rainfall and mild winters is best suited to pastoral farming, and the fields were enclosed direct from the wild. They still show the distinctive irregular pattern of little piecemeal additions as farmers took in patches of cleared land and enclosed them for grazing. Neither was the open-field system established in the South-East counties, for though the farming there was chiefly arable (Kent exported corn even in Roman times) the fields were separate clearings in the forest, and 'the enclosures', says Marshall, 'were made from a state of woodland, by following narrow lines of bushes or underwood and clearing up to these on either side'. The plants in such hedges were not the ubiquitous hawthorn of later official enclosure, but blackthorn, holly, hedge-maple, elder, crab-apple and the local plants of particular districts, and where such mixed and generous hedges still exist we can suspect an early enclosure. They make a distinctive landscape which we can still see in parts of the South-East. 'The inclosures are small', said Marshall, 'and the hedges high, and full of trees. This has a singular effect in travelling through the country: the eye seems ever on the verge of a forest, which is, as it were by enchantment, continually changing into inclosures and hedgerows.'

Although this old method of taking in land left plenty of trees, all farming was essentially by destruction of forest, and the open-field landscape was almost treeless. The fields were large, as much as a mile long for large villages, and were divided up, not by hedges, but by baulks of unploughed land; and these large open spaces were not

*Fields in Cornwall enclosed directly from the wild. The land in the middle distance is still open heath.*

*Fields in Sussex. Forest clearings with strips of woodland left as hedges.*

surrounded by woods but by the common grazing ground. This was often of huge extent, being virtually all the country which lay between the arable fields round the villages, and the boundaries were often marked only by stones. These were the commons Clare loved 'left free in the rude rags of nature', and often wet and marshy – 'low vallies of kingcups'. They were rough uncared-for land and we are now so used to fields everywhere made smooth by centuries of ploughing and harrowing that we forget how uneven is the natural land-surface. Molehills, in fact, were even valued as dry berths for lambs in marshy pasture.

This common-land was often badly over-grazed and the vegetation above grass-level was chiefly thorny scrub (gorse is most commonly mentioned, and was planted for fuel) while the trees which survived were cut for animal fodder as well as for wood.

With our wide modern range of materials and fuels it is difficult to remember the enormous importance of wood in pre-industrial Britain. It was the chief material for the construction of most things man made, and for centuries was his only fuel. This need of wood combined with the spread of farming produced a steady destruction of the original forest cover of Britain, and despite the Norman Forest Laws and the enclosure of private hunting-parks the long-term process was everywhere the same – the conversion of woodland to open country, whether arable or grazing. This increasing shortage of trees was recognized as serious even in the Middle Ages, and down the centuries responsible people tried vainly to prevent the wholesale loss of timber reserves. Sheep, however, were England's wealth in the Middle Ages, and sheep are most efficient converters of forest to grassland. Britain became grassier. The Black Death reduced the number of labourers for arable farming and pasture replaced corn. Britain became grassier still. The population recovered and farming spread into areas formerly wild like the North-West, destroying the forests as it spread. Britain became a naval power and more trees were felled for ship-building. Glass-making and iron-smelting became widespread and burned up the woodlands for fuel, until even the ancient impenetrable forest of Andreada on the Wealden clay was gradually eroded by the iron-founders.

Man's interference with the wild animal population also hastened

27

the destruction of woodlands, for he exterminated predators like wolves which checked grazing animals, and encouraged herbivores like deer. He also introduced aliens for which Britain is dangerously vulnerable as a habitat, like rabbits in Norman times.

To replace the lost forests and provide a continuing supply of wood for timber and fuel the coppice-with-standard system of woodland management was evolved. By this method twelve standard oaks were kept on each acre of land (twenty-nine per ha) and were underplanted with coppice wood, generally hazel but also chestnut and ash. These lower trees were cut back to the stool in rotation after a fixed number of years to shoot again and provide a steady supply of small timber and fuel, while the oaks developed into mature trees for major constructions like ships. This coppice-with-standard is still common woodland in much of southern England, especially on heavy land; some is still worked – especially for fences – but often it is neglected.

Despite such efforts, however, timber became steadily scarcer, even in the well-wooded South-East, and Londoners used 'seacoales' for fuel. This was coal brought from the North by ship up the Thames Estuary; it was cheaper than wood, but the smell of coal-smoke was much disliked. So serious was the shortage of wood that by the seventeenth century England relied almost entirely on imported timber, and John Evelyn in 1662 published his *Sylva or A Discourse of Forest-trees* as a rallying-cry to responsible people to plant trees for the good of the nation since 'the waste and destruction of our woods has been universal'.

Whether from Evelyn's influence or not there followed a wave of planting in the eighteenth and early nineteenth centuries; many of our present woodlands belong to this period, and there is an interesting account by the Duke of Portland's gardener of how they planted large areas of Sherwood Forest. Such woodlands are semi-natural, for the trees planted were generally those suited to the district since otherwise they would not have flourished, and the woodlands were left to develop with little interference from man except selective felling.

Until the eighteenth century the changes in the landscape were a steady process, disturbed only by temporary fluctuations. The population (apart from the Black Death reversal) increased by very roughly half each century, farming spread into less profitable land, enclosure went steadily forward, and the forests decayed. The eighteenth century, however, was pregnant with the various revolutions which continued through the nineteenth and produced our modern world. In the rest of Europe these were most obviously political, but in Britain, where at least the principles of democracy were already established, the revolutions were chiefly agricultural and industrial. Not that such categories can ever be distinct, for a hungry population is not free whatever political freedoms it may starve under, but nonetheless compared with the rest of Europe the changes in Britain were not primarily political, and it was the agricultural revolution which first affected the landscape.

The changes, however, were not as sudden as we tend to see them in our foreshortened backward view. Parliamentary enclosure for instance is often thought of as a swift and universal transition from one kind of countryside to another, but in fact half the farmlands of England and Wales were already enclosed by the beginning of the eighteenth century before official Enclosure began. As early as the first half of the sixteenth century Leland in his *Itinerary* comments on the country he passes through. Some is 'champayn ground' (unenclosed) but much is 'wel inclosid', 'inclosid with hegges', 'ful of enclosures'. (He also laments everywhere the lack of trees – 'placis sore decayed in wood' – though Weardale was still 'wel wooddid', and there were pines in the 'mountainous ground' near Gateshead.)

The merits of enclosure were early recognized, not only by filching landowners but also by practical farmers like the Tudor writer Thomas Tusser. Some of the land already enclosed had been taken in direct from the wild, and some had been enclosed from commons by agreement, as Marshall describes. 'During the last two centuries the feudal organization has been mouldering away. A great majority of the commonfield lands and commons have been inclosed; either by *piecemeal* or by *general consent* – the whole of the proprietors agreeing to commit their lands to the judgment of arbiters, who reparceled them out in a manner more convenient to the several proprietors, and laid each man's portion, which had consisted of numberless narrow slips, on one or more well-shaped grounds.' The process was not all sweetness and light, however, whatever the enthusiastic Marshall may imply. 'That covetous and insatiable cormaraunte and very plague of his natyve countrey', so an early writer describes the enclosing landlord, and though another says more calmly, 'There were several Commotions about the taking in of Common Field Land,' this is an understatement which covers centuries of sullen and sometimes violent opposition.

These early enclosures are the fields we can see in the background of Kip's bird's-eye view pictures of country houses at the end of the seventeenth century, a landscape not of the old open-field system but of the neatly-enclosed fields we know today. Whether Kip reproduced what he saw, or whether he put in as background the 'improved' landscape which his patrons would like to see it is hard to know, but clearly the idea of enclosure was well established at the end of the seventeenth century. British farming supported a population of roughly six million people.

The new methods of agriculture in the eighteenth century were essentially the emergence of our present mixed farming, including better cultivation and rotations, new crops and winter fodder, fertilizers and feeding-stuffs, and improved strains of plants and animals. (It is interesting that this advanced type of farming was developed in Norfolk, which with Lincolnshire had been the most prosperous and populated area before the Black Death.) These improvements, however, could not be applied to land which was farmed on the open-field system, for not only were new crops and methods impossible, but so was controlled breeding in animals which grazed all together on common land. For the good of the country as a whole therefore, if not of individual land-holders, Government accepted the policy of enclosing what was left of the old open farmlands.

This was done by private Acts of Parliament, and in the Midlands created a distinctive landscape which still partly survives and which we think of as typical farming country. It is a patchwork of fields roughly rectangular, mostly between five and ten acres (two to four ha), and divided by straight lines of hawthorn hedges with trees growing through them in regular rows. There are farms among the fields but most of the housing is in the old compact villages, and the land between them is criss-crossed by connecting roads and lanes.

This landscape which seems to us simple country is a highly artificial creation of the Enclosure Commissioners, and they produced it by the determined application of definite rules. It was not even an adaptation of what was already there, for the existing layout of the land was completely ignored, and the new pattern obliterated the old. It is a square grid of fields laid over the countryside, and indifferent to the form of the ground beneath, drawing-board planning worked out on maps and applied to the land as a logical system. Air photographs of the Midlands often show the ridges of the old strip divisions cut up by the new hedges as if they had never existed. Where new roads were needed they were laid out with the fields, in straight lines where possible, and with widths exactly specified for their different categories. With their direct and open character and their wide verges they are very different from the narrow winding lanes which developed from farm-tracks in country which was early enclosed. The Commissioners' hedges were equally businesslike, and each owner was required to enclose his allotment of land within a specified time – often a year. The usual enclosure consisted of a ditch three feet deep and four and a half feet wide at the top (1 and 1·5 m); the excavated soil was thrown up to make a bank, and on this was planted a row of hawthorn seedlings, protected from animals by hurdles or a dead hedge of brushwood or a post and rail fence (barbed-wire being an urgent need of which farmers were not yet conscious).

*Contemporary drawing of a section through the typical hedge and ditch of enclosure. Hawthorn seedlings are planted on the slope and protected from animals by the ditch on one side and a dead-hedge of brushwood on the bank.*

31

Thousands of miles of such ditches and hedges were dug and planted, and the few remaining trees were mostly felled as wood for the fences. To make up for the loss of timber the new hedges were planted with trees at regular intervals of 20 to 30 feet (6–9 m). These were chosen for their timber value; oak was especially prized, but also ash which is tough and quick-growing, and elm which lasts under water and was used for harbours and docks and the keels of ships. Small coverts were also planted both for farm timber and as game-cover on odd patches of land, but since both trees and hedges

*Three successive field-patterns in Gloucestershire. (1) Early Celtic lynchets (parallel lines right of centre). (2) Anglo-Saxon open fields (ridges bottom left). (3) Existing hedges superimposed at Enclosure.*

started as insignificant seedlings the new landscape must have been very unattractive. It was a ruthless reorganization of the countryside by business-efficiency methods, and no doubt looked what it was. Certainly it was thoroughly disliked at the time, and not only by the poor whose way of life it destroyed. Country-lovers used to the freer landscape it displaced disliked the new discipline and regimentation, the straight neat hedges and rigid enclosures, the rectangular pattern of fields which completely disregarded the land-forms, and above all the loss of the open uncultivated heaths and commons. The lamb-crowned molehills were levelled to sober fields, the king-cups were gone from Clare's valleys, and Bewick sighed for 'the beautiful wild scenery – all swept away'. Nor was it only countrymen who lamented the destruction of the countryside they had grown up in: eighteenth-century connoisseurs of scenery were equally united in reviling this new regimented landscape. It was 'disgusting' they said (a favourite word of the period) and above all it was 'unnatural' – that ultimate in abuse from any eighteenth-century man of taste. Nor was it only the raw state of the newly-made landscape they so thoroughly disliked, they objected to the fundamental pattern, and Repton, writing much later when the new countryside was beautifully mature and established, still feels it to be a crude imposition on the subtleties of the natural scene. Farmland, he says, 'is forever changing the colour of its surface in motley and discordant hues; it is subdivided by straight lines of fences. The trees can only be ranged in formal rows along the hedges; and these the farmer claims a right to cut, prune and disfigure.' The hedges he particularly dislikes – 'lines of confinement and subdivision' he calls them, and 'the line of a fence is unfortunately that which, of all others, tends to destroy the union of hill and valley'.

In fact a large anthology could be put together simply by quoting attacks on the new landscape of enclosure by all kinds of people from poet to peasant. Such a collection of abuse, however, would prove no demerit in the landscape – after all it is still there. We can see it and judge for ourselves. For the countryside they reviled is the one we cherish, and are now as anxious to preserve as those who saw it created were to keep the older countryside it replaced.

Yet its fundamental pattern *is* both unnatural and insensitive as they said. 'The patchwork of fields' – it is the inevitable metaphor for any extensive view of our farmlands – a patchwork of rectangles fitted ingeniously together on a map and laid on the ground like a quilt. But neither the surface of the land nor natural vegetation has anything to do with the ubiquitous man-made rectangle. The earth is a plane varied by hills, and the shapes of the landscape are subtle and irregular curves. But though the grid of enclosure is ruled on the ground regardless of natural contours, it combines with them in fascinating contrapuntal rhythms of squared fields and rounded landforms, and the combination of mechanical pattern and organic material is wonderfully satisfactory. Our old farming countryside is a centuries-long conversation between man and nature, a humanized, understandable, intimate landscape evolved through generations of compromise with our habitat, and even for our new urban population it is rich with associations and half-realized memories.

My own first landscape was the northern Pennines, and when I first came south I suffocated in the gardenish neatly-kept countryside, and pined for the open hills. But I have grown to love the lowland farming landscape above all others; I am homesick for it out of England, and would not change its gentle fields for all the dramatic prospects of seas and mountains. In our old farming landscape the natural and the man-made are beautifully balanced. The hedges may be planted rows of hawthorn but they are invaded by the local shrubs and flowers. There are local trees growing casually in odd corners, and the woods are mixed and semi-spontaneous, for though the natural ecology has been destroyed the new plants are ecologically suitable species. The farming landscape is *laissez-faire* in an ordered setting, a sensitive balance between the formal and the spontaneous, like good manners – like the very best manners.

When Marshall wrote, the landscape of enclosure was already well established in most districts, and his descriptions are a vivid picture of pre-industrial rural England. The new farms were flourishing, and he praises the prosperous state of their new crops and healthy animals and properly managed grassland. They are 'like large gardens,' he says, 'divided into beds, where before was only poor common-land with scarce a bush or tree'. Farms had grown very much larger, and though this increase in the size of separate holdings was not a new process it was greatly speeded-up by enclosure. Small landowners often could not afford to enclose their allotment of land, or if they did they found it could not support a family now that there was no common grazing for their animals. Many poor people sold their inadequate plot to become hired labourers or destitute paupers, and the new prosperity was at the expense of such small sad people. There are revealing figures of parishes losing their population, and heartrending accounts of helpless people driven away workless from their homes, which were pulled down to prevent their return.

In this way the holdings of better-off buyers increased proportionately, and large estates could be acquired and laid out in the new style of the landscape parks. Some of these beautiful extravagances still survive, though of others the only evidence left is a splendid cedar dwarfing a new housing estate, or an unmistakably ornamental group of trees in the middle of a workaday field. Of the parks which remain many are now public playgrounds, where their hard-pressed aristocratic owners now woo entrance fees from the prosperous descendants of the dispossessed.

Marshall, however, was more interested in the countryside than in landscape parks, and he travelled widely. He describes in detail the farming methods of different districts and the different variations of landscape they produced. Much of what he describes is the countryside we can still find in places where the Industrial Revolution has yet barely reached, but there are various differences, some very significant for the future of our landscape. One is the huge number of sheep which later declined with the import of wool from abroad, and large areas of the country, especially on the chalk, were perennial sheepwalks – 'a fine carpet down with a sweet close herbage of dwarfish growth', with few trees and almost no hedges. It was a landscape not only devoted to sheep but also created by them, as Marshall clearly recognized, pasture 'reclaimed from a state of woodland or heath merely by being hard-stocked with sheep, and has not passed through any intermediate stage'.

Most of Marshall's sheep-walks have now gone, and so have what he calls 'Watery Grounds'. Britain with its high rainfall on the uplands and impervious clays in the lowlands is a naturally marshy country, as everyone has told us from Tacitus onwards. The Anglo-

Saxon place-names are widespread evidence of our original damp condition, names with -fen or -car or -mere or -was or letch- or slough, or simply marsh or pool or water. Villages on heavy soils were commonly isolated all winter, and accounts of travel are of journeys made perilous by mud 'to the horse's belly', and pot-holes so deep that the unwary drowned in them. 'A ruinous state of foulness,' says Marshall of the roads of the Weald, 'such as no man who has not stept out of his cradle into them can travel without disgust; if he can without danger. The toll roads are rather better.'

In the newly enclosed districts some of the land-water was carried off by the miles of new ditches, but until piped drainage became common in the nineteenth century there were still large areas of marshy ground. The Fens proper were drained by the seventeenth century, and as the remaining wet areas gradually dried out, our marsh flora disappeared except in odd isolated patches, further depleting our vegetation, though botanists were probably the only people who lamented the change.

Another significant difference between Marshall's countryside and ours is the disappearance of wild areas near most large centres of population. 'A considerable portion of the lands,' he says disapprovingly of the Thames Valley, 'even within a few miles of London, remain in the same state of nature and neglect as that in which they were found by the first inhabitants ... Groups of ragged wild ponies are seen as on the mountains of Wales and Scotland,' while the people, he says, are 'as homely, in their dress and manners, as those of the more recluse parts of the Kingdom, and are far less enlightened and intelligent than those of many parts of it' (an opinion which Manchester still traditionally shares). It was only close in to London that the city's influence was felt, in the 'grassland townships of Marybone, Pancrass, Islington, Highgate, Hampstead and Hendon', where the farmers kept dairy herds and grew hay for London horses on land 'strongly-manured' with waste from the town.

Until very recent times much of the country south of London was wild and sparsely inhabited. 'Nothing strikes [a traveller in the Weald] more than the extreme fewness of its inhabitants; ... the villages are not only few, but small; and a man may travel for miles without seeing a hamlet or scarcely a solitary roadside cottage.' The now much-built-on sandy heaths were still almost uninhabited, for the land could not support an agricultural population, and there was as yet no other. 'A barren sand or gravel of the very worst quality. The present produce, if it deserves the name, is a sort of dwarfish stunted heath; in many places unable to hide the sand, on which it may be said to starve. The flat between Farnham and Godalmin is almost literally a barren waste, a sandy desert.' It was in this district, on Bagshot Heath, that Daniel Defoe was caught in the sandstorm which he so feelingly describes in his *Journal*.

As for our present wild areas in the uplands, they are probably little changed despite descriptions of mountains, precipices, wildernesses, deserts, wastes and so on. If we allow for the change of taste, the difference between then and now seems mostly the difference of outlook from an exposed position on horseback and a comfortable seat in a heated car.

However, there are plenty of other differences between Marshall's England and ours, for, although the Industrial Revolution began in the eighteenth century, the coming flood was no more than a trickle. The early source of mechanical power was water, and early industry was scattered about the countryside, often in the hills. Defoe has an enthusiastic account of the weaving towns of the Pennines, each with its own branch of the streams which tumbled down the hillsides, and Young insists that 'Mr Champion's copper-works about three miles from Bristol are very well worth seeing. They displayed the whole process [of making pins] and all the machines and wheels are set in motion by water.' Young was a curious observer, but even the most precious of the eighteenth-century aesthetes much admired the romantic effect of smoking iron-forges as a decoration of picturesque landscapes. It was not till the steam-engine was adopted and coal was used for power that the pattern of industry as we know it took shape. Coal was carried by canal and later by railway, both of which established industry on lower ground, and the huge superiority of coal over water-power led to increasing concentrations of factory workers in industrial cities, congregations of people living closely together in far larger numbers than ever before.

Since civilization develops in communities, society's evolution could be considered as the developing ability to live in communities of increasing size. Neolithic farming, by making communal settlements possible, began the long series of cultures based on cities: the countryside supplied the cities with essentials, especially food, while the cities provided services in exchange – government, religion, law, arts and crafts and the whole superstructure of settled civilization.

The size of cities in an agricultural economy was limited, however (like the size of insects), by their limited capacity for interchange with the outside world – by the distance supplies could be carried and by the exchange value of what the cities offered in return. Even for efficient capital cities the size was relatively small, and this vital restriction operated through thousands of years of man's history. It was industry which suddenly removed the size-limit, by making widespread supplies available both through new methods of transport and by producing in exchange manufactured goods which everyone wanted. Cities suddenly erupted at a speed which makes modern expansion seem trivial, and not only the old capital cities but new and independent concentrations.

This process we can trace in detail in England, where the natural tendency to gather into larger communities is evident from as far back as the Domesday Survey; for in this early census of a small population are recorded not only the names of most of the settlements which still exist, but also of many others which have disappeared. There are 1,300 known deserted villages in England (mostly in the Midlands and eastern lowlands) and more are constantly being discovered, for although the population steadily increased it also steadily congregated. But the units were still small, and at the end of the eighteenth century four fifths of the people of England and Wales still lived in the country.

By the middle of the nineteenth century, however, the urban population of the huge new congregations outnumbered the rural. The population as a whole had also doubled since the start of the century, and this despite a catastrophic death-rate due to appalling living conditions and to the poverty endemic in a system where 'the natural price of labour', according to current Malthusian doctrine, 'was the price which is necessary to enable the labourers (one with another) to subsist and perpetuate their race'. This they certainly did, though by ruthless survival of the fittest, and by the end of the century the population had trebled — a sudden rocketing rise of the former steady increase. It was a larger and also a changed population, for farming had lost its overriding importance now that cities were supported by overseas trade, and despite the disastrous effect on British agriculture the Government had no choice but to accept the policy of importing cheap food for urban workers.

Small wonder the landscape changed, for the cities mushrooming up in what had been tranquil green country were very different from the old local towns which had served as markets for a country population. The aesthetes ceased to admire the new industry, and now found that 'nothing can equal them [cotton-mills] for the purpose of disbeautifying an enchanting piece of scenery'. The effects of the Industrial Revolution, however, are too well known to need further description. Not only did cities spread, but the new canals and railways carried goods and people into formerly remote rural areas, and near cities 'the rusticity of the village gave place to a London out-of-town character' (it is a complaint we could now develop at length). However, although these new intrusions seemed overwhelming to a startled population whose rural way of life had slowly evolved through centuries, the new developments had surprisingly little effect on the actual methods of farming, which had as yet changed comparatively little from the earliest beginnings. The new-style eighteenth-century farmers had been 'Improvers' not revolutionaries, and the most fundamental change was in land tenure and farming structure. Farm equipment was also improved (Jethro Tull's seed-drill was a landmark), but animal muscles were still the source of power, horses for traction operations like carting and ploughing, men for more specialized manoeuvres like reaping and threshing: both were comparatively weak and easily tired (there was much concern about the horses, less about the men). Although therefore a combine-harvester was designed for the Canadian prairies, it needed huge teams of thirty to forty horses, and the power for the reaping and threshing could only come from the friction between wheels and ground.

The revolutionary new source of power which had transformed industry was steam, but this proved mostly unadaptable to farming.

*Ploughing and reaping – Egypt, second millennium B C (and still much of the world in the second millennium A D).*

*Ploughing, harrowing, reaping and threshing. France, fifteenth century.*

Steam-engines were too heavy for field-work and sank disastrously into the ground, and though ploughing was tried by hauling a plough with winches from a stationary engine the difficulties are obvious, and the engine needed rails to run on. Threshing was more successful since the corn could be brought to the machine, but steam did not widely replace animal muscles on the farm, and the early Industrial Revolution had little effect on farming practice.

The difference in fact between the first primitive farming and the methods still in use at the end of the nineteenth century is astonishingly small. There are wall-paintings in ancient Egypt and prehistoric rock-carvings in Scandinavia which show processes almost identical with those of Victorian farm labourers. Through the centuries the same muscles produced the same methods and the same implements – the drawings are cruder in Anglo-Saxon illustrations, the clothes

*Identical processes. England, nineteenth century.*

more attractive in the Middle Ages, but otherwise there is little change from the first beginnings to the twentieth century.

The breakthrough in farming was the internal combustion engine, and this is now transforming our landscape both through tractors and cars. For not only did steam have little effect on farming, but even as a way of transporting urbanism abroad it has limitations. Trains may carry the town into the country as Victorian clergymen complained, but they do so only along narrow strips of railway. Even if towns grew up round every railway station they were still only beads on strings stretched across an otherwise rural countryside. Between the thin lines of railroad the country was relatively undisturbed, for there was still no method of moving goods and people about the intervening areas except by the horse. Only group movement was mechanized, individual movement was unchanged: private travel was a little easier than it had been in preceding centuries because roads were better, it was a little more democratic because of cheaper public coaches, but that was all.

For centuries the urban towns and the rural countryside had been distinct. The towns had now changed their nature, but they were still on the whole distinct. The different populations of agriculture and industry still occupied different areas, for in an age when commuting was scarcely even a word in a dictionary, country workers lived in the country and town workers lived in towns. Industry had invaded the rural landscape and was firmly established, but it was still by our modern standards self-contained. Where it existed it dominated the area, but it did not infiltrate the surrounding countryside. The rural landscape and way of life were little changed for centuries, the industrial cities were new growths dependent on arteries of railroads and waterways: industry and agriculture were separate land-uses which existed side by side in more or less isolation. It was the first and simplest phase of our new industrial society.

# 3. Our Changing Society

All periods are periods of change to those who live in them, and throughout history various people at various times have been so impressed by the apocalyptic events they were living through that the end of the world has been forecast for a wide range of dates all now safely in the past. Nonetheless if we also fear coming catastrophe we have far more reason to believe it likely now that our new do-it-yourself methods of destruction make us independent of Outside Help.

We commonly talk of the Industrial Revolution as something which happened in the nineteenth century, whereas this was only the start of a new era in man's relationship to his environment which has barely yet begun. My generation was brought up to marvel at the wonderful factory where pigs went in at one end and came out sausages at the other, but no modern child is impressed by such out-of-date wonders, for after all the factory was full of workers who processed the unfortunate pigs, whereas future factories so they tell us will run themselves, with the workers off in their factory-produced cars eating factory-produced ice-cream at the sea-side. What more could anyone want? (Except more space at the sea-side.)

Mechanization, automation, electronics — these are still crude and early processes, but which promise a future of machines producing and manipulating other machines in hierarchies of non-human labour, with man only needed as lord and supervisor. Computers too are still far from rivalling the human brain (which, as one admirer points out, has the added merits of being small, lightweight, portable, working on simple fuel and being easily reproduced by unskilled labour). Nor do we yet use computers as powerful new instruments, but as substitutes for our own specialized abilities, and it is pointless to ask a computer to tell the difference between the two simple statements – Time flies like an arrow, and Fruit flies like a banana.

But as we learn to use them on their own terms the possibilities are unpredictable; as for instance a number of people using the same machine as a group memory and means of communication, computer and users together forming a new intellectual unit; or for storing and regurgitating as needed, by satellites, laser beams and so on, the vast amount of knowledge which doubles every ten years and which no human brain can now encompass. With such possibilities it seems probable that our blue-collar stage of industrial labour is only the first move away from the old muddy-boot stage of agriculture. Already office workers are increasing in proportion to industrial workers; in ten years in the U.S.A. for instance white-collar jobs have risen by six per cent while blue-collar workers have already fallen by two per cent.

But though the Industrial Revolution has barely begun, yet it has already produced world-wide changes more profound than any other event in man's history since the development of farming. It is creating in fact a new type of man and a new structure of world society. Industrial man is an urban creature who lives in communities – not simply in groups of relatively independent units assembled together for company and protection, but in close integrations of people whose lives directly depend on each others' activities, and whose communities in their turn depend on the activities of other communities all over the world. As this new type of man develops the integrations grow larger, with the fastest world-growth now in cities of over a million people.

'Rural people are a residual population', said an economist at the Food and Agriculture Organization. They survive from an earlier stage of society's evolution, and by using modern farming methods the whole world's food could now be produced by five to ten per cent of the world's population, freeing the rest for other production. It is part of the vicious circle of poverty in underdeveloped countries that most people are small farmers working the land by the old inefficient methods and therefore unproductively employed. And in the process they also eat most of what they produce, providing little to feed the cities which are their only hope for the future. For the food producers of the modern world are not large rural populations but machines from city factories, and it is not agricultural but industrial societies which now produce food surpluses.

The world population explosion which makes mechanical food production vital is itself due to an incomplete adaptation to man's industrial condition, and is therefore worst in the countries worst able to cope with it. In agricultural societies both birth- and death-rates are high, in industrial societies both are low; but the transitional societies of the underdeveloped countries still keep the old high birth-rate of agriculture with industry's new low death-rate. It is a combination so disastrous that even the most head-in-the-sand isolationist cannot be ignorant of the menacing facts – that three times more people have been born this century than in all man's existence before, and that whatever we do our numbers will double by the end of the century. Even the affluent West is in trouble, and our British birth-rate is expected to add another third to our numbers by the year 2000, though already in England and Wales we have the highest density in the world except for the marginally more congested Netherlands. Compared with our average figure of 825 people per square mile (318 per km$^2$), America has only fifty (19 per km$^2$), and even a country like Japan has only 640 (248).

Despite the congestion of modern cities, however, living-space as such is not the real problem. It is agricultural societies which suffer from land hunger: modern man hungers for industrial development – as well he may when he sees its results in the prosperous societies. 'The experience of nations with well-being is exceedingly brief. Nearly all throughout all history have been very poor. The exception has been the last few generations in the comparatively small corner of the world populated by Europeans.' So said Professor Galbraith, but we pay dearly for this well-being, and the disasters of the package-deal are already with us – the population explosion, the hydrogen bomb, the pollution of our environment by radiation, pesticides and all the disastrous rest.

As the birthplace of the Industrial Revolution, Britain's population was the first in the world's history to change from a rural to an urban society. We are still the most urban people in the world with eighty to ninety per cent of us living in settlements of over 10,000, and though to the future our present urban state will no doubt look

*The Marquess of Bath with lion cub in his park at Longleat.*

much like primitive farming to modern agriculturalists, nonetheless the social results are already profound. Ordinary people, as Galbraith says, are prosperous as never before, and though the benefits are still not shared equally enough, and a tour of our old conurbations would stir anyone's social conscience, yet compared with the have-not nations even the poorest of us are very much haves, and our commonest form of malnutrition, for instance, is over-eating. We are also highly educated, for by the usual egg-and-chicken progress of human affairs, general education is a democratic transformation which is both cause and effect of industrial development. In the old agricultural society only a restricted minority could read and write, and what existed for them to read was equally restricted. Not only therefore were the abilities of the literate limited, but also a vast amount of ability was submerged in an uneducated population. The intelligent poor remained imprisoned in their illiteracy, and only the

*Mr and Mrs Peacock with dahlias in their garden at Trumpington.*

outstanding escaped the limitations they were born to. The spread of general education during the nineteenth century which culminated in the Education Acts of the last decades was a social and also an economic revolution, for it meant that for the first time we were developing that most important of a modern society's resources – the nation's brains. The education might still be sketchy, but at least all the able could now read, and this is the fundamental irrigation system of knowledge. With accessible books in public libraries the gate was now open even if the way was arduous, and the humble origins of much of our modern meritocracy prove the wealth of formerly unused ability in the general population.

It is arguable that the Education Acts have had more effect on our landscape than all the tractors and cars and bulldozers put together; for machines are only the tangible products of our new knowledge, which even if it had not discovered these particular forms of self-

47

expression would have invented something else instead. Education produces progress and progress produces education in an ever more swiftly-ascending spiral (even though the merits of such progress may appear ambivalent, especially to those who were comfortable without them).

Those who complain that our society is still as class-ridden as ever would soon be cured by a course of nineteenth-century social history, for we have come a vast distance since 1844 when a 'Commission of Inquiry into the State of Large Towns and Populous Districts' found a death-rate four times higher in poor streets than wealthy. Such life-and-death class distinctions have gone, our present differences are of degree not kind, and our snobberies no more than inconvenience and inefficiency and a wry entertainment. Between duke and dustman (a splendidly old-fashioned confrontation) the gap has sensationally narrowed. They can both read and write. They will both live to much the same age. Any children either of them decide to have are almost certain to survive. They both have enough to eat (both may be equally concerned about the effect of their over-eating). They are both likely to live in houses with piped water and drains. They both have leisure. They both have, or soon will have, motor-cars.

Even on a less material level the homogenizing process is equally thorough. Books, newspapers, all kinds of journals – these are now accessible to everyone, and though tastes and I.Q.s vary the variation can be surprisingly random. Radio and television are even more powerful and universal equalizers, not only of class but of interests and ways of living. We even laugh at the same jokes – that acid test of equality, and indeed few people have proved more understanding in catering for public taste in recreation than the ancient aristocracy (though rivalled recently by a gardener and his wife in a council house who opened their grounds to the public with equal success).

This growth of mass communications is a new phase of our industrial development, and is fusing us into an urban-industrial democracy sharing not only prosperity and education but also leisure. To ordinary people leisure is a recent luxury, for the average working week in 1850 was just under seventy hours, and the intervals in such labour are not periods of leisure but simply of recovery. The $5\frac{1}{2}$-day week was a triumphant milestone, but now Saturday has been added to Sunday, and Monday too is confidently predicted. Holidays with pay are also new, for the system developed between the wars and is now not only universal but growing from the original fortnight to an increasingly common three weeks.

Nor is it only the wage-earner who has more leisure, but his wife as well; for though by Parkinson's law any time saved is a vacuum which draws in more work, yet the new tasks which replace the old are far less essential. Compared with the former subsistence house-work much of what we now do is gilding the lily – is not to support life but to make life pleasanter. The essentials are now mostly done for us by other people – our water brought to us in taps ready sterilized, our garbage and sewage collected and disposed of, our houses lit and our rooms and our cooking-stoves heated by turning switches, and so on. No one who has lived in the old-fashioned country without such services can have any illusions about the amount of solid drudgery they save us, nor of the comparative irrelevance of most of what we do instead. Nor now do we even expect to bake our own bread or make our family's clothes, or the dozens of other tasks which were once the common lot. 'Take the housewife's chores into the factory' – it was the slogan of the can-ning industry, and we are all of us now, not only housewives, and poor as well as rich, served by other people – by a huge array of workers and machines who wait on us anonymously and whose services everyone takes for granted.

This widespread sharing of the new ways of living is in itself a change as profound as the new ways themselves. When benefits were limited to the few their provision had an equally limited effect on the landscape, but their new democratic spread now produces problems as far-reaching as the industry which makes the democracy possible. The increase of leisure and of private transport are only the more obvious results, but we can now move about as never before, not only along restricted railway routes but all over the countryside by the network of roads and lanes. From the private car few places are isolated, and rural areas which for centuries were cut-off societies now make an easy day's outing on fine summer Sundays.

Living has changed in the towns, however, as well as the country, for our cities have achieved the first essential stage in recovery from the disasters of the nineteenth century. The old pre-industrial towns were small and developed slowly, so that though public health services like water and drains might be elementary, yet they were reasonably adequate when services and population developed together. But industry destroyed this balance by flooding the towns with huge numbers of people they were in no way able to cope with, and crowding them together at teeming densities – as high as 1,500 people per acre (3,700 per ha) at one stage in Glasgow. The inadequate services broke down completely, and living conditions in many great cities could better be described as dying conditions. Infected water, open sewers, inhuman housing – the horrors are well known both from writers like Dickens and Engels, and also from official reports. The death-rate in industrial cities was twice that for rural areas (though that was already high) and in Liverpool for instance a labourer's expectation of life was fifteen years, while in cities like Leeds and Manchester more than half of all children died before they were five years old. As a child in a poor family I grew up in one of the old industrial slums, and even then most of my friends had brothers and sisters who died in infancy. Dead babies were one of the facts of life we took for granted.

As late as the end of the last war there were areas in industrial cities with up to 600 people per acre (1,500 per ha) (modern planners consider 200 (500) a daring experiment) and there still remains a vast amount to do, not only in restoring the twilight areas of cities but also in taming the new menace of the motor-car. Nonetheless we have triumphantly solved the first and most desperately urgent problem of how to live together healthily in large congregations; our public health services have made our cities extremely healthy, and even in poor London districts the infant mortality rate (that sensitive index of living standards) is lower than the national average.

This is proof which we find hard to accept, however, for the old conditions have left us with a deep-seated faith in the healthiness of fresh air and spread-out living; and the still-surviving garden city ideal (how else account for many new housing densities?) is an obsolete legacy from the days when high-density living was both squalid and dangerous, and space was the only sweetener. But the garden city is a reaction not a solution. For though city living has many problems, low densities do not solve but merely dilute them, diluting too the big-city environment which many of us treasure beyond any other, and creating in the process new and equally intractable problems. We shall not have come to terms with our new urban state until we build high-density cities which are a pleasure to live in.

The effect of industry on the countryside has been much slower, since even the first and comparatively simple process of replacing muscles by machines only effectively reached farming this century with the tractor and its corollaries. The tractor is the landmark in agriculture as the steam-engine in industry, and the essential difference between mechanical and muscle farming can be summed up in two simple figures – a man and horse ploughed an acre a day (often less): a tractor ploughs an acre an hour – or five acres or ten – there are logically no limits, since the figure depends not on restricted power but on the size of machines and arrangement of land. For the first time since man became a farmer he is free from the limitations of animal muscles, a revolutionary emancipation which is transforming our farming landscapes.

As sources of power men are inefficient. They are not only puny and easily tired, but need high-grade fuel in the form of palatable food, and wastefully insist on doing all sorts of other things than work – like walking about and talking to their families and sleeping one third of every day. (Horses are marginally better on all counts.) Machines on the other hand are powerful, tireless, obedient, reliable, and round-the-clock workers, and unlike muscles they need no upkeep when not working – an important advantage to any farmer. By replacing men with machines farm output has been more than doubled and on less land, and the proper sound track for films of the country is now the roar of tractor-engines, not the usual passages from the Pastoral Symphony played by a city orchestra. (Not that music was ever suitable, but rather the earthy complaints of plough-men trudging all day in the freezing wind, or cursing cowmen up before dawn on winter mornings. It is only on townspeople's farms that the year is always summer.)

But machines are taking the drudgery out of farming, and the

*The farmer's Rolls-Royce.*

combine-harvester, so says one grateful user, 'has done more to ease the farmer's lot than any invention since the tractor. We still find sheaves of corn in church at Harvest Festival, but a few nicely-polished combine spare parts would not be out of place.' And what about electric milking-machine parts from the dairymen? And since church decorations already include tins of fruit with their supermarket prices, why not also the coloured advertisements of the fashionable new tractors? 'Handsome is as handsome does, and our colourful tractors are every bit as good as they look – orchid white, poppy red and metallic chocolate.' Farmers now delight in their machines as other men in their cars.

Yet even with machines to take over from weary muscles farmworkers are still leaving, and the so-called drift from the land would be better described as the stream to the towns, for it is a purposeful movement of people seeking a better life. Between 1951 and 1961 the number of agricultural workers dropped by forty per cent, with marked loss of population not only in the predictable uplands but also in lowland Lincolnshire and East Anglia, Cornwall and rural Scotland, where the loss is not masked by return-flow from towns.

And since it is the young and enterprising who leave, the old rural societies which still remain are dying; there are more old people than the national average, fewer young women, and though boys now in any case seriously outnumber girls in the population (106 boys born for every 100 girls), the surplus is even more marked in rural areas. When children leave school they also leave home, or if they stay on and marry then they are likely to leave in their twenties and thirties to give their own children a better chance in life.

Northumbrian Tweedside is a region of large-scale farming on excellent land where the long-continued exodus of country workers has reduced the population to critically low numbers. From 1851 to 1951 the population fell to half, between 1951 and 1961 another $12\frac{1}{2}$ per cent left the area, and since this is an example of rural decline uncomplicated by urban backflow surveys were done to find out the reasons for leaving. The complaints are not, as they once would have been, chiefly about housing, which seems adequate, nor even primarily about wages or working conditions. There have been vast changes in country living, but equally vast is the change in what ordinary people expect from life. There is little choice, they say, of occupation; living costs are high and public transport and services inevitably bad; housing is often in hamlets up to a mile from neighbours and the ' sense of isolation' is oppressive. In such conditions the reasons people gave for leaving are obvious: they want better and more varied employment, better education for their children, better social conditions, better shops and transport and all the rest, and most people want to live in a town.

'The condition of any real value in modern city life is holidays spent in the country.' So pronounced one typically urban writer, and I would like to hear Tweedsdale's down-to-earth country answer. For these people are not concerned with holidays, but with their basic lives and their children's future.

Yet it is natural for urban people to idealize the country life, indeed it is a measure of our distance from country reality. For every way of life has its own specific inbuilt daydream, and for city people it is country contentment snug in a cottage. 'This little unsuspected paradise,' said the poet Gray about Grasmere, 'where all is peace, rusticity and happy poverty.' But Gray was the Londoner on holiday, and Marshall the countryman had no such urban illusions. He describes a wretched cottage lived in by a family of poor farm workers and adds the acid comment: 'If superior happiness belong to the cottage, how supreme must be that of the hopper's hut.' Certainly the old rural life was not always as Cobbett describes it, 'misery walking abroad in skin and bone and nakedness', it even no doubt had its own delights, though country people have always been suspiciously silent. It is only the recreation of the comfortable we hear about – the Izaak Waltons and Gilbert Whites and Mr Jorrockses and their modern equivalents. One of our few English writers who expresses the sense of unity between working country people and their environment is Thomas Hardy, but it is significant that he describes an old agricultural society which was already disappearing, and also that he himself went off to London as a young man and when he returned to Dorset earned his living not on the land but as an architect.

One of the things I still vividly remember from living eight years on a farm is the mud – the ubiquitous, everlasting, all-pervading mud of long country winters on heavy clay. It was rubber-bootless wartime and the children were too young to pick their way, but generations of country people must have lived as we did, with shoes that never dried out and feet only warm in bed. Not that we minded unduly, but nonetheless we praise the merits of country life most eloquently as urban people with no intention of living it. For if we had there is nothing to stop us; there is a shortage of agricultural workers, and the wages and housing are now adequate for a healthy life. To argue that we can't find the work we are trained for is simply to reject the country. Our skilled work and wages are urban: the country has never provided them. It is one of the many reasons why people migrate to cities.

For if citizens dream of country cottages country cottagers equally dream of city lights and of setting out to seek their fortune. They dream and they also set out, and the success of the venture is convincingly proved by the fact that of the millions who leave the country very few ever go back except on urban terms. Or if they do they regret it, like the islanders of Tristan da Cunha. 'We didn't realize how barren the island life was until we got back' – it was a serious young school-teacher leaving again for the new-found world of opportunity. We don't sing the praises of cities – there is no need – and Doctor Johnson made a pertinent remark about the praise of wealth. 'Sir, all the arguments which are brought to represent poverty as no evil, show it to be evidently a great evil. You never find people labouring to convince you that you may live very happily upon a plentiful fortune.'

But though remote rural districts may be threatened by depopulation most lowland districts are not remote, and the old drift from the land is more than cancelled out by a new return from the towns. The first large expansion by railways was continued as branch lines opened up new areas, and later on public buses further increased public mobility as did the Underground around London, though the really alarming expansion has been through the private car. Between 1900 and 1960 the area of urban development doubled. With one car for every other family and a further three times the number predicted for the end of the century we are now a very mobile population; where we live is no longer dictated by where we work, and even as city workers we can make our homes in the old communities of the surrounding countryside.

And what transport is doing for the urban population it may equally do in reverse for the rural. The old-style farmworkers lived in tied cottages, mostly on the farms which employed them, but modern workers with alternative jobs no longer accept such conditions, and Tweedsdale is only a clear-cut case of the desire for the general urbanized standard of life which most of us now take for granted. With a small labour force on highly-organized farms it is possible for country workers to live in a community and travel out to work; such a system of rural commuting is already developing (in Cambridgeshire for instance) and is suggested as a possible solution for Tweedsdale, where a population of skilled farm workers with cars might travel out from key villages. This could well be a pattern for the future, and it is after all very similar to the old open-field system of workers living together in villages and walking to work in the fields. It is simply that the units are bigger now and so therefore are the distances; but ten miles by car takes less time than one mile by legs, and much less energy.

This new urbanized life of old rural communities is one of our new twentieth-century patterns of living. Another is the suburb, the large areas of new housing near urban centres which are not communities like the old villages but assemblies of separate houses in gardens. The suburb has been accounted for in many ways: by the influence of Ebenezer Howard and his Garden City ideal, by the growth of transport, by providing what Professor Myles Wright calls 'motorized accessibility at low cost', and so on. But though such reasons may explain the existence of the suburb they do not explain its popularity; and the fact revealed by opinion polls is that a majority of people if given the choice prefer to live in a detached or semi-detached house with a garden; that is, to live in a suburb. It therefore seems likely that this new pattern of housing corresponds to something new and fundamental in our new way of life.

The pre-industrial population was essentially static and for various reasons. First of course with horses as the only source of horse-power there was little scope for mobility, especially since most work was in agriculture, the most rooted of occupations. The general population was also poor, and except in extremes of misery poverty is a great settler. Only the well-off travelled, and most people lived and died in the place they were born, in a stable and closely-bound group.

But the new world is mobile, we are more prosperous and therefore more enterprising, and we are all conscious of the wider world and its possibilities. Above all our work is fluid as never before, and when we change jobs we often change houses. We also change house for social reasons – because we are richer or poorer, our families growing or shrinking, or simply because we fancy a change (not to mention the Joneses). Already the last census shows that eleven per cent of the people of England and Wales change house every year, and the number is growing among blue-collar as well as white-collar workers. In America it is already as high as a quarter of the population each year ('we change house when the old one needs a new coat of paint') and it is surely significant that America is the home of the quintessential suburb.

Most of us therefore are now no longer rooted in a settled community (for if *we* don't move our neighbours do) and our social life thus depends less on close and long-term friends and neighbours, and more on work and short-term acquaintances and the clubs and societies we join. These are looser contacts than the old, more transitory, more easily broken off, but also more easily renewed in different places. We still, however, need close and permanent ties with other people, and in the modern world we are making these increasingly in the intimate private family unit with the married partner and children. This is surely why young people now marry so early, despite the new sexual freedom and the lengthening period of education, both of which might logically be expected to lead to later not earlier marriage.

The basic social unit therefore is the separate transportable family; not the old ramified family clan which needs settled conditions, but the small individual household which can move as a whole. And for this tight and mobile group the setting is the individual house – the self-contained unit of a family in its private habitat. The Englishman's house has never been more his private castle than now, and certainly he has never been so house-proud. Their home is a chief concern of hundreds of thousands of people, and is the natural destination of all the shining new kitchen units, washing machines, central heating systems, mammoth refrigerators, acres of fitted carpet and 'exciting' colour schemes. This is the Ideal Home, set in the ideal garden, with the ideal $2\frac{1}{2}$ children in the nursery, and the ideal family car in the garage.

For such a unit a suburb is in many ways the natural setting, and is likely to provide the best value in houses – not only in bricks and mortar and gardens but also as compromise between incompatible benefits. It offers privacy without isolation; it is within reach of the city but far enough out to escape city pressures; it is in a setting of trees and gardens but not remote as the country is from schools and shops. Above all, and perhaps conclusive in the future for some form of near-urban living, suburbs and motor-cars are highly compatible. It is the car, whether private or public, which produced the typical suburb, and it is living away from the centre which in future may make car-ownership possible for people in towns (the car like the house is an ideal container for the new small family unit, which is no doubt why a car filled with parents and children looks such a natural and self-sufficient entity).

## New Lives, New Landscapes

Whatever our future living-patterns the effects of industry on our landscape are now all-pervading; for it is no longer only a matter of built-up cities or of the directly industrial areas of factories, mines, spoil-heaps and so on. Roads and bridges for instance on their present scale are industrial structures in the landscape, so are airports, sports grounds, large new buildings like hospitals and universities, and all the new developments which now surround our towns and cities. Whether or not they include industry as such these are new industrial landscapes which did not exist in the agricultural scene. The new urban-rural communities, the suburbs, the spread of urban recreation – these too are industrial developments, and so also, less directly but just as inevitably, are the changes in the countryside – the new farm landscapes and the depopulation of isolated areas by the magnetism of industrial cities.

Our society is changing from an agricultural oligarchy to an industrial democracy. The landscape which is society's imprint on the habitat is inevitably changing with it, and the rest of this section is an attempt to understand our changing landscapes in terms of our changing lives. The uplands and lowlands are considered separately, for the same causes produce very different effects in the different habitats – there has probably never in fact been a greater contrast between the desolate uplands and the thriving lowlands. The traditional upland land-uses are changing, while urban recreation is a new development, and the two are discussed separately. Changes in the lowlands are both more complex and more violent, for here are the growing populations both of people and cars, as well as the sites for industry and the farmland for food. The lowland changes are considered in three contexts: first the new developments in farming which are transforming our countryside; second the changes in rural areas caused by the presence of an urban population; third the changes due to industry itself and its many ramifications.

The built-up cities are not discussed: this is the realm of town-planners, and to join in their internecine battles is to perish on alien ground.

# 4. Changes in Lowland Farming

The townscape of the pre-industrial scene has gone. Its architectural remnants may survive, adapted to modern uses and shaken by modern traffic, but the close urban groupings surrounded by fields have exploded into modern cities, and the villages are often unrecognizable, with no more than a carefully-preserved centre to suggest what they were like before industry transformed our lives. As an environment the pre-industrial town is little more than a charming nostalgic scene preserved in old prints; yet until now the surrounding countryside has scarcely changed, and what we mean by the country in fact is still much what Jane Austen meant – winding lanes between flowery hedges, cows knee-deep in buttercups, cottages and cottage gardens, woods and farms and fields. Fields above all, the irregular patchwork of ploughland and hay-meadows and smooth green pasture, little intimate enclosures sheltered by walls of may-blossom. In this landscape of muscle-power farming everything, from the pattern of fields and woods to the smallest detail of flowery banks, has been adapted to the pace and scale of animal work, and it is exactly this – its scaling to man's capacities – which makes it sympathetic in a way that natural scenery often is not, and is why we feel at home as we do in a house or village. It is the landscape of Constable's paintings and Cobbett's eulogies: 'Talk of pleasure-grounds indeed! What that man ever invented under the name of pleasure-grounds can equal these fields of Hertfordshire?'

But though we still feel the same about just the same countryside, between Cobbett and us there is the profound difference of a century and a half of far-reaching social and economic change. The marvel is not that the old agricultural landscape is going, but that it should have survived at all into the last third of the twentieth century for anyone now alive to admire. Yet all over the country there are miles

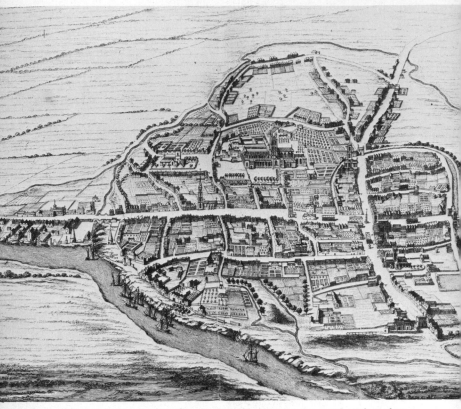

*Kip's plan of pre-industrial Gloucester, 1715. It was tiny, compact and mostly gardens: a vanished townscape. Modern Gloucester is an administrative and industrial centre of over 70,000 people.*

of farmland scarcely altered in centuries; farming's inertia has been astonishing, and all the thousands of tractors and combine-harvesters are only now beginning to drag it into the twentieth century.

We could take what until now has been a typical mixed farm of about 100 acres (40 ha). It is likely to consist of ten or more fields divided by hedges with trees growing through them, the field-drains are probably undisturbed since prisoners laid them in the Napoleonic wars, the farm buildings a picturesque huddle of old barns and sheds awkwardly expanded and newly supplied with electricity and piped

*Kip's view of the pre-industrial landscape. The countryside has scarcely changed today.*

water. The farming is mixed, with arable crops and grass leys on the easier land, and permanent pasture on heavy or otherwise difficult ground. There will be animals: a small milking herd of cows, perhaps a few store cattle, probably farmyard hens and even a few pigs or sheep. Since such a farm was laid out (whether by Act of Enclosure or earlier) to be worked by cheap animal labour the fields are a suitable size for their limited powers, the divisions are by hedge and ditch, the ditches cleared and the hedges laid by hand, and odd corners and uneven land kept tidy by hook or scythe. Everything is

61

small-scale and the mixed economy is therefore appropriate, and since such farms were chiefly self-supporting in the age they belong to, most of what ordinary people wanted was produced at home. They are the farms of our pre-industrial economy before machines and before intensive trade, and one expert unkindly describes them as 'a cross between a zoo and a botanical garden'.

Yet our countryside was created by such farms, and maintained by traditional methods about as well suited to modern life as a horse and cart to motorway traffic. They are the farms described two centuries ago by Young and Marshall, and still scarcely changed when war overtook our society in 1939 and our children and I found safety from London's bombing on just such a beautiful anachronism. Even

*Kip's landscape in the 1960s. The only difference is the trees in the hedges — most have gone, those left have grown tall.*

then, however, and even to my innocent but urban eye, the methods seemed astonishingly archaic. Harvest particularly was an impressive Breughelesque occasion with a group of sunburned men labouring till dusk each day in the big wheatfield. There was hedge-bottom lunch of bacon-roll and cider, and little girls (it was always the girls) bringing cans of tea from the village. The operation lasted for most of a week, with a final excitement of guns and dogs when the last central patch was cut and the trapped creatures it sheltered rushed out to death or freedom. The wheat was cut by a reaper-and-binder, and this was considered a highly-advanced machine whose ability to knot the string never ceased to amaze the old farmer. But the sheaves were still gathered by hand and propped together to dry in the field (most

63

beautiful of farming patterns), and afterwards were loaded and carried to the rickyard, and the field cleared up by a horse-drawn rake. One rainy summer of frustrated harvesting the sodden grain started to grow where it stood in the field, the stooks of wheat sprouting like rows of green bonfires and wasting the whole year's labour.

Today a combine-harvester with a single man would dispose of the field in a day or two, and would also thresh the grain into the bargain. For our sheaves were built into ricks in the yard (a surprisingly skilled operation) and thatched against the autumn rains, until one fine winter day an ancient steam-engine and threshing-machine would come snorting into the yard, and for a further week another bevy of dusty hard-working men threshed out the ricks, while the children burrowed in the soft heaps of pale-gold chaff, and lunched with the men on pickles and cheese, and at night the boilerman damped down his fire by laying a piece of slate just so across the funnel.

Yet this was a well-run efficient farm (top grade in the wartime assessments), it was less than forty miles (64 km) from London and the farmer was wise from generations of farming ancestors. In a corner of the sixteenth-century barn was a flail which his father used for threshing wheat by hand; it was dusty and the hinge broken, but by now the steam-engine too (and probably the wonderful reaper-and-binder) is no doubt similarly rusting in some field corner.

Yet it is the landscape of flails and horses (we had a horse for tedding hay and other light tasks) which still survives to delight us, for in the late nineteenth century the import of cheap food from the New World and the Antipodes plunged agriculture into a depression which lasted for over half a century. The 1914–18 war produced a partial recovery which did not last, but during Hitler's war the need to grow our own food or go hungry was a stimulus which roused farming from its long stagnation, and agriculture began at last to move into the industrial age where we have all been living for generations.

Government policy has continued the process, and the often-quoted figures of increased farm output (a further one third rise in the last ten years despite a one quarter decrease in farm workers) are proof enough of the efficiency of machines and modern methods. The

3,000 pre-war combine-harvesters have increased to 60,000 and the 180,000 pre-war tractors to half a million. Great Britain in fact has the highest tractor density in the world, with one per 36 arable acres (14 ha). But these are only unit numbers and machine size has increased almost as impressively; there are 8-furrow ploughs, 140-horsepower tractors, and sprayers with 60-feet-wide (18 m) booms. Machines have never developed so fast and as if to make up for its belated start agriculture is now rushing into the modern world, and our fathers can tell us how men are replaced and machines instead of workers multiplied. Though we do not need our fathers to tell us, we can see only too clearly for ourselves by the mechanical destruction of the old farm landscape.

Arable farming has been mechanized first since vegetable crops are more tractable than animals, and government subsidies have stimulated cereal-growing. With the new machines arable farming needs little labour and this too has encouraged its increase, especially as mechanization now makes it profitable in areas which before were unsuitable. For the powerful new ploughs can break up the heaviest land, poor soils can be fed with fertilizers, cereals will grow well even in the traditionally pastoral land of the North and West, and it has chiefly been climate which hindered arable farming. But ploughing, harrowing, drilling, rolling – these once long-drawn-out operations can now be quickly done in a spell of dry weather, and the harvest snatched in during a few fine days and dried out under cover, or stored wet and used for animal feeding.

The result is that arable has more than doubled in a decade in England and Wales, especially in the wet South-West. And though continuous cereal-growing could have dire long-term results, yields are still high. They depend on fertilizers – in 1956 half the world's supply was used in Europe and a quarter in North America. The chemical industry's synthesis of fertilizers and of sprays against weeds and insects has been only less important than machines in increasing yields.

Most of these developments are in arable farming, and so far therefore it is the arable landscape which has changed most thoroughly. On old farm maps the fields are small – often less than the usual five to ten acres (2–4 ha), this being a reasonable division of land for horse-power arable and for enclosing grazing animals. Though even in the eighteenth century Marshall did not think so, and said they wasted time and labour by constant turning of the plough and journeys between separate enclosures. But if small fields are inefficient for two-horsepower ploughs what are they for 100 horse-power tractors, and for huge combine-harvesters like moving factories which can thresh up to ten tons an hour? The answer is clear enough for the Government to encourage farmers to sweep away the old field-pattern by making official grants for removing trees and hedges. Ten acres (4 ha) is scarcely space to turn for big modern machines, and turning is in any case an extremely wasteful operation. Even in a field of thirty-three acres (13 ha) it is reckoned at seven per cent of working time, while the operations of drilling and spraying are mangled in the turning area, and the Rothamsted researchers reckon that in this way many farmers lose up to fifteen per cent of their possible crop. Forward-looking experts are already forecasting fields of 1,000 acres (400 ha).

About the virtue of larger fields there can be no doubt, but what of the hedges and hedgerow trees which must go to create them? Since as non-farmers we would like to keep them we therefore try to find practical arguments in their favour. In fiercer climates than ours hedges are barriers against erosion, but in Britain this is scarcely a problem and can generally be controlled by farming methods. Even in the Fens where wind-blow can be serious its true cause is the unstable condition of the newly-drained organic soils, and on the light land of the exposed and hedgeless chalk-hills it is not a problem. Trees and hedges are also urged as shelter for animals in bad weather, but the humblest shed provides better protection, while as barriers for controlling animals hedges are inefficient compared with barbed wire and electric fences. Hedges need attention to keep them stock-proof, and being immovable are unsuited to new grazing methods. Wire fences on the other hand can be put up at speed by machine, while electric fences are light enough to move by hand. Other hopeful arguments are that hedges check the spread of infection between fields (but does a three-foot-high (1 m) hedge prevent wind-borne infection?) and that they shelter birds which feed on insects (but they also shelter pests).

Judging by the continuing loss of hedges and trees — seventy per cent in the last ten years in some Midland areas — farmers are more convinced by the arguments against them. For as well as their inconvenience to machines they take up large areas of valuable land, trees rob crops of food and water, their roots hinder the plough and clog the drains, they shade the crop, prevent it drying out, produce uneven growth and ripening, and cause wind eddies which flatten crops in patches. If the hedges are kept low there is the cost of constant cutting, and if there are trees they hinder the cutters, and all this apart from the loss of the land they grow on.

'There is an unnecessary prejudice against trees and hedges,' so pronounced the Government *Report on Hedgerow and Farm Timber* in 1955, 'and if those who dislike them were better informed they would be more alive to their advantages and less fearful of their disadvantages.' But would they? Or should the reporting Committee be better informed about the facts of farming? And we can guess before we even look at the list that the evidence will chiefly come (as indeed it does) not from farmers but from amenity representatives. Of the ten reasons the report gives for valuing hedgerow timber the last is the most convincing — that ' properly tended trees on the farm contribute to the beauty of the countryside and their presence increases the amenity value ... of many farms'. Yes. And as non-farmers we may well feel that this outweighs all the disadvantages, but if so we must say so frankly and fight for our convictions. It is useless trying to justify trees in terms of farming, for such unreal arguments are no protection against ten-ton bulldozers, and our wartime farmer had no illusions about the trees on his farm. Every one of them, he said, lost him money every year; he kept them because he liked them, and because he had no children and could afford to indulge his old age.

One farmer who recently grubbed-up his hedges and trees for the sake of efficient machine-working was surprised to find how many other benefits he gained as well. He gives figures and prices for the operation. On a farm of 600 acres (242 ha) he had two miles (3·2 km) of hedges and these cost £150 a year for maintenance. The cost of removing hedges and trees and piping the drains to fill in the ditches was £80 an acre (£200 ha) for the area involved, and partly paid by government grants. The land was worth £1,200 and increased the total farm yield by seven to eight hundredweight an acre (870–1,000 kg/ha). And all this in addition to the more efficient and therefore less costly working of the land which was his original motive. How can the old countryside pattern survive such results? Future farmers will not use their precious land to grow unprofitable trees and hedges, and their present survival is partly due to the fact that on rented farms in England and Wales hedges and trees traditionally belong to the owner, with the tenant not allowed to disturb them without permission. Even now their removal needs either the owner's consent or compensation, and a farmer I recently talked to as he bulldozed his hedges said it had taken him fifteen years to get round to doing it. Yet his thirty rented acres (12 ha) were divided into ten almost useless pocket-handkerchief fields, and his chief crop was the trees and hawthorn bushes he was burning on a mountainous bonfire. But as farmers acquire their land the hedges are going, and already in 1961 owner-occupied land in England and Wales had risen to forty-nine per cent compared with eleven per cent in 1919, and the proportion is still rising as leases of farms fall in.

At present thousands of miles of the old hedges still criss-cross our countryside (half a million miles (800,000 km) it was reckoned a few years ago but they vanish like vapour-trails). Almost everywhere now, however, they are cut by machine not laid by hand, and machine-trimmed hedges make a different landscape. Since they are cut frequently they never grow into the old tall leafy barriers arching well above eye-level (whatever the farmers intended) and dividing the countryside into visual as well as actual enclosures. Machine-cut hedges are low and smooth, disconcertingly gardenish, and at one sixth the height round fields six times the size are no longer divisions of space but merely lines of darker green across the countryside, boundaries simply, with no three-dimensional effect on the landscape. And even more important, they shelter no young trees to replace the old ones planted with the hedges; for where men will leave likely young saplings to grow on, machines knife indifferently through everything they meet. Already there are fewer trees in the hedges and soon there will be fewer still, for many of those remaining are reaching the end of their natural life, and over miles of the

Midland landscape in particular the only trees are stag-headed ancients decaying in the hedges, with dead upper branches rising starkly like horns through their leafy crowns.

Since in the old agricultural system labour was cheap, not only were the hedges laid by hand, but odd field corners were scythed and rough banks hooked: it gave the country an intimate, small-scale, cared-for-but-casual quality which is endlessly delightful. But modern labour is too scarce and expensive for such operations, and a man scything a road-verge is as extravagant as a gardener paid to cut a lawn with shears. Odd patches and corners must now be streamlined for routine machine-maintenance, if not there is nothing delightful about them, but thickets of nettles harbouring litter.

Then the flowers. The old landscape was flowery. Not only every odd corner, but arable land was bright with poppies and cornflowers and mayweed and corn-marigolds — much to the farmers' disgust — and farmland was more flowery than it ever seems likely to be again with our new chemical controls.

As well as the flowers and hedges and trees, the woods are also going. In the old economy timber was essential, and since transport was difficult much was grown where it was to be used. Thus there were many small woods scattered on farms and integrated into the countryside, providing the complementary mass in a landscape of fields, and tied into the pattern by the hedges and hedgerow trees.

But for us none of this is efficient any longer. Hardwoods are less profitable than conifers, coppicing is extravagant of labour (a little survives for chestnut fencing) and few farmers any longer fell and process their own timber. Small scattered woods are a nuisance now that the advantages of large-scale mechanical timber-working outweigh the cost of transport, and many of the old woodlands are derelict through long neglect or are disappearing. Successive surveys of woods under five acres (2 ha) show a steady decline, and farmers are unconvinced by arguments that it would pay them to grow timber on odd areas of land. Far from planting afresh, even the trees felled with the hedges are often sawn up and burnt on the spot (though one farmer I know paid for central heating in his farmhouse by timber felled in his hedges).

Farmland is changing with new farming methods and so too are the farmsteads. The old barn is too small for the new combine, the old cowshed unsuitable for conversion to electric milking, and the old house too uncomfortable for the new farmer's wife. It was just such a deserted Tudor farmhouse which we rescued and lived in through the war, without gas or electricity or drainage, and surrounded by farmyard cows and pigs and chickens, and by sheep at lambing time. It was much the most beautiful house we have ever lived in and much the most uncomfortable, and I realized afresh every day why the farmer's wife (and both the farmhands' wives as well) had refused to set foot in it.

All these are changes we already deplore in our countryside, but so far they are comparatively piecemeal and local, and much of the old landscape still remains. Farm change is slow, there are many factors which make it difficult, and until recently the production of milk which is the most important single product of our farms has scarcely been mechanized, and dairying has continued by much the same methods in much the same countryside. Traditionally dairying is the small man's farming: the outlay is small and the returns immediate; the extra work involved produces more profit from less land than arable farming; imported cattle-food in effect enlarges a farm; and in the past it has been possible to work up gradually from one or two cows to a herd. But perhaps most important for the survival of dairying in its old-fashioned form is its suitability to the old landscape pattern of small enclosures of permanent grass still inbuilt into many farms. Various new developments have also helped these small dairymen to survive in the modern world, such as the policy of the Milk Marketing Board, and swift transport of profitable milk to large urban pint-a-day populations instead of the old conversion to less perishable but less profitable butter and cheese. Better handling and preserving of milk have also led to collection from remoter areas, and though Wiltshire and Somerset are still with Cheshire the chief producers (the railway route from the West to London was christened the Milky Way) more milk now comes from Wales and the South-West.

The West has an excellent climate for grass and therefore for dairying, and in Hardy's *Tess of the D'Urbervilles* there is a living description of a prosperous Wessex dairy-farm. On many small farms the methods have scarcely changed since Tess's day, and until recently the benefits of industry (imported cattle-food, good transport, increased markets) have been of no overwhelming advantage to the large farmer compared with the small. But this seems unlikely to continue with new methods of dairying, and small farmers may in future find themselves at the same disadvantage in dairying as they already are in arable farming.

At present herds are limited by the land for summer grazing, but as grass management and stock feeding improve so the number of cows the land can support is increasing rapidly. Two acres per cow (0·8 ha) have been reduced to one, with talk of two or even four cows per acre (0·4 ha). Also a single cowman managing a hundred milking animals is not uncommon, though in 1963 the average for one milker was only nineteen. Some experts consider the ideal herd is about 200 cows, and it is significant that recent ten-year figures show 16,000 fewer dairy-farmers though much the same number of cows. The electric milking-machine in fact may well have been the beginning of the end for small dairy-farmers and equally for the old pastoral landscape. Modern herds are large and mechanized, not only with milking-machines but with milk-handling apparatus of pumps and pipelines (our wartime cowman carried buckets suspended on chains from a wooden yoke) and elaborate equipment for cooling. The cowsheds too are of factory-like efficiency, with automatic feeding and cleaning and pumping of slurry.

But none of this is for the small farmer. The most gruelling human labour cannot compete with machines, yet the capital cost of setting up a mechanized dairy-farm is prohibitively high. Nor do machines and cowmen cost less if they work at less than capacity, yet it is increasingly difficult to work up gradually as in the past. Even a 200-head herd may soon seem uneconomically small, and in West Germany for instance 1,000 cows are permanently housed and milked round the clock in shifts thirty-three at a time on a revolving platform – a new-world life which the cows appreciate by giving more milk than ever before. (The German public watch the process from an overlooking restaurant. One imagines them fat.)

But alas for the old unregenerate days of sweet-breathing cows knee-deep in buttercups (buttercups are anyway noxious weeds and taint the milk). And alas, too, perhaps for the cows – but about them we have no way of knowing. Certainly factory-farming can have serious abuses, such as overcrowding and needless discomfort, and these should be strictly controlled. But in the early days of factory-industry the treatment of humans was even more horrible than the treatment of animals now; the remedy, however, was not to abolish the factories but to reform the abuses, and so it must be in farming. A start has already been made with recent legislation following the Brambell Committee's report. As for the animals' feelings in the matter, our own anthropomorphic emotions are a less reliable guide than milk yields and the fact that unhappy creatures never flourish. And a first essential of factory-farming is the stock's increased prosperity – there is less disease, far fewer die, they are sheltered from harm and disturbance. Certainly when the gates were left open on our wartime farm the cows chose the shed not the field, and it is possible that from choice our domestic animals would spend much the same time out-of-doors as we do ourselves, which is very little. Our climate is no more ideal for them than for us, and though the optimum temperature varies (50°–60° Fahrenheit (10°–15° C) for cattle, 60°–70° (15°–21° C) for chickens) it can only be maintained in insulated buildings with controlled ventilation, and the most efficient animal husbandry is therefore under cover with balanced feeding.

Meat production is much simpler than milk to mechanize, and already there are plans for housing vast herds of up to twenty thousand animals, with automatic feeding, tower silos and mechanical unloading. Feeding six hundred beef-cattle, says one farmer, 'is a one-man part-time job, and if fully mechanized takes seventy-five minutes daily'. This is the two-part mechanization of animal farming, both by machine-servicing of stock and by using the mechanical methods developed for arable to grow forage crops to feed them. In fact if meat is to remain part of ordinary people's diet it must now be produced by economic methods, and as in so much else the choice is not what we like or don't like, but which we dislike less of two undesirable alternatives: not animals housed or animals in fields, but animals housed or no animals at all.

What fundamentally disturbs us in factory-farming is having to face the now obvious fact that farm animals are not a larger version of domestic pets, but a food crop for our consumption. Yet whether in fields or cowsheds they always have been, and the conversion of grass to milk and meat is an essentially unsentimental process. In less temperate climates than ours animals have always been housed, and the ubiquitous Marshall describes similar methods in the eighteenth century; not only cows and pigs, but even lambs were kept close-penned 'to restrain their natural propensity to playfulness and inordinate exercise'. There were elegant multiple pig-houses and an early version of battery hens, but despite his passion for efficiency, Marshall himself rather shamefacedly kept a mixed flock of free-ranging chickens and ducks and geese for the sake of what we should now call amenity.

But amenity or not, animals are coming indoors: it is the latest development in a long process which has changed them (like us) from wild creatures to indoor dwellers. And such changes, whether zero-grazing or small dairymen crowded out by large mechanized competitors, will have profound effects on the landscape. They mean that all farmland will essentially be arable land, and that the trees and hedges will logically go in the old pastoral landscape as they are already going in arable. But so far the changes – even in arable, let alone pastoral – have only begun, and as we travel about the rural lowlands we gradually discern three types of farming which give their character to the scenery of their different areas. The types are not distinct, for most farming is compromise between old and new and between efficient methods and local conditions, but nonetheless the three kinds of countryside are recognizable. One is intensive arable as in the Fens, New Holland in Lincolnshire, and on much of the chalk; there are few or no hedges or trees, but open country with no sense of enclosure or division. Simply the land surface with level crops emphasizing the smoothness of the worked earth.

The second type of rural landscape is the traditional mixed farm (the zoo and botanical garden), but mechanized and often enlarged. This is common in the Midlands in the parliamentary enclosure areas; the smaller fields have been run together and evened-off, but the old pattern is still recognizable in its new mechanized version. There are hedges still, but low now and neatly clipped, many of the small woods and copses have gone, and most of the trees in the hedges are the ageing survivors of enclosure planting. It is only a matter of time before they die (hard winters mean death to old trees as well as old people, especially two cold years in succession), and there are few new saplings in these machine-cut hedges to replace them, even if farmers wanted them.

The third type of landscape is the predominantly grass farm with animals on permanent pasture, and this is still common in a belt running north—south from Lancashire to Dorset and into the South-West. Here the fields are small (the average Devon field is a quarter the size of the average in Essex) and the hedges often tall and deep, leafy with trees of all ages as hedgerow saplings grow up to replace the dying giants. A survey of hedgerow trees shows more in the South-West than any other truly rural area (the South-East is leafier but urban) and looking across such country from rising ground the effect is of broken woodland with the fields screened by the luxuriant hedges — a lush and leafy landscape, beautiful in light mist with the outlines silhouetted in receding planes across the landscape. It is the least mechanized of our farming scenery, the least efficient, and the most resistant to change because of the multiple ownership and the often rented holdings.

These are not clear-cut categories of farmland but rather three tendencies of lowland landscape, and most farmland is intermediate and often in process of change. Nor do they cover land where urban influences disturb farming, nor regions of poor soils where farming is doubtfully profitable and the vegetation therefore nearer the natural tree-cover, as on the poor sands of the South-East, where hedgerow and park trees are nearly double the average. But in truly agricultural areas these are three discernible landscape types, and our lowland countryside can mostly be analysed in terms of them. Their distribution is very roughly from east to west and so too is the size of the holdings. The large arable farms are chiefly in the East and South-East, for this is the drier side of Britain and many of the soils are easily worked, like the light lands of East Anglia and the thin soils of the chalk. The farms are highly mechanized and these are the areas of really large holdings, many are over 500 acres (200 ha) and in East Anglia and on the chalk some are over 1,000 (400 ha).

The mixed farms of the Midlands and their extensions north each side of the Pennines are intermediate both in type and size between the arable of the East and the pastoral of the West, where most of the holdings are under 100 acres (40 ha) and many are much less. Indeed a map of the size of lowland farms can be used as a rough guide to the scenery we are likely to find in any area, though there are various exceptions to this general pattern. In the Fens for instance the holdings may be extremely small, and equally within reach of large cities like London there are more small farms than average, run part-time by people who like a home in the country and do not depend on farming for a living.

Land gets the farming it deserves – it is one of the sayings handed down the generations, and in the past, other things being equal, land was farmed according to its inherent qualities – arable on good ground, permanent grass on heavy clays, light land good for little, and so on. But other things are no longer equal, and unless we redefine land the saying is no longer true. For land must now include the farming structure inherited from the past, and this has become increasingly important with modern methods. Mechanized arable is now the most profitable and least demanding type of farming, but since machines need space, land without subdivisions either of hedges or (far more important) of owners, starts off with important advantages, and even 2,000 acres (800 ha) is considered by some to be too small a unit for future mechanized arable. The soil on the other hand is now less decisive, especially light land fed with fertilizers which is easy to work. In the past the holdings on poor soils were necessarily large to support a working family, whereas good land by the same economic argument was commonly held in small units. This is now a serious drawback, and the better farm-structure of much light land makes it more suitable for modern methods; it may even be more productive than better land in small unworkable holdings. This is so on the ancient sheep-walks on the chalk, miles of thin soils without trees or hedges, dry and easily worked and often in very large holdings. This has proved excellent land for machines and fertilizers, growing thousands of acres of profitable barley for the 'Barley Barons', and in the consultants' reports for the new town in the Swindon area chalk hills are considered good agricultural land.

There are new assessments of land which include farm structure as well as soil, the highest category being where good land combines with good structure as in much of East Anglia, and the lowest where poor land and poor structure go together, as in the clay vales of Buckinghamshire. This is a significant modern reversal of the old values, for one area of Buckinghamshire clay was once treasured as the finest grazing in England, and fattened beef for Queen Elizabeth's table, while in Young's account of farm prices in the eighteenth century the rent for permanent grassland is commonly double that for arable.

The structure of farms is very resistant to change, since a number of holdings must necessarily be reorganized together. Our British farm structure still mostly goes back to horse-plough days (it is worse in much of Europe), farming is like a modern industry awkwardly housed in little cottages. We have over two hundred thousand full-time farms, and almost as many part-time holdings. Of these only 2·4 per cent are over 500 acres (200 ha) only 5 per cent over 200 (80 ha) and more than half are between 5 and 50 acres (2–20 ha). This in an age which reckons that a 100-horsepower tractor needs 500 acres (200 ha) to pay for itself, and that one man suitably mechanized can farm 300 acres (120 ha) of arable single-handed.

William (large-field) Marshall was very percipient about the most suitable size for farms, and wherever he went he studied the acreage in relation to the management. Small farms, he says, 'fall into the hands of the ignorant or indigent,' while large farms mean distances too great for horses. 'From 200 to 300 acres (80–120 ha) is the most political farm,' he says, 'and it is chiefly among the cultivators of farms of these sizes that we find the three principal requisites of good husbandry, namely CAPITAL, SKILL and INDUSTRY.'

This was for farms still worked by horses, yet two centuries and half a million tractors later the structure is only now beginning to change. The number of holdings has only decreased by ten per cent since the war and thousands of small farmers are still trying to make a modern-world living on patches of land too small for modern-world methods. Which may be excellent for the scenery but not for the farmers, who try to replace machines by their own and their wives' unceasing labour (their children leave home), yet still earn less than a living wage. For their labour is wastefully extravagant compared with machines, and one observer has worked it out with ruthless clarity: if one man generates one eighth of a horsepower, then at wages of 10s. an hour he costs £4 a horsepower-hour. With a 40-horsepower tractor on the other hand he produces the same power for 3d. (1·25p) an hour plus the cost of the tractor.

This *reductio ad absurdum* nonetheless proves the point that man's place on the modern farm is as brain not muscle. As in any other industry the most efficient farmer is now a manager not a labourer, and his most important work is to keep up with new methods and markets and to organize his farm for the best use of its resources. This needs increasing skill (already firms offer computers to help with the planning) and modern farming methods and machines also need specialized knowledge. The headings of a recent agricultural supplement in *The Times* show how farming has changed since the dog-and-stick days – Machinery, Fertilizers, Irrigation, Information Services, Plant-breeders, Veterinary Surgeons, Geneticists and so on.

Mechanization for instance has scarcely started, not only in that much work is still done by hand, but because we have barely yet begun to rethink our old muscle-power farming in terms of machines. The tractor was a source of all-purpose energy which replaced the horse in its old tasks of dragging farm implements like ploughs and carts. But it did exactly that – it replaced one source of power with another in the same centuries-old methods. The actual processes of farming were still the same, and in many cases they still are, though grain-harvesting has now been rethought from first principles. At first, however, a tractor replaced a horse and pulled a reaper-and-binder which replaced men: the old animal methods were mechanized but they were still the old methods (even to tying-up wheat-sheaves with pieces of string). Combine-harvesting, however, is a fundamentally new process worked out in terms of machines – the grain is threshed off the stalk as it grows and mechanically dried elsewhere. Grain-handling too has been revolutionized: for centuries men carried it in sacks, for a generation or so machines carried the sacks, but now grain is moved like a fluid, sucked or blown loose through pipes like large and slippery sand.

Another much-discussed innovation is so-called chemical farming. This is a method of growing crops without ploughing, for after all natural vegetation flourishes on unploughed land, and the fact that farmers have ploughed for centuries does not prove that it is a necessary operation or even that it improves the growth of crops. It is possible that the chief use of ploughing, as of hoeing, may always have been to destroy weeds, and certainly one reason for letting land lie fallow every so many years was for weeds to be destroyed by summer ploughing.

But why plough when weeds can now be controlled by herbicides? There are new substances which destroy all vegetation but become inert on reaching the soil. These can be sprayed to destroy the remains of the previous crop instead of ploughing it in, and the new crop then be drilled into the undisturbed ground with the necessary

*'Chemical' farming without ploughing. The slots where the seed has been drilled are just visible through the dead grass.*

fertilizers and only a light harrowing to cover the seed. The advantages are obvious – operations are reduced to a quarter of the time, and are relatively independent of weather, the soil structure is undisturbed and the ground surface better for grazing, grassland is easily improved by reseeding and so on. Already results have been hopeful enough for the mass-production of a combined machine for cutting slots and drilling seed, and if such methods became common arable farming could quickly spread to many areas where permanent pasture has been the rule for centuries.

In animal breeding even more revolutionary new methods seem possible. Artificial insemination may only be an old process mechanized (with computers to arrange suitable marriages and frozen bull semen sold in lots by auction), but new work by biologists suggests processes quite alarmingly new. Transplanting of fertilized eggs, for instance, or of cell nuclei, to breed animals like plants from cuttings, or extracting and injecting the nucleic acids which control development, or altering the actual genes to produce animals tailor-made to our requirements. By such means the chosen perfection would be achieved in a single generation – a very different process from the trial-and-error methods of hybrid breeding. Farmers would clearly be delighted to be able to reproduce some paragon milch-cow in unlimited numbers of identical twin sisters, though the rest of us may profoundly mistrust the non-farming possibilities, and even scientists are alarmed – those commonly untroubled devotees of art for art's sake ('art' in their case being knowledge).

The future of grassland appears much less sinister and is probably the greatest undeveloped potential in our agriculture. Grass is our chief British crop, and in England and Wales covers one quarter of all farmland, not counting rough-grazing. Until now the management of grass has advanced comparatively little, and much of our milk still comes from old unimproved pastures of very low fertility. The Grassland Research Institute considers that sixty per cent of our permanent grass is potentially arable land and could yield three times more food than at present, while less cautious enthusiasts talk of increasing the produce of grassland by as much as eight or nine times. Such results can only be achieved, however, if grass is treated as a crop to be sown and cultivated, and 'taking the plough round the farm' is already accepted as good farming practice (destroying the fritillaries in a meadow we knew where they grew as thick as dog-daisies in the ancient pasture).

Modern grazing too is no longer the wasteful old-style process of animals eating the ground-cover of the fields they live in. Grazing of new improved grass crops is by animals controlled by movable fences to eat off the vegetation of one area at a time before they trample and foul it. Simply to control grazing in this way and give the grass a resting period will in itself enormously improve the pasture, and even in pastoral landscapes of the future hedges and trees may have no more place than they have now on arable land, wire fences having the same effect as the tractor of stripping down the countryside to bare earth and crops.

In any case 'grazing is the enemy of production' according to one impatient modernist, and harvesting crops by peripatetic animals may well belong to a past which lacked machines to move the crops instead. Other writers are equally scornful of the 'horse-age practice' of haymaking, and grass has more food value made into silage than has hay, more still if mown young and dried. Nor is grass necessarily the best forage crop, but only perhaps the most tolerant of trampling, and there are suggestions for lucerne and for cereals cut young at their grass stage. Such methods would again change pastoral to arable landscape, and whether or not we like the change in terms of either landscape or animals it may well be inevitable. Farmers cannot afford to use valuable land unprofitably ('land's not for exercising cows at present values') and neither can the community. As our numbers grow and our cities spread we need ever more food from ever less land, and the spectacular rise in food production has been achieved almost entirely by using good land more intensively. This will in any case become economic necessity as the cost of land continues to rise. Already at present prices the rent for good land should be £15 an acre (0·4 ha) (the English average is £4), and in some recent sales the return on investment is only two per cent.

Modern intensive farming needs about £50,000 capital per person employed, and the developments which now make small farms impractical seem likely in the future to make them impossible. Medium-sized farms may prosper by changing their old mixed husbandry for specialization, there may even for special reasons be some small farms as there are small shops; but the future of agriculture, like other industries, is with large units which can profit from the new techniques of mechanization, mass-production, automation and all the not-yet-invented rest. Everywhere in industrial societies the future of small farms is a problem, and other European countries are also seeking ways of achieving the change to larger units with least hardship to the people concerned.

One method encouraged by government help is farm syndicates and cooperatives which share overhead costs like machines and marketing, and in effect combine separate small farms into one large one. But there are practical difficulties as well as farmers' individualistic temperaments. Specialist contract services are another solution and are developing fast (and in new spheres like silage-making and secretarial services). But all these are essentially arrangements for achieving the benefits of large-scale farming; they are roundabout ways to the true goal of larger units.

'Farmers will improve their position when the number of producers falls and the average size of units increases.' 'The modern trend towards larger and larger units applies with equal force to farming.' Commentators agree about the need, and the structure of farming is now beginning to change, with small farms like small fields combining in larger units. Four thousand farms now disappear yearly and the new process has even acquired a name – amalgamation – an unsympathetic word with suitable business overtones. Amalgamation is as essential for the new industrial revolution in farming as enclosure was for the earlier agricultural revolution, and indeed the two processes have much in common. Both are a logical reaction to new methods of farming, and both began as a slow change long-developing but gradually gathering speed (there were bitter arguments against enclosure in Tudor times and against amalgamation in Cobbett's – 'one farmer in Hampshire occupies what was formerly forty farms'). Both processes also are associated with hardship to small farmers, and both began with prosperous and forward-looking private individuals and were later adopted as government policy.

'The Government believe that one of the more important problems facing agriculture today is that of the small farmer trying to
win a livelihood from insufficient land. As time passes his difficulties
will increase. He will find it harder to keep pace with technical
advance. He will find it more and more difficult to maintain a standard of living in keeping with modern times.'

This clear warning was followed by measures suggested either to
help small farmers to enlarge their holdings, or to encourage them to
sell by an added gratuity or pension for those who 'want to give up
an unrewarding struggle'. The intention is clearly stated and is
the amalgamation of small farm units, yet this is a completely
new attitude, and the exact reversal of even quite recent policy
when small-holdings were provided for ex-servicemen, agricultural
workers, the unemployed and so on, and 'the aim was to foster a
peasant economy'. The aim now is to rescue the same people from
the peasant economy which cannot support them.

Coke of Norfolk in the eighteenth century complained that ideas
only travelled a mile a year, but changes now are swift and sweeping,
and already it seems inconceivable that so informed an observer as
Dudley Stamp could state in *The Land of Britain*, republished in
1962, that a farmer could make a family living on twenty to fifty
acres (8–20 ha) of land, that ten acres (4 ha) was the most flexible
field size, that fifteen cows were a suitable herd for a man and
assistant, and that new changes in farming had little effect on the
landscape! But his well-known Land Utilization Survey is interesting
not for the future but the past: it is a detailed picture of pre-industrial
farming surviving into the twentieth century.

Amalgamation is a new pattern of land organization and ownership which is producing a new kind of countryside, and again, like
enclosure, non-farming country-lovers thoroughly dislike it. But it is
a harsh truth that much of what we love in the old countryside
depends on poverty – either of poor returns on the land or of poor
farmers. Below a certain acreage labour seems never to have made up
for lack of land, and small farmers probably never enjoyed the
Golden Age we like to imagine. Certainly eighteenth-century observers had no such illusions. 'I consider these small occupiers as a set
of very miserable men,' said Arthur Young. 'They fare extremely

*The unrewarding struggle on Folly Farm. Sagging roofs, rotting woodwork, broken implements, gap-toothed fences, rubbish, nettles, and neglect. Even the name plate has since disappeared.*

hard, work without intermission like a horse, and practice every lesson of diligence and frugality without being able to soften their lot.'

The beauties of the old farming pattern in fact depended on a large class of labourers who worked at subsistence level with no hope of anything better. But like manual labour such inherited class distinctions are now disappearing, and as they go in society so they must in the landscape. Already we can guess a country's development from its field-pattern, so that even flying miles up over Europe we notice how the large simple fields of the prosperous West change to a small-scale irregular patchwork as we cross East Germany, and we know that the farmers must be poor, and spend their lives in what Cobbett calls 'break-back and sweat-extracting work'.

The new developments are inevitable, and no matter how we lament or resist them they will nonetheless be the basis of our new

83

scenery: it is why it is essential to understand what is happening before change overwhelms us. For whatever we hope to make of our future countryside farming is its raw material, and any viable landscape design must start from the organization of the landscape for modern agricultural methods. It is a pattern we may modify or adapt or add to, but first we must accept it; for if the countryside changes because of new farming methods the change is intrinsic. It is not a controllable outside influence but a transformation of the organism from within, as a grub to a chrysalis or a chrysalis to a fly. Resistance will not stop it nor will preservation preserve the old pattern, for the new developments will still happen inside the protected areas, or if we prevent them then farming will decline, and farmland without farmers degenerates as swiftly as gardens without gardeners.

Yet we seldom believe in change till it happens, for the known is our norm and we commonly dismiss future forecasts as science fiction. But what about aerial crop-spraying? To us it is no more than another new and noisy farm operation, but would the men who made our countryside ever have believed for a moment in such ridiculous fantasies? – To fly in machines which rise in the air by roaring engines, and to spray fields with magic fluids which kill the weeds but not the crops?

*The logical landscape of amalgamation in Lincolnshire. Fortunately neither land nor farmers are often so logical.*

# 5. The Urban–Rural Countryside

In Britain we are the least rural people in the world. Only 3·5 per cent of us work on the land compared with 6·4 in America, 18 in France and Denmark, 25 in Japan and 75 in countries like Turkey. In England and Wales the average rural population is only 60 per square mile (23 per km²) (the all-in average is 825 or 328 per km²) consisting of 40 employed on the land (the primary rural population) plus a secondary population of 20 who serve them, such as agricultural engineers. This is too low to survive as a community since the small villages it produces cannot support modern services, and two thousand people has been suggested as a likely minimum for a viable village. But clearly there can be no single answer since much depends on neighbouring development, and much smaller villages can survive as residential satellites. In small towns too there is likely to be a critical number for modern services to be feasible in the future, and 120,000 has been suggested.

Since little of anything can be provided at sixty per square mile, people are still leaving remote rural areas, but as remoteness is rare in lowland Britain their loss is completely masked by backflow from towns, and Wiltshire for instance now feels the influence both of London and Bristol. People find cottages for week-ends or retirement or increasingly for commuting – for why not travel an extra half-hour to work, and live in the country? Fifty railway miles may even be swifter than five congested street miles from the suburbs. This is the park-and-ride pattern of America (or the kiss-and-ride, depending on whether the car is parked at the station by the rider or the rider parked by his wife). In the Midlands and South-East, South Wales and the North-East coast eighty per cent of people in rural areas have nothing to do with the land, they are the adventitious rural population who keep the old agricultural settlements alive in an industrial society; for the early purist policy of rural settlements has gone – to be truly rural is also to be doomed.

The newcomers are the descendants of the poor illiterate labourers who left the land, but the cities have transformed them to an urban industrial population at home in the modern world, and the able have changed their status in the process. The new rural life is chiefly middle-class and prosperous – the country on urban terms to enjoy not labour in – and these newly-trained and educated people with their confident insistence on the benefits an industrial economy can provide are transforming the old way of life for everybody. The difference between urban and rural which survived the first phase of the Industrial Revolution is now chiefly of emphasis not of kind. New-style country people are increasingly like their urban cousins, and the chief surprise of travel is to find the familiar wherever we go. Certainly away from urban centres new fashions can look very undigested, but wherever we see a television aerial, no matter how thatched the cottage, the difference between town and country is mostly the view.

But the changes are by no means all gain, for the lively newcomers overwhelm the old static societies, and the old village life withers in the brisk new urban atmosphere. Certainly the landscape suffers, for the only ' real' people in any area, so said our chief planner, are those who work there, and equally it is the settings of our working lives which create ' real' landscape. Farm people living among fields, foresters in woodland hamlets, sheep-farmers in the hills, fisherfolk in coastal villages: these create unselfconsciously authentic environments, but all in pre-industrial terms and therefore disappearing.

New country workers prefer a new council house to a picturesque old cottage, and so would anyone who considered them at the same level of non-improvement. Thatched roofs and colour-washed walls may be beautifully integrated with their setting (being of the same mud and straw they should be) and are certainly charming to look at. But to live in? No damp-course, little light, no electricity or gas or drainage or piped water, no proper kitchen much less a bathroom, the roof almost certainly leaks, the floor is surfaced earth, and un-worn shoes will be green with mould in a week, as ours were on the farm.

In the past poor people lived and died (early) in poor cottages – no

nonsense about choice and no problems about services – and the old rural scene was undisturbed by the 'necessities' of living. But new country workers live in brick-built 'semis with all mod. cons' – with plastic pools and multi-coloured rose-trees and garden gates from catalogues. Splendid – for living in. But not country cottages. Even the few remaining local workers therefore no longer produce local landscapes, and for most country-dwellers the countryside is simply the backcloth of their transported urban lives. The original character of old towns and villages has often gone completely, submerged in a flood of new development or swept away ruthlessly for routine new layouts and easier motor-travel. Yet surely in this irreplaceable heritage we could make-do and mend, patching-up and filling-in as everyone else has through the centuries, and there are now promising new policies for protecting whole areas instead of separate buildings.

*Old country homes, abandoned by new country people.*

*New country homes for new country people.*

*Urban-based newcomers rescue the country scene. All three pictures are from the same village of Haddenham, Oxfordshire.*

*Old town plus new amenities.*

But old villages now can never be more than old shells for new ways of life. Farmhouses are sold without land 'strictly for non-tilling farmers', and equally it is urban people who save country cottages from demolition. This is a problem in the National Trust properties, for though their policy is to let cheaply to the local people they were built for, the Trust often cannot afford the necessary renewal. Neither can the villagers, and the cottages go to prosperous outsiders who can. The old country character of the village is lost, but what better solution? If the villagers stay the cottages fall down: if the cottages stay the villagers go.

This is one reason for the Trust's increasing interest in land rather than buildings. A fine landscape is not simply treasure preserved

*Old town plus new amenities plus new amenity movement. Lavenham before and after the anti-wire campaign. Constructive preservation. Commended in the Civic Trust Award Scheme.*

from the past but a still-living part of our environment, and our irreplaceable countryside is now as urgently in need of care as its buildings. Here the Trust is the best protection we have – widely respected, dedicated to long-term amenity, and resistant to change like the landscape. But the National Trust is only the earliest of the societies which have grown up everywhere – the Council for the Protection of Rural England (and others for Wales and Scotland), the Civic Trust and its associated bodies, and a host of local amenity societies. On average a new group is formed every week, and most of their members are urban-orientated. This is certainly true of the excellent conference on 'The Countryside in 1970', which was primarily a study of the urban influences which now affect it, and this

91

growing concern for our environment is in itself an extremely important new urban influence.

Our amenity societies, however, are still a very new phenomenon, and exist at every stage of evolution from the first blind resistance to change (a Canute-like role with little effect on the tide) to the realization that change is not only inevitable but is also for the ultimate benefit of those who resist it. (This is the kind of uncomfortable truth which makes adult attitudes so much less enjoyable than the single-minded convictions of youth.)

Societies at present exist in three progressive stages, as Reversers, Shunters and Translators. Reversers are simple: they want to put the clock back. They would like us all to live happily in a beautiful pre-industrial world, despite the fact that no one would now tolerate the pre-industrial life. The Shunters are more realistic but less sympathetic: they accept that modern living means unattractive developments like cement works and pylons, but propose to shunt these into someone else's territory. (We are all to some extent Shunters in private.) The Translators are the most advanced and therefore most useful: they appreciate the past but accept the future, and aim to incorporate the inevitable changes with least harm, or even with benefit, to the environment. Most serious societies (whatever the still-blinkered attitudes of some of their members) are now reaching this advanced stage of realism and responsibility. An offshoot of these are the practical action groups of energetic people who work in conservation corps, remove landscape eyesores, restore old canals, act as wardens in National Parks and Nature Reserves, plant and protect trees on spoil-heaps and run all the voluntary schemes which now find enthusiastic supporters.

But such potential urban good is at present outweighed by the actual harm of an urban population in an unfamiliar rural environment. 'I get a good deal of stick,' said a farmer whose land borders a new housing estate; for town people know little of farming, and simply through ignorance can do great damage to crops and animals perilously exposed to their unconcern. Their dogs chase cows and worry sheep, their children make gaps in hedges and fires in ricks, they play football in hayfields, make love in wheatfields, fill ditches with rubbish, steal tools from tractors, leave gates open for straying cattle – and all the destructive rest. 'To have children roaming about would have a disastrous effect on the running of the farm. The same applied if the mansion were used for old people who could be expected to have visitors.' This is a witness in a recent case resisting the public use of a stately home, and whether we like it or not urban people and farms are a bad combination for the farms.

Hundreds of thousands of people now living in the country know no more about the farming which surrounds them than they did in towns. Why should they? They have other and equally valid preoccupations. Even most modern country-lovers are now several generations out of touch with farming, and therefore see the country as a charming view, not as working land carefully maintained in balance between the processes of natural growth and the man-made operations which exploit them. There is still the unformulated belief that the country is 'natural', that it is what is there when towns are not. 'The country's where trees are left not planted,' says my Londoner husband, whose second greatest pleasure in life is the country landscape, where a 'left' tree is rare, and most were deliberately planted for practical uses. But he is in excellent company and Le Corbusier (who is never more urban than when admiring nature) felt exactly the same. His 'Nature' is simply the view, a beautiful green setting for life and architecture. 'Your room is installed before the site. The essential joys have entered the dwelling. Nature is inscribed in the lease. The pact with Nature has been sealed.'

But it is pacts with farmers we need, to live amicably together in the same countryside; and if living is difficult, playing is very much worse. The problem of urban recreation in the countryside is already becoming acute, for the farming landscape makes little provision for recreation. In the past the nobility and gentry pursued their pleasures (mostly various sorts of hunting) on their private land – royal forests, warrens for lesser men, and later on coverts for foxes which were (and still incongruously are) hunted over farmers' fields. This indulgence of man the hunter has always been a nuisance to man the farmer (even when combined in the same person) but since the hunters were tolerably few and intolerably powerful they were only gradually driven from land needed for food production. As for the recreation of ordinary people, there was no definite provision. They pursued their humbler (and often illegal) versions of country sports discreetly, and since they were country people trained to farming the farming countryside absorbed them as its own.

But our new mechanized farmland absorbs no one. She'd had a lovely holiday in London, said a farmer's wife from Bedfordshire overheard by Sylvia Crowe in a train. 'Lovely to have all that grass to walk on in the parks. At home you couldn't set foot off the road.' For modern farmland is no place for walking; much grass has been ploughed, many footpaths have gone on arable land, and even where hedges survive, tractors now plough close up leaving no unused borders for walkers and wild flowers.

Yet leisure in the countryside is vastly increasing – already five million campers and caravanners, three million anglers, a million golfers, half a million sailors, huge numbers more skiers, climbers, riders, shooters and so on, as well as the uncounted numbers of walkers. The constantly increasing figures show one thing very clearly – we are spending our extra leisure and prosperity in active not spectator sports, and most of them out of doors.

Upland farming can to some extent accept such extra uses, but the lowlands which chiefly surround our living areas cannot without special provision, while an even more acute problem are the people who simply drive out from the towns for a day in the open. Since the sea is an unsurpassed attraction, all coasts within reach of city areas now suffer unmanageable numbers of holiday-makers, but even so a Whitsuntide traffic survey found that forty-five per cent did not travel more than twenty-five miles (40 km) from home, and another twenty-five per cent not more than fifty miles (80 km), which often means a local beauty spot, or simply the countryside wherever we can find somewhere to park. The country is a different environment which we need for our recreation, whether it 'calms our souls – no less', or whether it provides green space in the open air for family ball-games. In our new economy it is an essential function of the rural eighty-five per cent of our land to provide a liberating environment for the urban eighty-five per cent of our population.

The English have a particular gift for enjoying the country – so Henry James considered, and what particularly impressed him in London was the way its citizens rushed out of the town at the least excuse of holiday. We are still a race of country-lovers, and not only James's landed gentry but the thousands of present-day urbanites who cherish a flowery dream of a country cottage; while even without cottages to call our own, a day in the country still means holiday for millions of city-dwellers. But the difficulties are serious, both because efficient farming creates an unsuitable landscape for recreation, and because recreation may hinder efficient farming and harm the countryside.

Double the number of day-trips is forecast by 1985, and the character is changing as well as the volume. The newcomers are more thoroughly urban than the former few, with no childhood background of holidays on farms or in seaside cottages. Fields are parks to city children, and the country a wonderfully extended playground for all. 'A day in the country' is the new prosperous version of the old charity outings for children from city slums which I used to look forward to every year. It was how I discovered the unimaginable country, on a Whit Monday treat packed in a charabanc with fifty other excited children; the boys with larded-down hair (it really *was* lard), the girls in new white frocks, and all of us with enamel tea-mugs dangling round our necks on strings. We drove through the streets waving and shouting, through the diminishing city squalor and out into the green.

To me the country was a sudden stupendous revelation. A lavish day of early summer, warm and moist and growing. I remember it still as a long green delirium like a vision of Paradise. I had never imagined such beauty existed, and I must have been at the age when small children make bargains with God, for I remember deciding that I would believe in Him ever after if He performed the miracle I offered – that next day I should walk down a dark city street I particularly hated, and find cowslips growing between the tram-lines (not that I then knew their name was cowslips, nor now remember whether I went to look).

I doubt whether any modern children are as cloistered as I was (though cloistered seems scarcely the word for the wild rough-and-tumble street life of poor industrial cities), but such city dwellers are clearly urban, as are only less obviously so the inhabitants of luxury outer suburbs and all levels of semi-detached rural living between.

And for none of them is modern farmland a suitable place for recreation, with its crops and sprays and costly equipment and valuable stock — all the developments which have doubled food production for the hungry cities.

Yet farmland is commonly regarded as semi-public, or at least as a different sort of private from private gardens. It is not a view farmers share. They would prefer to have neither 'those who visit the countryside simply for recreation, nor those whose concern is primarily with its natural features'. (This is Government tact.) Those who use farmland as playground are quite simply destructive (and that they are often unwitting merely means they don't realize why farmers don't want them). But the country-lovers can cause equal difficulties by cherishing a landscape pattern which for farmers is inefficient and wasteful, and when I crossed a field to photograph hedges being bulldozed the farmer rushed up in a fury to drive me away — Was I the Press? He'd had endless arguments about trees with local societies and he wanted no pictures in local papers. He'd had more trouble than enough already and he'd got to get on.

Urban animal-lovers also campaign indiscriminately against any kind of intensive rearing, and alternate between attacking farmers as 'vandals', 'inhuman', 'mercenary', or as idlers living on subsidies and 'feather-bedding'. Not that farmers are any more complimentary about their critics — 'out-of-touch', 'sentimental' and above all 'ignorant' — that all-embracing abuse which includes lack of manners as well as of knowledge. (And if farmers add 'Mind your own business' we can scarcely blame them since they are so efficiently minding theirs.) Strangers on a farmer's land can bring no possible benefit and only too probable harm. Any farmer would rather they stayed away, and is unlikely to encourage them by preserving at his own expense the landscape they come to admire. They are no more welcome than on a building site or shipyard or any other working area, and urban workers would certainly object to casual strangers on their own territory.

We all need a better understanding of each other's attitudes in the countryside we have all got to share, and though farmers are fewest in number they are certainly the most important for landscape. Farmers, however, are not articulate: we see their activities but we rarely hear

*Urban visitors to the country (posed by themselves) make dangerous neighbours for farmers.*
*'Now let's go and chase them mini-cows' (the calves in the next field).*

their point of view: it is why this book may seem to give it dispro-
portionate emphasis. The country-lovers are a larger group though
still a minority, but they are highly articulate and any discussion re-
flects their views in a way out of all proportion to their numbers
(it is equally why their case is often here taken as stated). Since they
are clearly on the side of one kind of angels this is all to the good,
but nonetheless it is important to remember that most people are not
country-lovers in their select meaning of the word. (And even among
dedicated naturalists there are tensions between botanists who want to
keep nature reserves open ground for flowers, and bird-watchers who
welcome scrub for cover.)

As well as more understanding we most of us also need more
education in country matters, for it is unrealistic to condemn city
people because their dogs run wild in an ecstasy of green fields, or
because they leave country gates open behind them like city swing-

97

doors. But just as our Whitsuntide bus-load needed intensive education before we were fit to let loose on the countryside, so will the
millions like us who will soon be driving out of the cities, and have
never heard of the Country Code of basic Dos and Don'ts on
farmland. There is no reason why those trained to live in a city (an
increasingly specialized and exacting skill) should also know how to
live in the different rural environment. Country people equally have
to learn to use a city – the bus routes and subways, lifts and esca-
lators, the crowds and the traffic and the pace. But cities are tough
where the country is vulnerable: in a city the careless may end the
day in hospital, in the country it is not the careless who suffer but the
countryside.

For part of the necessary education the need is already recognized,
and what we might describe by the old-fashioned name of nature
study is well provided-for by schools, museums, excellent books, and
large numbers of natural history societies. Since it fosters care of
wild-life this is all excellent, but as an approach to the actual countryside it is quite unrealistic; for it is concerned with an environment
where farming scarcely exists, and where the chief rural land-use is
as nature reserves. It is as if we studied cities by considering the wild-
life of bomb-sites (unexpectedly interesting) without ever mentioning
that cities consist of roads and buildings where people live and work.
Most of the countryside is likewise working farmland, but if there is
any general education about agriculture we hear little of it. Yet we
need to understand at least its essentials before we invade the farming
countryside, and what more pertinent study in ecology than man's
control of his habitat to produce extra food? Or in genetics than
plant and animal breeding? Or in biology than the effect of chemicals
on wild-life? Or in technology than new methods of using crops of
plants and animals to convert the raw materials of earth and sunlight
and rain to human sustenance? Such subjects would attract many
children who sigh with boredom at the very name of nature study.

And why not model farms run as show-places for paying visitors –
with properly-housed animals, machinery demonstrations, eggs and
fruit and vegetables for sale; and for children pony rides and rural
adventure playgrounds, with piles of straw and old farm machines
made harmless? Such farms would be a refreshing change from the

present round of stately homes, and to be told about the eggs and milk and meat we eat every day would mean far more than the usual stately-home chat about who married who in the aristocratic past. The commentaries might include a tactful amount of Country-Code-type exhortation, but understanding alone could prevent much damage done simply through ignorance. We readily identify with man's ancient role of farmer, and seen with a knowledgeable eye the farmer's land would be twice as safe as well as twice as interesting.

Farmers themselves, however, are certainly not blameless. That they are destroying the countryside we love there is no question, whatever the exigencies of the matter. But the valid grounds for disagreement are not change itself, but whether some changes are unnecessarily ruthless. Certainly on every body to do with the countryside there should be a farmer as representative of the land-use which creates the country landscape. This seems self-evident but is

*'You realize there is a cover charge of course.'*

*A well-planned caravan site, Cannock Chase. Large numbers of caravans are lost in glades between birch trees. An attractive setting for occupants, an attractive birch-wood for the landscape.*

often not so, and my bull-dozing farmer bitterly complained that in an agricultural area there was not a single farmer on the local council, and that country affairs were now run by urban newcomers who knew nothing of farming.

*Country Life* is an excellent but thoroughly urban journal: to understand the working countryside we need the *Farmer's Weekly* or the *Farmer and Stockbreeder*, or perhaps more pertinent still for the future, an alarming journal called *Power Farming*. These are what a farmer reads who depends on the land for his living, and any group without him is one more *Hamlet* without the Prince of Denmark. Such a down-to-earth spokesman of agriculture could prevent a great deal of unrealistic urban thinking about the countryside, while he in turn could be helped to realize what urban people legitimately want from the countryside besides cheap food.

Urban recreation in the country also has its urban misunderstandings, for walkers commonly consider themselves superior to car-riders and country-cottagers to caravanners (though where are the cottages for the $3\frac{1}{2}$ million caravanners?). But snobberies apart there are fundamental differences, and like farmers the less-articulate need better representation. For though there are lively groups for preserving every aspect of our rural past, and protecting everything from birds to mountains, yet we also need equally articulate groups for what will be the main body of future users – a Council for Better Caravan Sites, societies for More and More Attractive Car Parks, for Country Playgrounds, for Motoring for Pleasure, and for Enjoying the Countryside without Feeling Virtuous. People represented by organized bodies are more responsible as well as more communicative, and the Caravan Club has proved that, given the goodwill, camping and caravan sites can be well designed and camouflaged in the landscape. (Though couldn't they also encourage quieter caravan colours by giving the suitable drabs unsuitably glamorous names – Spring Dawn for light grey, Summer Twilight for dark, and Autumn Ploughland for mud?)

Good neighbourliness depends, however, on good planning as well as good intentions, and the less the space the more need of planning, as with neighbourliness on roads. The earliest recorded traffic disaster for instance is Oedipus killing his father at the cross-roads. They met. They were obstinate about priorities, and in these uninhibited heroes the misunderstanding ended in death. On the uncrowded roads of classical mythology such fatal congestion was crass bad planning, for with even the most elementary traffic arrangements Jocasta's husband could have lived to prevent all the family scandal. Certainly we shall have to manage better in the crowded modern world, and on our roads we are learning reasonably fast. The mileage we travel without mishap increases steadily, for despite our appalling accident figures they only in 1966 reached the former peak of 1934, and since cars were then less than one fifth of our present numbers the skill of pre-war drivers in road-sharing must have been minimal. The figures are even beginning to fall again, and we now more-or-less accept the necessary rules: we move to an agreed pattern and we keep to our own side of the road; or if we don't we realize we are flouting a fact we know to be true – that cars travelling in opposite directions are incompatible users of the same area of land.

The problems of sharing roads, however, are now inherent in our wider environment, and we urgently need new methods of avoiding friction between parties with different viewpoints. The simplest way is not to meet, and this worked well for town and country in the past; but since peace by isolation needs maximum space and minimum transport it clearly will not work for the future. There is also the method of quarrel and compensate, and there are already suggestions for compensating farmers for damage. But apart from the obvious practical difficulties, peace by compensation is only a truce between enemies; it is a form of tinkering with the past, not a solution for the future.

The only hope of peace at close quarters is agreeing to differ and respecting the differences. This is peaceful coexistence and the space it needs depends on how carefully we coexist. The fostering of mutual understanding already suggested might work wonders in some happy future, but at present friction is more evident than co-operation (and even official policy has a muddled left-hand right-hand quality, with instances of farmers given grants to plough up classified Sites of Special Scientific Interest, and advice on how to level barrows scheduled as Ancient Monuments).

But even if sweet reason reigns at every discussion (how dull) human nature is still only relatively perfectible. Even though the careless may be educated to virtue there will always be vandals (for though the young men with shotguns who pepper the flanks of cows may well be ignorant, it is not of the damage to cows). We shall never all be virtuous all the time, and the most realistic hope for peaceful coexistence is the old disillusioned maxim, 'Good fences make good neighbours.' With a fence between us the area of potential disagreement is reduced to a boundary which both sides accept, and all the effort of tolerance and self-restraint is transferred to an impersonal barrier.

In the countryside urban recreation and farming now need this clear-cut division, for though there will always be country-lovers who find their own country way and keep their peace with farmers, urban recreation as such needs its own legitimate areas. This is now officially recognized, and the proposed Country Parks are to serve three purposes: 'They would make it easier for town dwellers to enjoy their leisure in the open . . . they would ease the pressure on the more remote and solitary places, and they would reduce the risk of damage to the countryside – aesthetic as well as physical.'

Such parks should contain their users, and provided their boundaries are efficient, adjoining land can be safely farmed. The two land-uses would exist intensively side by side, for coexistence by fences is also the most economical use of land, like a river channelled between containing banks instead of turning a whole valley to unusable marsh.

There are other positive suggestions for leisure in the countryside, as by better use of water – reservoirs, lakes, rivers, wet pits, and especially by developing canals as 'cruiseways'. Also plans for more camping and caravan sites and for better use of commons, and for a coordinated network of footpaths and bridleways. Many of the ancient rights-of-way are now little used and overgrown despite efforts to preserve them, for since old paths were the working routes of people whose transport was legs, they are only by chance satisfactory routes for enjoying the countryside. A new network of old and new is therefore proposed, which 'being more regularly used could be more readily kept fit for use'.

Which is fine for walkers but what of the farmers whose land provides the network? Footpaths to farmers are legalized trespass inviting all comers onto their defenceless fields. And it will no longer be a question of a few country-walkers who can be ignored: with inviting paths leading from public gathering-grounds as suggested, we shall come in large numbers of assorted townsfolk to enjoy our country rights – it will after all be the purpose of the exercise. On marginal land clear sign-posting in the right direction might be sufficient, but not across lowland country intensively farmed. The present Please Keep to the Footpath notices will certainly not be enough protection, and some physical barrier will be essential. But though fences may make good neighbours they don't make good landscape – certainly not the prison-perimeter type needed to contain small boys and dogs. Some footpaths, however, may already be hedged, there are also 1,800 miles (2,880 km) of towpaths ready-made along canals, and 3,000 miles (4,800 km) of abandoned railway track already enclosed, as also the old green ways so seductive and mysterious in our countryside, and which as part of a footpath system might be saved from the ubiquitous plough.

For damage is not entirely one-sided, and the new footpaths will equally need protection from farmers whose huge new machines destroy any walking surface. The Berkshire Ridgeway for instance is an ancient track along the chalk which till lately survived all comers including the Romans: a green ribbon of turf with pasque flowers in spring and gentians in summer between the White Horse and Wayland's Smithy. But the turf has gone now and the chalk is churned into ruts a foot deep by the tractors and combines which work the miles of arable on the hills. Farmers' machines must be kept off footpaths and so clearly must cars, and even horse-riding needs separate tracks since it cuts up the grass and makes walking unpleasant.

Definite recreation areas will please not only farmers but also those who like their country lonely; for more people in one place mean fewer in another, and if the two places are separated the users cease to annoy each other. The survey of the Norfolk Broads sponsored by the Nature Conservancy is a pioneer study in possible coexistence, for the Broads are both a famous wild-life habitat and a popular holiday area with a yearly turnover of £10 million, and the survey shows how pleasure-boating and wildlife could exist side by side in specific areas.

Future town and country must similarly learn to live together, for they are now essentially interdependent, and only the wealth of old towns and villages from our agricultural past disguises how thoroughly life has changed within them. An old village for instance in undisturbed farmland has nothing to do with the harsh and spreading ugliness of industrial Britain. Or so we might think. But if we do we are like city children who think that milk appears in bottles without benefit of cows. Such a village makes full use of everything industrial Britain has to offer; the cars outside the medieval church were made in the Birmingham conurbation, their petrol came in through a dock in a National Park (or didn't come in and fouled the coasts of Cornwall), the goods in the quaint old shop-window are imported from half the world, the welcoming fire in the pub burns coal from northern mines, the red-shaded light uses electricity carried on miles of country-striding pylons, the dinner plates were made in the Potteries, the knives in Sheffield, the clothes, the furniture, the goods of all kinds were made in hundreds of factories all over Britain; telephones, books, papers, water, roads, railways — the village makes full use of everything an industrial economy produces.

To assess the effect of such a village on the landscape it is no longer enough to notice how snugly it lies in a hollow of the hills, how the church is set on a slight rise and perfectly framed in trees, how the old cottages grow into an organic whole which is the High Street, how they are built in the local stone and style, contained by a curve of the stream on one side and the rise of the hill on the other, with fields flowing up to the back gardens.

If that were the whole of the picture then the life of the village would still be the subsistence farming it was for the people who built it — 'nasty, brutish and short' as it still is over much of the world. As a setting for modern life the village is as unreal as a coach-lamp wired for electricity. It is also a form of environmental cheating, of preserving one landscape at the expense of another, for if its life were fairly represented in its landscape the village would be surrounded by its own proportion of all the industries and services it lives by. It would have its own part-share of a hundred factories, its part pylon, part coalmine, part spoil-heap, part dock, part oil-fouled beach, part motorway, part urban sprawl and part everything else we don't like. The fields and stream would no longer encircle its charming gardens, and its views would not be rural. For every one of us now is a destructive urban influence on the countryside whatever we do and wherever we live. Our modern Arcadian comforts are provided by industrial areas, and if the view from our windows is still Arcadian we are living at the expense of someone else's landscape.

# 6. The Disturbed Landscape of Industry

In the pre-industrial landscape there were two elements: an agricultural countryside and compact settlements. The countryside supported the settlements and they in turn provided services like markets and shops for the countryside. Everything in such a scene had meaning and relevance in the same fairly simple context, and this created a strictly coherent landscape pattern of great natural harmony.

This long-developing unity was suddenly disturbed by the Industrial Revolution, and in the last two centuries we have produced a large variety of new land-uses which only have one thing in common – they seldom create valid new landscapes. In time industrial use may achieve its own landscape identity, but at present it is little more than destruction of the old pattern, and is therefore most usefully discussed under the non-committal name of disturbed landscape.

The first and most violent disturbance was the early industrial cities based chiefly on coal, and these are the 'dark Satanic mills' of Blake's 'Jerusalem' (that hilariously unsuitable theme-song of Women's Institutes). Their expansive nineteenth-century prosperity has declined in the twentieth, and these areas of the old heavy industries are now the saddest places in Britain. There are many poor people, thousands of houses are classed as unfit for human habitation, and the nightmares still linger of mass unemployment and the exploitation of poverty.

I grew up in the West Riding of Yorkshire during the Depression, when the men were out of work on street corners and all my friends had bow-legs from rickets (fortunately for our own family legs my mother had a mystic faith in milk), but since conditions are better now I went back recently to find how much things have changed. I wanted especially to find what had happened to a sinister place in a deep hollow where very high buildings made of half-rotten planks rose shakily out of the dampness and gloom. In a room at the top sat rows of pale women with sewing-machines, and I used to climb up to collect the shirts they made for our family, treading warily on the side of the sagging stairs for fear the whole flimsy structure should collapse with my extra weight. The shirts cost 1s. 3d. to make for my father and 9d. for my brother, which was cheaper than ready-made, and it seems odd that shirts were made to order at both ends of the economic scale.

But things have improved, and that perilous edifice no longer exists (except in my occasional nightmares of buildings collapsing beneath me), replaced by brave new blocks of flats already grown shabby. The street where we lived is still there, however, and surprisingly self-respecting; though our back-to-back house had only one small room and a scullery downstairs and one bedroom and a bed-sized cupboard up, and our back-to-back neighbours' daughter practised endless hesitant scales on a piano against the flimsy party wall. The lavatory was in the street and we shared it with various neighbours and this my mother minded more than all the rest. As a small child I was very happy in that house, I liked eating my meals on the doorstep and shouting to my friends across the street; but as I grew old enough to realize my surroundings I also grew to loathe the ugliness and dirt and depression I could not escape. I once went to Nottingham and was overwhelmed by its beauty – it was the only place I had ever seen where trees grew in the streets, and I must be one of the very few people whose *Ville Radieuse* is Nottingham.

Our house was clearly a model home compared with the conditions it replaced, for we had sewerage and clean piped water, and even if the sewerage was outside and the water a single tap over a stone sink, yet beside these fundamentals of healthy urban living the rest is trimming. Refinements like bathrooms and hot water may add to the *douceurs* of living but they don't govern the survival rate.

The North-West, however, still has twice the national average of slums, and my West Riding the highest percentage of all, as well as one of the highest proportions of derelict land, for where early industry was based on mining it has left a hideous legacy of land-

*Part of the 150,000 acres of derelict land and one of the millions who suffer it (two if we count the depressed-looking dog).*

scape destruction — 60,000 acres (24,000 ha) of heaps, 60,000 (24,000 ha) of holes and another 30,000 (12,000 ha) of assorted dereliction. In some areas of the North, the North Midlands, and South Wales as much as a quarter of all land is derelict; the minerals have been wrenched from the earth and the waste spewed out like suppurating wounds on the landscape. They might heal in time like the old spoil-heaps in Cannock Chase now cheerful with willow-herb and feathery birches, but it would be an intolerably long time, for much large-scale nineteenth-century dereliction is still hideous a century later: it is solid and made to last like the nineteenth-century town halls it helped to build.

There is a current fashion for admiring all spoil-heaps as 'exciting', but it is confined to the fortunates who have never had to live with them. Those who have 'want to be shot of 'em' or at least their brutal starkness gentled into the landscape. This is the scenery of violence, and in the narrow troughs of the Welsh valleys the menace is overwhelming, as the steep hillsides are piled up threateningly higher and the valley-floors sink above the worked-out coal seams collapsing beneath them.

Yet even the Aberfan tragedy may not be entirely loss if it stirs the public conscience to action. We now have the techniques for restoration – huge earth-moving machines, an increasing knowledge of what plants will grow on waste, methods for 'making' soil, and hydromatic seeding of difficult areas. The Civic Trust has published an excellent and encouraging book on reclamation, and among other projects a study has been made of the $3\frac{1}{2}$ square miles (6·5 km²) of nightmare dereliction outside Swansea – so excellently viewed from the railway. Things are now even slowly beginning to happen: the Coal Board is anxiously reforming, the Forestry Commission planting tips, the Government makes grants of up to eighty-five per cent of the cost in Development Areas, and where local authorities start improvement schemes private firms will often help.

As important as reforming the old, however, is to prevent new dereliction, which still increases by 3,500 acres (1,400 ha) a year; though some new workings can be organized surgical operations, controlled and clean, leaving healthy wounds which quickly heal, like new-style open-cast mining, and gravel and ironstone working. But there is still new spoil to dispose of, and since it is essentially inefficient that by-products should be wasted (and no doubt a sign of our still-primitive industry) the ideal disposal is efficient use. This is now happening increasingly, and just as city dust-heaps were used to make nineteenth-century bricks, so nineteenth-century slag-heaps now make roads and tennis courts and even produce low-grade coal. Domestic waste and sewage sludge are also increasingly converted to compost, and the five million tons of pulverized fuel-ash produced yearly by modern power-stations makes building material, road embankments, 'soil' for agriculture, and near Peterborough is restoring 2,000 derelict acres (800 ha) of old pits.

Solid waste, however, is not the only form of pollution, for we also foul, and irretrievably, our air and water. Air pollution is a human rather than landscape problem, though it limits the species of plants in cities (the Kew Arboretum has moved out to Surrey) and produces the famous dark variety of moth to suit sooty tree-trunks and delight entomologists. But most city air is now cleaner if not purer, and our rivers too are slightly less polluted; though if we shall only be civilized, as one critic holds, when salmon come back up the Thames, then this still seems some time off, since the only thriving resident of the putrid lower reaches is a small red worm. Yet this was once a good salmon river, and Henry II had a polar bear which he let out on a rope from the Tower of London to fish for itself, and even in the eighteenth century the ditches round Westminster were full of water-lilies. However, there are hopeful portents, and the filters for the cooling water at Fulham power station now catch live fish as well as rubbish. Fortunately too the swift run-off of Britain's water to the sea mostly prevents the disastrous build-up of pollution which is happening in Lake Erie. In *Man and Environment* Robert Arvill shows with horrifying clarity how man is everywhere fouling the world he lives in.

Some pollution of our environment seems at present inevitable since it is the end-result of processes our economy and way of life depend on, like carbon dioxide; but a vast amount of landscape pollution is completely unnecessary. Industry has developed an attitude of criminally careless squalor and of using the public landscape as a private rubbish dump; old buildings and machines, derelict huts, decrepit fences, battered oil cans, old hard-standings, rotting dumps of building and industrial rubbish – all are simply abandoned when no longer needed and remain to foul the landscape for generations to come.

The Armed Forces are scarcely better. It is bad enough that they commandeer beautiful areas (why not use derelict land?) and seal them off behind a smoke-screen of security, but it is intolerable that when they give them back they should leave behind the sorry mess of old huts and concrete and so on that everyone knows too well as eyesores in beautiful places. Tens of thousands of acres are due for return, and old-fashioned precepts about leaving things as we found them are valid whatever the scale.

At every level we despoil our environment, for as private citizens we equally spread rubbish and spread it increasingly widely. People have always dumped, but old-style rubbish was perishable and new-style is not, and hollows and roadside spinneys are now sordid with old tins and bottles and worse. Are there still Councils who don't collect ordinary domestic waste? Otherwise why do people carry it abroad to be rid of? Not all can be gypsies, and certainly anything not collected officially at doors is likely to be found unofficially in ditches.

Large-scale rubbish from old cars to old radios is even more intractable, for though the affluent society encourages us to buy new possessions it has declined to rid us of the old ones, and though prams and mattresses and television sets may be expendable they are not disposable, and it is scarcely surprising that they finish as landscape litter. The recent Civic Amenities Act enjoins local authorities to collect abandoned cars which should now disappear as common elements of our scenery. Councils are also to provide tips where tidy citizens can dump their larger cast-offs. But we still have to take them there, and if tips are distant and virtue frail won't near-by ditches still tempt on dark nights?

Much of housekeeping, like gardening, consists of keeping our environment tidy, and our urban and rural landscapes are like a huge-scale house and garden which need a huge-scale tidying-up. This alone would make an astonishing improvement, and once clear our landscape needs keeping so – by persuasion, coercion or any way which works – if need be by simply collecting everything without question and putting the cost on the rates: it could scarcely cost more than the present policy.

Derelict land and litter are anti-social destruction of our environment and the need for reform is clear, but most recent landscape disturbance is the legitimate, even if often not the appropriate, spread of urban development. The population explosion of the nineteenth century was far more violent than ours, and trebled the population, but its incidence was far more concentrated; the cities spread but were still held together by the gravity of their central mass. For cities are pools of people and spread like water, and without easy transport are like water in a hollow. As gravity holds a lake together by the difficulty of moving uphill, so the old towns were held together by the difficulty of travel, and the need to keep in touch with the centre was a powerful centripetal force. When population increased it was like adding water to the lake – deeper, more concentrated at the centre, and the least possible spread because of the uphill effort of travel.

But modern transport has removed the effort, like levelling the hills round the lake, and our new mobility is a centrifugal force which has scattered new development over the countryside in a thin film of living like water on flooded fields. The doubling of urban areas between 1900 and 1960 spread to $4\frac{1}{2}$ million acres (1,800,000 ha), and this extravagant use of land has often left inner districts half-developed, with too few people to make true communities. For it is easier and cheaper to start with an empty field than to fit new development into an existing framework; small projects mean small profits, limited elbow-room makes action difficult, and new fields have therefore been taken in quantity, leaving the odd bits and pieces of land unused. Round every city there are areas which may be vaguely classified as open space but are often quite simply waste land accumulating litter, and I still remember from my childhood the squalor of the patches of ground where we played between houses and factories. (Not that we minded: to us they were adventure play-grounds and these are commonly successful in direct proportion to their ugliness.)

This uncontrolled 'clutter and sprawl' is the development attacked in books like Ian Nairn's *Outrage* and Lionel Brett's *Landscape in Distress*. All sense of an urban environment is lacking, but we are certainly not in the country; it is disturbed landscape, where every kind of unsuitable misuse is mixed up with what Lionel Brett acidly describes as 'twentieth-century residential development in its pure form undistorted by planning'.

Yet not all unplanned residential development is bad, and despite the scorn of intellectuals the suburb is the one authentic new type of landscape which our century has created. Much of Surrey for instance is excellent suburban landscape; farming was never profit-able on these hungry soils (Marshall said even the rabbits starved) and since farming resists invasion by other uses in proportion to its own prosperity, this almost unused and well-drained land was an obvious site for London's housing and recreation, turning much of the area into an extended residential park and country playground.

It is fashionable to decry Surrey; Cobbett was an early sneerer ('the buildings consist generally of tax-eaters' showy tea-garden-like boxes') and much criticism is just such irresistible catch-words

*The edge of Leeds from the air. As much land is wasted as used. A littered landscape even at this distance, and worse still at ground level.*

(Stockbrokers' Tudor and the Scampi Belt). I have never liked Surrey since I first came south and suffocated in its suburban countryside after the bleak northern Pennines, but that is unfair. Surrey has done many things extremely well, and done them as a pioneer without earlier experience to profit from. As urban life in a green setting it is many people's ideal environment, and despite mass invasion from London the Surrey Hills are still an official and real Area of Outstanding Natural Beauty.

But Surrey is highly prosperous and heavily wooded – an excellent beginning for any residential landscape. Most of our suburbs have no such advantages, and at a less expensive level suburbia is less successful. There are few more depressing landscapes than sliced-up rows of houses with skimpy gardens and more fence than green; nor does spreading out such suburbs improve them but merely makes them draughty. This is the landscape of William Plomer's *No Identity*:

> . . . a shallowly-rooted community, a huddlement
> Of not very settled commuters, interspersed with retired
> Couples, tending to dwindle to widows,
> Little communal sense or parish pride,
> And the usual private or commonplace fears
> Like that of being moved to some distant branch
> Of one's place of work, or of cold old age.

Identity apart, however, we quite simply have not got space to house us all in garden-suburb style, and existing low-density areas near cities are already regarded as valuable future sites when the houses can be pulled down as obsolete, like the eighteenth- and nineteenth-century villas.

Resistance to spread became firm in the 1947 planning controls, with the heartening result that eighty-five per cent of Britain is still classed as rural. But though this sounds wonderfully reassuring we should rejoice with caution, since land-use on paper and landscape on the ground can be disastrously different, and planner's Rural may well be country-lover's Disturbed. 'Country' is a concept which depends not on land-use percentages but on our reaction to the scenery, and our countryside is invaded by all kinds of developments which may cover little land on paper but which disturb the rural character for very large areas. It needs after all only a scatter of footprints to change untrodden snow to trodden, and eighty-five per cent of Britain is not untrodden country.

Ribbon-building and scattered non-rural housing are obvious examples, since farmland, especially in its increasingly treeless state, can absorb only a small number of even the most inoffensive houses discreetly sited, and most of our houses are not discreet and are not lost in the rural landscape; on the contrary it is the rural character which disappears. Yet houses are small and human and potentially sympathetic: if even they obtrude what hope is there for the rest? Pylons for instance, however well designed and carefully routed, are too large, too alien, too unmistakably organized for a mechanical world ever to be absorbed in small-scale organic landscapes. They stride across our intimate countryside like files of linked giants. Though our very dislike of course is proof of our prosperity, and developing countries cherish their pylons as we do our pylonless landscapes. Even here, incredibly, I meet people who admire them, but I am not one. I abominate pylons as I do the Eiffel Tower and the old Forth Bridge and all such fidgety criss-cross Meccano-like constructions. I accept them in the landscape only as anyone would who brought up a family without electricity or gas and with only the wartime coal-ration for part-time fires and cooking. Even now I never quite believe that simply by pushing buttons I can have hot water and a cooking stove and a warm room to sit in, and rather than lose my miracle buttons I could welcome the largest-size pylon in the middle of the garden.

Of pylons and other landscape problems the Central Electricity Generating Board are acutely conscious. Much of their recent work is exemplary, as is their patience with customers who complain in the same breath of cuts in power and of the pylons to carry it. Certainly undergrounding is not the answer except in exceptional places, for besides many technical difficulties the extra cost is up to a million pounds a mile (1·6 km). Those who cheerfully demand undergrounding seem to feel it would be paid for by some quite extraneous fund, whereas all the millions would go on their electricity bills, and on those of people who can barely afford their own cooking stove, much less other people's scenery. In any case under-

*Except in superlative scenery, putting cables underground is a poor way of spending money available for amenity. The whole of this landscape in London's Green Belt could be rescued and restored for the cost of getting rid of the pylon. Since this was taken, the car has gone and the tree died completely. Nothing else has changed.*

grounding is very poor amenity value for money, and at up to £200,000 per pylon we could get rid of far worse eyesores.

Pylons moreover do not disfigure the permanent landscape, and they can quickly disappear if new research makes them obsolete, and this we should insist on. Farmers are less disturbed by pylons than by undergrounding, especially since new designs give clearance for machines. Roads are a far worse disruption of the farming pattern and new roads necessarily slice up lowland farms. The old roads often evolved from farm-tracks (their meanderings show how carefully they are skirting Farmer Jones's field) but since new motor-roads are not laid out in right-angle bends for the benefit of field-corners, they

117

dismember farms ruthlessly, as railways equally did, slashing across the carefully worked-out landscape of enclosure. Visually too roads tend to disrupt the country, not in themselves, since good roads enhance the landscape, but by attracting other development like filling-stations and lamp-standards. (Architects commonly detest lamp-standards, but why? Inevitably there are bad designs, but the best are elegantly simple, and their much-abused verticals are only the natural verticals of tree-trunks in stylized form. There are plenty of uglier things to campaign about, like discordant advertising on railway property in country places.) Nonetheless lamp-standards good or bad are unmistakably urban and can change a rural road to a city tentacle; they would certainly transform our motorways if continuous lighting were ever adopted.

Urban leisure is a further disturbance, not only all the mobile paraphernalia of modern holiday, but holiday bungalows, caravan sites, filling-stations, cafés and so on built permanently into the landscape. The coast suffers most with double the average urban development, and only a third, so Enterprise Neptune considers, is still worth fighting for. Two thirds of what we inherited little more than a century ago is now too sick to recover, yet for its size Britain has a longer and more variously beautiful coastline than almost any other country.

The coast is particularly at risk, but its fate is only an exaggeration of the widespread disturbance of the countryside. Wherever our new land-uses spread our landscape is in trouble, and near urban areas is like a house occupied haphazard without a plan, simply by unloading the arriving furniture into the nearest space. Far more rooms are cluttered with ill-assorted belongings than would ever have been needed in a properly-planned occupation, and where areas are undisturbed it is chiefly because they were inconveniently distant from the source of clutter. The cause most commonly blamed for our landscape shortcomings is profit – that the land has been callously exploited to make money for its owners. But profit is neither good nor bad, it is simply a motive; it is a legitimate purpose of most development, a form of functionalism which can produce excellent results, as in the old farming countryside. But to do so it must be interpreted both widely and long-term. It is proverbially unprofitable to kill the goose that lays the golden eggs, and equally so to defile thriving industrial areas so that new development shuns them. 'Where there's muck there's money' is a brutal adage now proved disastrously false.

But short-term profit has only been part of our trouble, and the lack of planning is at least as important. The first explosive spread of the new land-uses was completely beyond the control of individuals; planning could only come from above, and the necessary powers were lacking. So was the necessary knowledge, for the new-powered industry was an utterly unfamiliar phenomenon whose coming was swift and violent, destroying the old society and bringing a new one to painful birth. We are only now by deliberate study beginning to understand what is happening to us, and to plan the control of our development.

In terms of landscape there is a further reason why our new land-uses have not produced good scenery, and this is a new difficulty inherent in the industrial use of land. In industry land-use means something fundamentally different from land-use in agriculture, for it is a term which covers two quite separate concepts – one is the use of the area as a site, the other the use of the actual ground. These may be the same, in which case 'land-use' covers both as it does in farming – where an area of country is classed as agricultural (the site-use) and the process of farming uses the earth itself (the ground-use). But with industrial uses this is commonly not so, and if the same area is used for instance for urban recreation, then this is a site-use only: the recreation makes little use of the actual land, it is not a ground-use, and this must therefore be provided by other methods. Many industrial uses are chiefly site-uses. A factory or a generating station for instance covers only part of the land (the ground-use) and the rest is a site-use only: the installation needs land simply as elbow-room, but unless the unbuilt-on ground is otherwise maintained it deteriorates. It is like an unoccupied room in a house – since no one uses it no one cleans it or keeps it tidy; it is a backwater which silts up with all the litter of living.

Such neglected ground now covers surprisingly large areas round our cities, it is a new negative form of dereliction, of dereliction by default, a potential ill of much industrial landscape which can only be cured by a deliberate policy for using the ground. The past cannot help us here since pre-industrial land-uses were almost entirely composite site and ground-uses, not only farmland but also pre-transport towns which covered their sites compactly, and the maintenance of industrial land in its widest sense is an urgent new problem which we have barely yet recognized, far less solved. In itself this is difficult enough, but it is also greatly aggravated by our patchy and incomplete use of land, and also by 'planning blight' on land scheduled for future development and meanwhile neglected. We now have thousands of acres with no more landscape coherence than the debris following an explosion, and seen from the air the comparison is inescapable – our new development has exploded in the old agricultural landscape, destroying the old pattern without producing a new.

In Britain industry has got what industrialists would call a bad image. And no wonder when we look at most industrial areas. 'Evil communications corrupt good manners' – they certainly have in industry. We have treated it like a pariah and not unnaturally it has behaved like one. It is the usual vicious circle of bad making worse. In the old agricultural economy, where work was done by a separate working class, the non-workers lived civilized lives in civilized settings while the workers lived in whatever settings the work produced. Since, however, the old ways of farming created a civilized landscape, workers and worked-for lived in the same environment. But this was the countryside's good fortune; farming was nonetheless governed by profit not aesthetics, and when the same attitude was transferred to industry the results were very different. At first there was no suspicion of the horrors ahead, and it was in this early and innocent stage that the Wedgwoods built their new family mansion opposite the factory at Etruria in Staffordshire, living on their working estate as landowners always had done.

But the subsequent history of Etruria could serve as a parable of the rest; for the factories proliferated; coal was mined in the earth below, piling out waste on the land above; the worked-out seams collapsed and carried the potteries ten feet (3 m) below the level of the canal, narrowly missing the mansion; outside the windows a steel-works mushroomed up, and a neighbouring field is used for special research in toxic pollution. The once-proud stately home long ago ceased to house Wedgwoods and is now the headquarters of the mill which dominates it, overlooking a devastated landscape which stretches to the horizon when the air is clear enough to see. In this ravaged environment the workers still live, but the local people I asked for directions to the mansion had never heard of the Wedgwoods.

As the industrial revolution progressed, work and leisure thus existed, not only in separate classes as they always had done, but also in separate areas — a far more dangerous division for the landscape. For the separate worlds were now so incompatible that those who might have alleviated the horrors avoided the ugliness they could no longer control. Work and leisure still largely do exist in separate landscapes, for who spends their spare time among slag-heaps except students of the old conurbations and writers taking photographs? Most people still work in ugly places, and leisure is escape both from work and its setting, as if man at work and man at play were different species in different worlds. It is an attitude we have inherited with the derelict land which is one of its consequences, and like derelict land it is essential to rid ourselves of it before we can create good landscapes for land-uses now almost wholly industrial. In our new society we all work: we also all have leisure in the areas where we work — all-the-year-round evenings and week-ends, quite apart from escapist annual holidays. It is therefore no longer even an efficient much less a humane solution to divide the scenery into good and bad and ignore the bad — we cannot ignore industry in an industrial economy.

And if we look dispassionately at any installation it is seldom the essential work which is unsightly, but the casually-accumulated squalor of its surroundings. In such a setting a palace would be degraded. But manners can be reformed, old sites cleared up and made seemly, and new ones planned as self-respecting concerns. What has made the old conurbations so depressing, however, is not the dereliction but the inertia. The dereliction could be restored, what is lacking is the new life to carry the restoration. But already the new efforts are beginning to show, and it is this first almost imperceptible progress which needs most faith and takes most energy — to check the downward drift and reverse the decline. Like a tide turning there is a long period with seemingly little change, yet once started the process can gather momentum at exhilarating speed. Hope feeds on achievement, and one laborious improvement can beget ten confident others and bring new life.

Happily much new industry is more tractable than the old. Nuclear power for instance produces no mass waste nor air pollution and needs no large supplies of dirty fuel, while planning controls can help to reform the inconsiderate, both by making permission conditional on careful development and by considering the past record of applicants like gravel companies. Nor has much of the new manufacturing industry any reason to degrade our environment. Clearly light industry is little problem and belongs in living areas with schools and shops and other public buildings, adding interest and variety and cutting down journeys to work.

Even some larger industries with their new reforming manners could well be sited in living areas with mutual advantage to both; though public opinion still resists this, and there may be valid objections like noise, or too large scale for the domestic landscape. Nonetheless new factories can be palaces of marble and plate glass and tropical plants in the old world of pits and derelict land, with workers who 'walk about resplendent in white coats and hats like a congress of cricket umpires pressed into service. For many the main job is to make sure the machines do the right things.'

Since the products of modern industry are increasingly highly processed, the most important raw material of new-style enterprises is often the skills of its workers. Unattractive industrial areas will therefore be increasingly inefficient for the future, since it is the skilled élite who particularly avoid them. A bad environment creates a disastrous brain-drain, and the old conurbations are increasingly anxious to be rid of their 'soot and shirt-sleeves image', and to 'soothe the anxieties of southern-based executives who feel only horror at the thought of a spell somewhere north of Barnet'. Durham's clear-sighted aim is 'to improve the image of our region, which means more than anything else upgrading the quality of the landscape'. This has long been the policy of the German Ruhr, where large restoration schemes are undertaken to keep workers in the area and attract new life, and our Imperial Chemical Industries is currently spending £165,000 on six TV commercials to enhance its image.

The very structure of modern industry is changing its nature, for size now means efficiency, and industries tend either to grow or to disappear (the 'eat or be eaten' law of nature); and in huge modern firms the simple personal profit motive of most early industry is replaced by concern for prosperity, of which profit is only part. To appear prosperous is to attract not only customers but investment and skilled workers, and therefore good architects are employed for new development, and even landscape architects to design its setting. For, as the Director-General of the Cement and Concrete Association frankly announced, 'good landscape is not only necessary in the public interest but it is also good public relations and therefore good business'.

'I think that our architecture is still slightly apologetic' said Sir Christopher Hinton of industrial building. But it should not be. Modern architects and engineers can build excellently for industry — are in fact better at working design for Martha than luxury for Mary. Industry suits the technical imagination of the modern world, and it is surely a portent of dawning pride that the *Financial Times* now makes an award for good industrial architecture. Why not also an award for the good industrial landscape we equally need to encourage?

# 7. Local Land-Uses in the Uplands

After the lowlands the uplands are astonishingly empty: wide expanses of bleak and barely-habited hill-country where the commonest buildings are ruined cottages. From Caithness to Cornwall the empty hills are dotted with the empty homes of their lost population, some long abandoned with sheep lying against the tumble-down walls, others so newly deserted that glass still shines in the dark windows, but all of them part of the past like the life they sheltered.

The Highlands of Scotland are one fifth of the land-area of Britain, yet their population is about a quarter of Glasgow's, with hundreds of square miles of mountains where no one normally sleeps. The Highlands are an extreme case where the land and the climate are worst and the isolation most destructive, but they are only an exaggeration of conditions throughout the uplands. As early as 1773, Boswell in his *Journal of a Tour to the Hebrides* tells of glens deserted as the Highlanders left for America, and the depopulation has continued since with only minor variations. Despite active efforts to prevent it the numbers are still falling; in the four Highland counties (excluding Caithness with Dounreay) the 222,500 in 1951 fell to 214,000 in 1961, and the figures for Mid Wales show a similar loss.

Roughly 18 million acres (7,200,000 ha) of Britain are classed as mountain-moorland, mostly above 800 feet (240 m), and although this is over a quarter of our land area it produces only four per cent of our agricultural output, varying from one sheep per acre (0·4 ha) on 'good' land to 10–15 acres (4–6 ha) per sheep on bad. Even the good land is marginal and therefore vulnerable to economic changes, and bracken-invaded fields and ruined walls show where the valley farms once reached higher up the hillsides.

Hill farming is by no means homogeneous: holdings vary from a few acres to vast areas of mountain, and problems vary in the Yorkshire Dales, or the Cheviots, or grassy Wales, or the barren Highlands. But the underlying conditions are the same – a poor habitat producing a poor living – as little as £4 to £5 a week for crofters. 'Crofting is not a way of life but a way of death,' says one observer, and though crofters are an emotional conception rather than a group with significant numbers (one-fifth of the sparse Highland population) their life is little worse than that of many small upland farmers. Hill farming was scarcely affected by even the agricultural much less the industrial revolution, and has changed little through the centuries. It is here that the old local traditions are still remembered, the old languages and customs, all the local colour in fact which we admire as urban visitors.

The structure of hill farming is very distinctive; sheep are the chief agents for extracting what little virtue there is in the poor land, with cattle as an alternative on better ground, and in Scotland the much-discussed and mostly patrician deer. The profit from hill sheep is chiefly in the sale of lambs bred on the upland grazing during the summer and sold in the autumn sheep-sales to lowland farmers for fattening. Ewes are also sold for cross-breeding with lowland strains, and young cattle are sold in the same way as lambs. Wool is a further product, but it is not high quality and is now threatened by synthetic fibres. This traditional system profits very little from modern methods, so that whereas on lowland farms production per man has soared and can therefore support a rising standard of living, in the uplands the same labour still brings much the same return. Sheep are still managed by shepherds on the open hills as they have been for centuries, and an average flock for one man is 500 ewes, which on poor land means a daunting area of ground to cover, necessarily on foot and in all hill weathers.

Hill farmers thus grow steadily poorer, and the chief effect of new developments is not to improve their lot but rather to increase the already wide gap between uplands and lowlands. No one supposes (least of all the farmers) that hill farming could survive without support in the modern economy. In the crofting counties sheep bring 4s. 6d. per acre (56 new pence per ha) a year, and of this pittance

125

sixty-six per cent is subsidies, while for cattle-raising the subsidies are 123 per cent.

Even so hill farming has not prospered but is now in serious trouble, and the present decline seems far more fundamental than its past vicissitudes. Prices for sheep and cattle have been falling steadily even though costs have risen – 'The last few years have separated the men from the boys,' said one Caithness farmer, 'and this year (1966) is separating those with resources from those without.' Many farmers did not cover their year's expenses, and had to sell at a loss because they lack winter grazing to keep their animals; few could afford the essential lime and fertilizers for their land, and excellent hard-working men were facing bankruptcy. Conditions have since improved with the easing of credit, but essentially a system which does not benefit from modern methods cannot prosper in a modern economy; there is also the more immediate problem of an all-eggs-in-one-basket structure dependent on lowland buyers.

'There are changes in consumer demand' is the ominous explanation, for lowland farmers are losing interest in upland sheep. 'Where there's stock there's trouble' says one, and, as hill farmers are finding to their cost, other and more mechanized crops than sheep are being used to vary mechanized lowland grain-growing. The future of hill farming is therefore debatable, and there is little encouragement in the *Report of the Land Use Study Group* for the Natural Resources Committee. This questions 'the justification for sustaining the sparse population eking out its precarious existence in uneconomical hill areas largely at the expense of the nation', and its depressingly revealing figures prove hill farming's basically unprosperous nature. Even these figures are over-sanguine since they 'cannot take account of the willingness of the small farmer and his family to devote time and energy to their enterprise far beyond what is expected of ordinary industrial workers, and the small farmer does not have to cost his own, or his wife's hours of labour'. Small farmers and their families, however, are proving less willing to work for nothing, and the question then arises whether the money and the land could not also be better used in other ways. Sweden with similar problems believes they can be, and is concentrating labour and investment in more productive areas.

In Britain, however, we regard the continuing depopulation of the uplands as a continuing tragedy. But why? For despite our romantic urban notions the mountains are not the home of free and independent spirits but chiefly of depressed and poverty-stricken people, and the Good Life is not lived in desolate hills on National Assistance. All poverty is a prison, but poverty in the uplands is prison in a wilderness. The old way of life, whatever its antique virtues, is now rejected by those who know most about it, and improved local conditions have not persuaded hill people to stay. Piped water and electricity are now common, and the motor-car has vastly improved life on more prosperous farms, but such limited benefits are also a glimpse of what modern life offers and are therefore a stimulus to move. It is why new roads and bridges are equivocal remedies; they make the lowlands accessible as well as the uplands, and if easier transport reverses the movement of population it will be reversing history.

Of various experts asked for reasons for keeping people in the uplands only one cynical (Tory) planner gave a straightforward answer: 'safe seats for Tories'. But even with a Labour government, and for whatever reasons – the four per cent of our food-production, ancient tradition, local colour for visitors, maintaining the upland landscape as we know it, preserving a resident population for potential future development – official policy is still support, and was clearly restated in a recent White Paper. The grants for improving land are to be continued, so are the subsidies on animals sold. Also, as in the lowlands, amalgamation is to be encouraged by special powers and grants. For many hill farms are impossibly small; more than a quarter of all Highland crofts are less than five acres (2 ha), and in Wales the old law of inheritance called gavelkind divided the land between the children at every generation, resulting in holdings of sometimes a single small field.

It has been estimated that about $3\frac{1}{4}$ million acres (1,400,000 ha) of hill land might be improved, and one farmer in north Pembrokeshire for instance has done what he calls 'a creative job with a bulldozer', flattening seven miles (11 km) of the local turf walls and making thirteen small farms into one 500-acre (200 ha) unit. The improved land now supports pigs and turkeys as well as store cattle and lambs, production has doubled and the farmer is naturally delighted. But we

127

once shared a cottage there on the cliffs in the old days of water fetched from the spring and candles to go to bed by, and with our only company in the sandy bays the Atlantic seals and local ravens. And now our much-loved holiday landscape has gone with the seven miles of turf-covered walls and their short sweet flowery grass and the apricot-scented gorse of South-West summers. As Londoners on holiday we grieve for vanished beauties – but the people who live there live twice as well. For improved hill farms are not picturesque, and if upland farmers are to stay, then the upland landscape will change. The old countryside and the new life are incompatible here as everywhere else.

For better or worse, however, much of the uplands cannot be thus improved, and sheep remain their chief product. If lambs cannot be sold to the lowlands the alternative is to fatten them in the uplands; but hill farms lack grazing, especially in winter. Some land has been enclosed and improved, and experiments tried with quick crops of rape and fodder radish, and of seeding grass direct on to peat with the necessary fertilizers. But hill sheep have been bred for hardiness; they are not good lambers nor good at converting food into meat, and many changes are discussed for the future – Finnish Landrace crosses, housed ewes, stimulated fertility, feeding with silage, lambs fattened on good pasture, stall-fed sheep and so on. The possibilities are various but one thing they all have in common – they have little to do with half-wild sheep on poor mountain grazing, where up to a million hill lambs die each year and the losses in ewes can be catastrophic in bad winters. Red deer not sheep are the indigenous animals naturally adapted to the harsh conditions, and it is considered they might produce more meat than do sheep on the worst land. There are suggestions for raising herds for venison, and some is already produced and exported to Germany.

But other uses for poor land are likely to increase, and in Britain as in other countries commercial forestry is a promising alternative. We grow only eight per cent of our timber, the rest being our highest import after food and oil, and the Forestry Commission was formed after the 1914–18 war to avoid this dangerous dependence on imports by growing more home supplies. Whether or not we still suppose any future war would leave us time to run out of timber,

*The past and future in the Highlands. In the foreground an abandoned croft: in the background new forestry and a telecommunications aerial. Rumster Forest, Caithness.*

future world shortages and high price are other and convincing arguments. It is estimated that up to one-third of hill land could grow timber (though in the Highlands it is nearer one tenth) and our mild wet climate produces the fastest growth in Northern Europe. Forestry is therefore a profitable use of much poor land, and (although current targets are not being reached) the aim is 5 million acres (2 million ha) of public and private forest by the end of the century, sixty per cent on land now bare.

This policy has roused violent opposition both from those who dislike forestry in upland landscapes and from local hill farmers who see loss of land as a further threat to survival. But forestry also brings them advantages like part-time work, while in inaccessible areas forestry roads are a vital benefit. Even unmetalled roads cost £5,000 to £6,000 a mile (over £3,000 a km) and some landowners have given land for forestry in exchange for sharing such expensive lifelines. The shelter of the new forests can also directly benefit farming; the grazing period is lengthened, animals find protection from the worst of the weather, and in the Highlands, despite loss to

129

trees, some areas now carry up to twenty per cent more sheep than the former windswept hills. When properly integrated, farming and forestry benefit each other (open land prevents the spread of forest fires and infection) and the Natural Resources Committee recommends this combination as the best use of marginal land.

Less convincing is forestry's role in restoring the upland population, though hopeful figures once seemed to prove that timber production would employ one man per eighty acres (32 ha) compared with one man to several hundred for sheep on similar land. With families added this was to mean a large increase, but repopulation by

*A new-style and beautiful Forestry Commission landscape in Wales.*

forestry has proved very meagre. In the whole of the Highlands in 1952 the Forestry Commission employed only 2,152 people, and by 1962 even this number had fallen to 1,708. In Mid Wales the figure rose by 356 but this did little to offset the loss in the same period of 2,767 employed in farming, and whatever its effect on the landscape forestry is not replacing farming in human terms. Forestry workers are now housed, however, in existing communities instead of the early separate villages. These were not successful, and workers with cars moved to larger centres and commuted to work (even the horses commute by lorry in Kielder Forest).

The early farming opposition to forestry is now calming down, and their integration is an important function of the Rural Development Boards proposed for more coherent planning of the use of land. The Boards are to draw up programmes for large areas as a whole, with the necessary powers to carry them out if persuasion fails. The National Farmers' Union on their side urge smaller areas of planting intimately combined with farming instead of the early block afforestation, and this is in any case future policy, based both on new forestry methods and the smaller areas of land available.

These changes will also largely answer the second objection – that forestry spoils the hill scenery. Many people dislike conifers, but these are the trees best suited to poor upland areas and in any case it is softwoods we need. And conifers can be excellent trees like any others, clothing thousands of miles of splendid scenery in North America, and creating some of the most beautiful of all Highland country in the natural pine forests of Scotland. What we dislike is conifers grown by crude commercial methods, and some of the early Commission planting was unfortunate to say the least. The Commission do not deny it, and the harsh fact is that the most profitable way of producing timber (as other crops) does not produce the most sympathetic landscape. But when planting began amenity was still a word of the future, and since cars were few, few people in any case cared about remote hill areas they would never see. The Commission's given task was to produce timber not scenery, and everyone knows the results—crude and unnatural patterns of straight lines and sharp angles in flowing hill landscapes, block-planting of geometric patches of forest on bare hillsides, chequer-board arrangements of different species, straight rows of trees ruled up and down slopes, and extraction roads like wounds slashed across the hills. Worst of all to many hill-lovers is blanket-planting in small-scale scenery, smothering the landscape in a uniform dark fleece of trees (though even here, as one forestry officer ruefully forecasts, there will be an equal outcry against felling when the trees are mature).

Whether by extraneous pressure or endogenous virtue the Forestry Commission is now wonderfully reformed since those pioneer poverty days. Much of its bad work is early, and much recent planting is reassuringly landscape-conscious. The problems are still real, however, and even if block and blanket planting are avoided, lines of land-ownership on maps have nothing to do with a natural forest edge. Trees grow on hillsides as snow lies on mountains, in irregular bays and promontories governed by the slope of the land and the local micro-climate. But forest fences cannot follow such wavering outlines, and however carefully the boundary is suited to the land-form it can never be the irregular fraying-out of a natural forest edge. Trees do not grow solidly up to a predetermined line and then abruptly cease, as if the plantations had been edged by some kind of monstrous mowing machine. In large-scale planting, however, the boundaries may be hidden in folds of the hills, or otherwise softened with deciduous trees which merge the forest into the farming or natural landscape.

Much of the planting (the rows for instance) is governed by efficient methods of working, but often quite small variations are making an impressive difference in the new forests – aligning the rows to avoid a viewpoint for instance, or inflecting the divisions between compartments in sympathy with the land, not only improving the distant views of the forest, but avoiding the end-to-end vistas between military ranks of trees. The compartments are also smaller, and harvesting is less often by clear-felling of large areas but by smaller sympathetic clearings, or even by selective felling, producing more natural-looking forest. 'In the husbandry of nature there are no fallows,' as Marsh said in *Man and Nature*. 'Trees fall singly not by square roods.'

The Forestry Commission now accepts that good scenery is part of its job, and the appointment of Sylvia Crowe as landscape consultant is a highly promising sign of future intentions. But however well managed, forestry on the scale now planned will transform our upland landscapes. So far only a proportion is planted, and much is too young to be more than faint rows of regular dots combed across distant hillsides, but as the dots grow to trees our mountain scenery will become very different from the bare hills we are used to. Since farming too will change, a general pattern is likely to develop of fields and farms on the good land in valleys, flanked by rising wooded hillsides with open mountain grazing above the trees. It is a pattern common in Switzerland where the forests protect valley farms from avalanches as with us they protect them from mountain weather, and when farming and forestry are sensitively integrated they produce a balanced and beautiful landscape. Kielder Forest for instance on the Scotland–England border is 72,000 acres (32,000 ha) of large-scale rolling country once uniformly stripped by sheep. Here forestry with its changing patterns of woods and open hills has made a far more varied and interesting landscape.

But there are fashions in mountains like everything else and the fashionable mountain today is bald. There are people who prefer all hills everywhere grazed smooth like lawns, and resist all planting on principle as unnatural. Certainly bare hills have their attractions – an austerity and absoluteness, a stimulating violence which is blurred and softened by trees. But natural they are not. Mountains are only naturally bare above the tree-line, which in Britain now averages about 1,500 feet (455 m) but is potentially higher. The present ubiquitous denudation of our uplands is a man-made and man-maintained landscape; we have stripped the hills of their natural vegetation and reduced them to desert; cold and wet instead of hot and dry but desert nevertheless – dead landscapes scattered with dead cottages. In parts of the Highlands the sense of destruction is overwhelming, mountains murdered twice over by ice and by man.

Our current passion for sheep-mown mountains may well seem an aberration to future generations who grow up with the new forests, and certainly landscape lovers of earlier periods much disliked tree-less hills (though that did not stop the felling). Wordsworth lamented the lost woodlands of the Lake District when a squirrel could travel for miles without coming to ground. Not that he liked the new plantations: 'vegetable manufactory' he called them, and so are all trees grown for timber. But so too is farming and kitchen gardening, yet a ripening wheatfield is beautiful, and plenty of people prefer rows of runner-beans to any flowers. We could admire timber trees in the same way for their straight stems and healthy even growth.

Farming and forestry are not, however, the only land-uses in the uplands, and demonstrably more important than either roast lamb or timber is water. Since the populous lowlands lie chiefly in the rain-shadow of higher land to the west they depend on upland gathering grounds for much of their water, which nature obligingly collects and carries both in water-bearing rocks and in rivers whose course has often decided the site of the dependent settlements. But the settlements have grown to cities, and as our use of water increases yearly so we need ever-increasing supplies from the hills. Water-collection in the uplands is chiefly by the natural run-off of rainfall stored in reservoirs, and these are the chief effect of water-gathering on the landscape. Often they are fine additions to the upland country, like the new man-made lake at Treweryn in the Snowdon National Park, where a man and wife who sat in their car watching the sunset over the water told me that they drove out every Sunday from their home in nearby Bala simply to sit and admire it. For lakes are universally loved, and lakes are water held in a hollow by some obstacle to its flow – whether a moraine made by a glacier or a dam made by an engineer makes little difference to the lake. The problem is less whether the reservoir will look natural, than of deciding the best height for the water, of a suitable design for the dam surroundings, and of the rise and fall of level which can produce unsightly shore-lines. This is a basic difficulty and a chief reason for resisting the use of existing and beautiful lakes.

In the harmonious integration of such new developments landscape architects are invaluable, and are now employed in schemes both for water and electricity. These are often combined, though power alone may be the object, as in the pumped-storage scheme at Ffestiniog where water is electrically pumped in off-peak periods to a deep cwm high up the hillside (an ingenious use of glaciated mountain country) then released at times of heavy demand to flow back through the generators. The loss of power through pumping and regenerating is twenty-five per cent, the gain is in using otherwise unwanted output from a full-time generating plant, and also in the swiftness and ease of control to meet sudden peak loads, like the end of a popular television programme when millions of people all at once turn on kettles and fires to go to bed. And it is odd to realize that the solemn-looking graphs of output remote in the mountains are really a form of programme rating, and that a favourite funny is a national emergency in the generating world.

Other technical developments also seem likely in the uplands.

*The Highland desert.*

Nuclear power stations for instance need load-bearing rock for foundations, large supplies of water for cooling, and until now remote situations as a nervous safeguard against dangers declared non-existent. Such conditions are likely in the uplands, as are the sites for defence installations like Fylingdales, for radio and telecommunications masts, and a whole range of new developments which we have not yet invented but certainly shall. We may not welcome such structures, but there seems little chance of avoiding them; what is essential is to prevent them becoming nuclei for the spread of other

136

*Man-made lake at Treweryn in Wales. The dam (out of sight) is shaped into the hillside and turfed. The generating station is inconspicuous in the hollow below.*

development, and to remove or otherwise screen the surrounding clutter they engender. To keep them in fact remote non-human presences in the large-scale upland landscape.

Mineral extraction, if we judge by recent activity in Ireland, may well become more important, and strict control will be essential to avoid the dereliction of past workings. Anyone in fact proposing to disturb the hills should first spend a wet winter week among the 700 acres (280 ha) of waste from slate-quarrying which are the heart of the Snowdon National Park, a grey desolation of shattered rock dumped in the valleys, and even more depressing than soil-heaps from coal. Something could surely be done to make this area less hideous, if only for practical reasons of holiday trade. Has anyone tried to establish vegetation, perhaps by hydromatic seeding of local plants? There are hopeful green wisps here and there already; even a little help might start an accelerating process of natural regeneration and veil the ravaged landscape in merciful green. The tiered workings on near-by hillsides are a different matter and will doubtless be treasured by industrial archaeologists.

137

*Slate-waste at Blaenau Ffestiniog. The centre of Snowdonia National Park: slate rubble reaches to the far horizon.*

But whatever the drawbacks of industrial development to upland scenery, to upland life it means very definite benefits in new population and prosperity. The newcomers bring new ideas and vitality, and the Fort William area of the Highlands for instance is prospering not only from the 750 jobs at the fine new pulp-mill but also from the stimulus to the whole district. Outsiders bring a fresh approach to old problems, and in the far North it is the newcomers at Dounreay who are experimenting with new ways of upland farming. The Highlands and Islands Development Board are very conscious of the benefits of attracting industry to the uplands, despite acrimonious arguments as to whether the Highlands should be kept as 'the playground of businessmen and the preserve of local lairds', as one unsympathetic observer described it (though with a quarter of Glasgow's population in one fifth of the area of Britain it seems less a question of either-or than of and-and-and).

To industry, however, the benefits of such a move to Ultima Thule are much less obvious, and the Moray Firth plans are making slow progress, to put it mildly. In general, industry in remote areas needs high-quality low-bulk products to make transport costs economical, yet for such products the uplands lack the essential skilled labour. It is hill farmers who want work, not highly trained industrial crafts-men, and even if skilled staff are persuaded to move to the heather they bring new problems with them such as children needing educa-tion to modern standards, and there are already rumours of discon-tent. But if industry is only a partial answer, in some areas it could help to create centres where industrial staff lived with foresters and farmers in communities large enough for modern living, travelling out to work by the increasingly democratic motor-car. Such centres and the countryside round them would also attract people from urban areas, some as holiday visitors but also for week-ends or retirement or even as commuters. (Few people want to be completely remote from either neighbours or services, and 'getting away from it all' really means *half* away from *some* of it – as is proved by the thousands of empty cottages in away-from-it-all places.) In Scotland the demand for convenient cottages is growing fast, and in Wales, where the whitewashed farmhouses dot the hillside across the estuary from the garden terrace at Bodnant, only two, so a local Welshman told me, were lived in by farmers, the rest were urban people who liked the country.

Urban recreation already provides a useful secondary income for many farmers. Bed and Breakfast notices are now common along most upland roads and in the holiday season an empty bed is hard to find. Farmers also take campers on their land, crofters are allowed to take three caravans, teas and the sale of milk and eggs and other produce can also help, and some farmers hire out ponies for trekking.

Not only, however, is the future of hill farming by no means clear, but forestry too, though the doubts are longer-term, may face new problems in the future; for our modern commercial forestry is a completely new development and we therefore lack any experience of its long-term effects. Until now man has cut down trees where he found them, destructively for centuries, with more care recently by selective felling, but never before has he systematically planted and harvested timber. In terms of food production our past forestry has been mostly food-gathering; we are only now moving into the farming stage of growing trees as a planted crop, and we do not know what will happen to the land we grow them on. We do know, however, that continued farm crops depend on fertilizers, and also that first crops on old pasture land produce high yields from the stored fertility, though later the land must be managed like any other arable. Might it be the same for trees? Most forestry land has been pasture of a sort for centuries, and most of the first trees are doing excellently. But will the next do as well? Trees are a taller, slower crop than grain (forty-five years is an average rotation) but perhaps not essentially different, and already in some areas there are difficulties which might be ominous, like slower growth and undecayed conifer litter in a sterile blanket over the mineral soil. Deciduous trees with their more fertile leaf-fall are now being tried; alder and southern beech have done well, and in landscape terms such deciduous planting would avoid the common objections to massed conifers.

But if tree-growing proves to need increasing amounts of fertilizers, less profitable rotations and so on, then might much forestry, like farming, in time prove uneconomic? The uplands need to share the benefits of our industrial economy in more positive ways than by grants and subsidies, and since prosperity must come from the lowlands the hills must sell their produce for profit as in any other commerce. 'The staple of the district is in fact its beauty,' said Wordsworth of the Lakes, and the upland produce most precious now to an urban population is not sheep or timber but scenery. It is therefore essential that the proposed Rural Development Boards should accept urban recreation as a potentially valuable land-use, and the White Paper in fact specifically includes recreation and tourism as 'other uses of land' – proposing grants for camping-sites and holiday accommodation as well as for roads and electricity. This controlled development of the uplands for lowland leisure might end for good the long struggle to live on the inadequate produce of their niggardly soils.

Such proposals, however, always bring moral objections about wasting farmland in a hungry world, and here the telling answer is an easy sum I worked out in round figures to help my poor calculation. The agricultural production of the uplands is four per cent of our whole. We grow half our food. Our human population is 50 million. Our dog population is estimated at 5 million (without counting an estimated 4 million cats and unknown numbers of horses). If four dogs eat as much as one man then by my reckoning our dogs eat the food production of the uplands (not counting the acres of good lowland pasture for horses and the large dairy herds for milk-drinking cats).

We may not relish the uplands as urban playgrounds but while we keep pets we can scarcely be moral about it. This is their logical development in our modern society; it is their true *industrial* use, and where the process is already established it has brought unmistakable new life. In Wales for instance popular centres like Betws-y-coed and Dolgellau are as snug and bright as well-kept dolls-houses. Wales is also triumphantly Welsh, with thriving male-voice choirs (the farmers drive down from the hill farms to practise on winter evenings), with sheep-dog trials, and a national Eisteddfod which looks very serious locally, with HOME RULE FOR WALES painted on bridges in truculent bad lettering, and customers in chemists' shops gossiping in an unselfconscious stream of Welsh punctuated by 'OK's' and 'Kodak film'. In people who love their homeland as deeply as the Welsh love 'purple Wales', well-being can nourish the old traditions as well as poverty and isolation.

This new dependence of the uplands on the lowlands is becoming evident in most developed countries, and Switzerland, for instance, long ago realized that she must sell her scenery. There the poor mountain farms and the thriving tourist centres belong to utterly different worlds, and only meet on the mountain roads where holiday cars from the cities sweep past local country carts dragged by human beings whose life is slightly worse than that of the cows it depends on. The two types of upland inhabitants are like trees growing side by side – one dying of local drought while the other flourishes because its roots have reached the general water-table of industrial prosperity.

# 8. The Uplands and Recreation

There is nothing new in town-dwellers' liking for mountains; it is a natural reaction to the organized comfort of urban living and has developed in direct proportion to the comfort. Celia Fiennes was an early tourist, but curious rather than appreciative, since the seventeenth century was not yet comfortable enough for mountains to come into their own. Horace Walpole is the typical early admirer of rugged prospects, for the eighteenth century was beginning to provide both the easy life essential for contrast and the necessary roads for coach journeys to remote areas. Mountains, however, were still fashionable luxuries for the privileged few, and it was the wider prosperity of an industrial economy combined with the new democratic railways which first brought people in large numbers to find in mountains 'all that is beautiful and sublime'.

Along railway lines through the uplands and to a lesser extent along roads, the new urban visitors spread through the desolate hills, establishing their prosperous urban standards of living side by side with the old hill-farming poverty. It is a contrast especially vivid in Scotland, where Victorians followed their Queen to the newly fashionable and kilted Highlands, and along the old London Midland and Scottish Railway barren mountains make an unlikely backcloth for comfortable Victorian villas in shrubberies of evergreens. This was the setting of the nineteenth-century travel books and amateur water-colours of misty peaks, and this discreet and limited tourism has continued since. Until recently in fact the typical mountain visitor was comfortably off in a comfortable hotel and likely to be middle-aged or more.

These early-type tourists were joined this century by a new kind of mountain-lover, mostly younger, poorer, and in more direct contact with the countryside – walkers, climbers, campers, youth hostellers and students of the natural sciences. This third stage of upland recreation lasted roughly until the last war, and was the happy state of the Lake District as I first knew it in my university days, when we went fell-walking each spring, sleeping (by private arrangements of keys under stones) in empty youth hostels still officially closed for the winter. The sun always shone, there was untrodden snow on the shining hilltops, we never met anyone but local farmers, and cars were so rare that we waved when we saw one.

To know the Lakes at this idyllic stage was an extraordinary privilege. We were 'active', as biographical dictionaries say, at the single moment in time when the Lakes were accessible to poor students (we had holiday leisure, cheap trains and youth hostels) but not yet within recognized reach of everyone. The only relevant comment, however, is how lucky we were to coincide with the tiny span of social history when such conditions existed: a generation before we should never have reached the hills as playground, a generation on and everyone will be there. It was an idyll as brief as the early days of motoring, when the whole undisturbed countryside lay open to any car owner, and towns were places to drive round for pleasure and park where one fancied, and nobody dreamed of our present tribulations.

Everyone now realizes that this Golden Age of motoring has gone for good, but so too has the era of easily reached mountains for our solitary pleasure. The early railways created the first popular centres, and Wordsworth complained that 'the Lakes had now become celebrated, and visitors flocked hither from all parts of England [and the scenery] was instantly defaced by the intrusion'. He waged an angry campaign against the Windermere railway and its effect of 'transferring at once uneducated persons in large bodies' to the Lakes, for Wordsworth only liked uneducated persons as solitary reapers or leech-gatherers or similar examples of local colour and preferably hard at work, certainly not as 'parties of pleasure out-of-doors'. But his angry letters to the *Morning Post* checked neither the growth of railways nor the taste for mountains, and the irascible Cobbett declared that 'the facilities which now exist of moving human bodies from place to place are amongst the curses of the country'. (This from a man who moved his own body from place to place in most thorough-going fashion, and indeed is chiefly remembered for his extensive *Rural Rides*.) What Cobbett wanted, of course, was to travel himself while other people stayed at home, and so do we all, however unreasonably. Ideally mountains would be inhabited by local people, and though easily reached yet still undiscovered by other urban visitors like ourselves.

The National Parks are a first attempt at a policy for the uplands in the age of tourism, and rereading now the commissioned report of 1945 and the others which followed, it is impressive both how exactly they reflect the attitudes of the period and how swift the changes have been since. The reports are statements of excellent intentions for democratic urban leisure by idealists who never dreamt just how very democratic and urban that leisure was going to be, and are written from the viewpoint of a public-school country-lover who foresees everyone using the Parks as essentially like himself. 'Camping is an adventure in itself . . . a way of escape from the cares and complexities of everyday existence into the simple life of the nomad. Much the same can be said for caravanning.' A modern caravan site would certainly surprise him. Nor is there much patience with ' visitors from towns . . . so careless, ignorant or loutish as to leave gates open, take uncontrolled dogs around with them ' and so on, and one wonders what splendid invective would greet the far worse crimes of some modern visitors. Yet the early reports foresaw very clearly the difficulties ahead: 'If the Parks . . . are too few, or too small, the concentration of visitors . . . will lead to the most serious consequences – in damage to amenities, in overloading and dislocation of transport, accommodation and other facilities, in objections by the resident population, and in initial discredit to the National Parks administration.' The trouble has already started in the Lake District and in Snowdonia, small and beautiful areas, long popular, and now within perilously easy reach of large urban congregations.

The original policy of the Parks was clearly stated: to preserve the natural beauty of the chosen areas and to ensure public access for everyone to enjoy them. The Parks were therefore designated and the public encouraged to come and enjoy. And come we have in overwhelming numbers, for a liking for mountain scenery, like the other good things of life, has spread from the once-privileged few to the now-privileged many, and John Smith enjoying Snowdon from his motor-car is the direct descendant (though without the wit) of Horace Walpole enjoying the Alps from his coach. The crucial difference, however, is not the wit but the number of Smiths compared with Walpoles, and looked at by hindsight it is easy to see that a joint policy of preservation and easy access is keeping our cake and eating it, and that the natural beauty of remote places does not survive the mass arrival of holiday admirers.

Like all our landscapes the uplands are in transition; the old pattern is disturbed by new and uncontrolled forces, and the necessary future policy has not yet been worked out. The Parks have struggled to preserve their unique landscape character despite overwhelming pressures, but far more positive action is needed if they are to survive as anything like the Lake District I knew, and also if they are to provide, as they should do, a prototype for the future management of recreation elsewhere in as yet undeveloped areas.

The problem of people in the Parks arises from two chief difficulties: that there are too many of us, and that we come for different and often incompatible types of recreation. Thus one solution now being planned is to recognize the different uses of the Parks, to provide elsewhere for those whose pleasure does not depend on the mountain scenery, and to reduce friction among the rest by attracting different categories into suitable areas. For if planned for specific uses the Parks could take far more people with far less disturbance both to Parks and people than they suffer from the present haphazard invasion.

The first reports on the Parks were concerned with nature-lovers, and whether from limited love or limited transport there were not many of them. Being also natural Country Coders they were little problem to farmers and easily absorbed in the countryside. Such people are still the chief protection of the Parks, but they are far from being the most numerous visitors, and shade off through steady gradations into those who use the Parks as pleasure-grounds with the background scenery only more or less important. Rock-climbing, pony-trekking, group-walking and so on may be ways of exploring remote mountain country or forms of outdoor exercise with the

Parks as open-air gymnasiums, and such free-form sports merge into more organized skiing, boating, ball-games and the always popular spectator-sport of watching other people enjoy themselves. Which was very pleasant on a sunny summer Sunday sitting on a bench on the crowded shore of Lake Windermere, eating ice-cream and watching the mishaps of amateur sailors.

How much the mountain setting adds to such pleasures is not easy to judge. 'Super view', said the pretty teenager sitting beside me and gazing appreciatively at the waves of flowing blue hills across the level water, and she went on to tell me about her home in a poor part of Salford. And whether we quote Book II of *The Prelude* or say more succinctly 'super view' may well be a matter of background rather than response. Nor does everyone approve of the more eso-teric pleasures: 'Too much education beyond this age (fifteen) pro-duces too many social isolates', so one sociologist considers, and who is to say that communing with Nature on a mountain is 'better' than sailing a boat on the lake below? Or that botany is better than ball-games? (As exercises in social living they are clearly worse.) Nor are they mutually exclusive, and from a rare childhood holiday at the seaside I remember with equal delight finding a new flower on the Yorkshire cliffs (it was Grass of Parnassus, as beautiful as its name) and wriggling to the front of a crowd on the promenade to watch a man roll the letters into Scarborough rock.

Whatever way we take our pleasures, in terms of the mountains we are in any case all urban visitors of only slightly different sub-species, and though I would classify myself as a part-time nature-lover living in London, the essential is that I live in London and read (occasionally) the Lake poets, not in the Lakes, and read the London papers. Much less do I live on a poor hill farm with time for neither poets nor papers. No one who reads Dorothy's journal of the Wordsworths' life at Dove Cottage can doubt that their feeling for the mountains is on a different level from our own as mere ordinary mortals. They walked alone in their beloved hills in all seasons and weathers and at all hours of the day and night, and the mountain solitudes fostered the highly ambiguous intensities of their emotional life together. As writers they could even be said to earn their living as local people by exploiting the natural resources.

*Ice-cream by Windermere. How much do the mountains matter?*

Our own status as urban holiday-makers is in any case implicit in the Parks' conception; what matters is how directly our pleasure depends on the Parks' distinctive character. For whole-hearted nature-lovers it depends entirely; for outdoor sports enthusiasts it presumably depends less; and at popular centres it is only one part of the general enjoyment which also includes ice-cream, capsized sailing boats and talks with pretty strangers. Its degree of dependence on the scenery is therefore one factor to consider in planning recreation in the uplands. Equally important is the effect of the recreation on the landscape – whether for instance it needs inbuilt changes like widened roads, lavatories, car-parks, surfaced paths and so on, which destroy the region's character, or whether like walking it is simply a temporary use of the existing landscape. Also important is whether a particular area of country is unique as landscape or whether it exists in quantity elsewhere. Also how vulnerable it is to use. Also how many people the type of recreation will provide for in a given space – the pleasure per acre, which varies from hundreds on sea-side beaches to logically none in mountain solitudes.

What we need is a classification of landscape areas to correspond to the categories of users, so that the two can be matched with least harm to the landscape and most benefit to the users, and American research suggests that six types are needed:

1. High-density areas near cities for day and week-end leisure.
2. Lower-density mixed-use areas in more natural settings.
3. Natural environment areas for walkers, campers and so on.
4. Unique natural areas to be protected.
5. Primitive areas without roads or permanent shelter for what the Americans call wilderness people.
6. Historic and cultural sites.

With the types of recreation areas thus spelled out it is clear that they cannot all be provided in the Parks, and this is one reason why the National Parks Commission has been extended to the Countryside Commission. Provision for leisure is a nation-wide need, and one cause of the Parks being used unsuitably is that suitable alternatives do not exist. We need far more areas in the first two categories – Pleasure-Grounds and Country Parks – to divert from the uplands those with no particular interest in the scenery; or who, if they have, might well prefer groves of flowering cherries and thickets of rhododendrons and roses to bare stony hillsides with four times the rainfall. Even a marginal preference for mountains might be outweighed by the increasing effort to reach them and park the car, and provision of other areas nearer home could greatly diminish the numbers who reached the Parks, like those games in little glass-topped boxes where a ball must be rolled past a series of holes to a finishing-point which only the most determined players ever reach.

But for those who still come despite both deterrents and counter-attractions the uplands should surely provide, and in our cramped islands such vast stretches of little-used land offer obvious sites for large Country Parks carefully contained. Fortunately this is a problem largely solved by our natural gregariousness, for as a general rule the more popular the activity the more communal its enjoyment, and in this lucky law of human nature lies our landscape's salvation. Most of us, even from crowded cities, don't in the least want to get away from other people; on the contrary crowds mean 'we've come to the right place'. Much of the general gaiety depends on the cheerful company of our fellows in holiday mood, and recreation areas are therefore an excellent way of collecting us in a single place and discouraging our spread, as also of providing a large return of pleasure per acre.

The place of such Pleasure-Grounds in the Parks, however, is debatable, though Windermere is there already. This can never again be a 'wild' landscape, but it could be properly developed for far better value on its own established terms. There are plans already for Windermere, and in return (for there must be two sides to the bargain) neighbouring Grasmere and Rydalwater should be protected absolutely from playground uses, as they now are not. These are withdrawn and intimate lakes, and a very little urban invasion destroys their essential character. They are numinous waters, and should be preserved as a memorial to the Lake Poets who made this area world-famous. Cheerful water-sports should be firmly diverted to extrovert Windermere, car-parks and their picnic parties be moved elsewhere, and the irreplaceable landscape guarded for those

*Wordsworth's Rydalwater.*

whose pleasure is simply to come and look. For, as well as its beauty, this area is America's category 6 – a cultural site: there is plenty of other water for boating.

Or if not it can be provided, for the new reservoirs we shall need in quantity are in future to be combined with recreation, as the White Paper on leisure makes clear. 'Arrangements usually are and certainly should be made at the planning stage so that the full recreational possibilities can be taken into account and the appropriate facilities included in the plans.' There are to be no more Water Boards shutting off large tracts of fine country like the Ladybower reservoir near Sheffield, where water and landscape equally are sterilized by edict. Purification by isolation is surely obsolete now that water engineers can deliver to us pure from our London taps water

150

which has already passed through the sinks and baths and washing-machines of Oxford and Reading and goodness knows where else besides.

New reservoirs can therefore be developed as gathering grounds for people as well as water, for whether we accept the Freudian explanations the fact is clear that water attracts us, and on every scale from sea to garden pools. In any landscape it is a magnet which draws us, so that only a few miles inland from crowded beaches beautiful country is commonly deserted. The Dartmoor National Park for instance attracts only five per cent of the annual holiday-makers to Devon compared with eighty-five per cent on the coast; which may be a nightmare problem for coastal planners, but their ill wind blows good to inland country.

Organized tours whether public or private are a further way of channelling visitors in the Parks. Most people like a definite place to make for, and the new mountain centre in Brecon Beacons was swamped from the start with ten times the intended numbers. The hydro-electric schemes are suitable destinations in terms of both visitors and landscape and are increasingly popular; North Wales is particularly enterprising, and the Central Electricity Generating Board boasts a certificate 'for conspicuous services to tourism in Wales'. The leaflet describing the nuclear power station in Snowdonia is in six languages, there are helpful pamphlets with route maps, and eloquent posters selling the Board's work as a tourist attraction – 'A shiver of blue water and the white swing of sculptured concrete – dramatic new vistas await the visitor to the R HEIDOL HYDRO-ELECTRIC SCHEME'. Glamorous Rheidol indeed has won a Civic Trust award for its new bridge and weir, where an unbroken film of water spills over the curving lip like a gleaming sheet of cellophane and shatters on the rocks below.

There is also an ingenious fish-lift to carry the salmon to higher levels, now freed of pollution from the old mines, and a viewing platform for watching the fish leap against the current. (Though there is no satisfying the perfectionists, and ' I don't approve,' said a Welsh voice behind me. ' It encourages the lazy types and the virile ones get crowded out. The stock's bound to degenerate.')

But whatever the future of salmon the future of public interest seems assured (Pitlochry is one of similar attractions in Scotland) and like the Central Electricity Generating Board, the Forestry Commission is valuable in channelling and providing for visitors. It is now accepted here as in America that forests should produce recreation areas as well as timber, and in the Open Forests the Commission has a policy of positive welcome. There are now eight Forest Parks with sites for camping and caravanning and with services like water and electricity laid on, and these have provided hundreds of thousands of camper-nights at an average charge of about twenty-five pence. There are sailing, skiing and signposted walking-routes over forestry land (by no means all forested), also bridle-paths, nature trails and increasing numbers of picnic sites in woodland glades. (Four million people are said to have used these – one wonders who counted.)

A landscape of varied forestry has many advantages for recreation, particularly its capacity for absorbing visitors, and if we feel there are both too many people and too many trees in the landscape we can at least use the trees to screen the people. Forests give us privacy at both landscape and personal level; they also temper the upland climate for humans as well as the sheep, and with trees as windbreaks the sun shines warm in spring and autumn weather which would send us shivering home from exposed hillsides. Forests also provide new interest by vastly increasing the wildlife of the uplands, for much of our wildlife everywhere, lowlands as well as uplands, has gone because we have destroyed its habitats. In their varied stages of growth the forests create a wide range of new environments lacking for centuries in the open hills, and when an area is fenced off for planting there is 'an explosion of wildlife' as one Commission naturalist describes it. The ungrazed vegetation immediately grows taller and voles and mice soon appear *en masse*, providing food for stoats and owls and kestrels and harriers. As the trees develop these move away to other new areas and are replaced by forest birds like robins, finches, firecrests, siskins and crossbills, and by squirrels, badgers, foxes, and the rarer pine-martens, polecats and wildcats. There are also more deer now in England and Wales than since Tudor times, and even in Commission woods on the edge of London there are fallow and roe deer, and muntjacs escaped from Woburn.

The Commission's policy is enlightened, aiming to protect the trees rather than kill the attackers, and even where control is essential, as with deer, there is no indiscriminate killing. Rare creatures like polecats and pine-martens are protected, and harmless ones encouraged; birds for instance by introducing food-plants and thousands of nesting-boxes, and badgers by providing swing-gates through forestry fences which badgers can push open but not rabbits. The new forests in fact are extensive new nature reserves, and the Commission hires out hides to visitors.

In Britain there is probably nowhere undisturbed by man, but in the uplands his influence is thinly spread, and any large areas still more or less natural are likely to be here. Also, since the British uplands were the birthplace of modern geology, there are the classic exposures of ancient rocks which have given their names to similar formations all over the world, and prove such a trial to Russian geologists struggling to pronounce Welsh spelling. Such areas are of essential value no matter how few people visit them, and if their intrinsic and often vulnerable character is once destroyed it can seldom be restored. Many are National Nature Reserves and are officially protected, often requiring a permit to visit them.

A similar policy would protect from over-use equally vulnerable and irreplaceable areas of country, but public resistance would make it impossible. The illusion is widespread that National Parks are national public property, everyone's birthright of fine mountain scenery; even with Nature Reserves there are murmurs of 'undemocratic' and no demands for permits could prevent the mass-ascent of Snowdon. In the nationally-owned National Parks of America entry is limited to suitable numbers and further arrivals are turned away, but our parks are simply designated areas of the general working countryside, privately owned and lived-in and accessible to all by public highways. Nonetheless the greatest pleasure of the greatest number is a self-defeating policy which would destroy the very source of the pleasure. But how do we sort the more suitable from the less? Wordsworth had a conveniently arrogant belief in an absolute difference of kind between the worthy few who could appreciate mountains and the unworthy many who could not – 'artisans and labourers and the humbler classes of shop-keepers' who should not be encouraged 'to ramble to a distance'! But facts prove Wordsworth wrong. The higher the level of general education the more people seek the less gregarious pleasures (the 'social isolates') and thousands more city-dwellers must even now be nurturing a still-undiscovered passion for the still-undiscovered hills.

Access to the uplands is chiefly by road, and in our car-borne society the nearer-the-road-the-more-the-people is a rule which now applies not only to family picnic parties but to walkers and climbers and everyone èlse. Simply therefore to build no roads is an obvious protection, and at present vast stretches of the uplands are thus preserved from our enthusiasm. But where roads exist it is difficult to close them (despite Polperro's brave example) and the measures for controlling traffic in towns are surely a more hopeful possibility. Cars in towns are now restricted by the difficulty of driving and the even greater difficulty of parking so that we can get out. This is control by frustration, and though it clearly has disadvantages, it works in reducing numbers in a way which society accepts as reasonably democratic. It also favours those who care enough to overcome the difficulties (an excellent limitation in the uplands) and a similar policy might control numbers in the National Parks.

It would mean three things – a determined refusal to widen roads or build new ones in vulnerable areas, the provision in suitable places of car parks appropriate to the roads' capacity, and the prevention of casual parking anywhere else. Access and parking should be charged to the users, but how they are paid for is only important if one way of transferring money from private pockets to public services works better than another. So long, however, as the services are partly dependent as now on local rates, progress is likely to be slow, for a penny rate in the average Highland county, for instance, provides less than £4,000 a year. Parking might be controlled by a combination of fines and physical barriers against leaving the road – walls and hedges, or in open country ditches or banks or local boulders. This is already happening piecemeal in other areas; many commons for instance and parts of the Downs are now protected by banks and ditches easily crossed on foot, and many woodland areas by tree-trunks. There are also suggestions for limiting and charging for access to the New Forest, where increasing numbers are causing serious damage.

But even if access were limited in the too-popular places there are still vast stretches of empty hill country for those who genuinely want mountain scenery. We cannot in the same breath complain of the loss of the solitary places and the tragic depopulation of the uplands; but we nonetheless do, and it is chiefly those who lament the one who lament the other. Yet it is only the popular places which have become more popular, the solitudes have never been more solitary. We must simply travel further to find them. We may even have to walk. The North Pennines, the Border country, Central Wales and most of the Highlands are oppressively solitary, emptier now than they have been for centuries. 'Scotland, the Land that Likes to be Visited' – it is the touching title of the official guide to the lonely North.

But before large areas of undisturbed country are made accessible we first need efficient answers to the problems already troubling the National Parks – diversion of unsuitable uses, access control, proper siting of necessary development, and the general protection of the landscape. There are obvious things like care on farmland and guarding against fire in forestry plantations (the first fifteen years are the most hazardous), and also the earnest but essential task of helping visitors to enjoy the uplands with least harm to the countryside and most pleasure to themselves. The National Parks already do their best with information centres, mobile caravans and so on (the Peak Park is particularly lively in this as in other spheres), but their budget is ludicrously inadequate at slightly over a fifth of a new penny per head of the population. The Forestry Commission and the Central Electricity Generating Board are also good at explaining their work to an increasingly interested public, but could not the Forestry Commission find a more persuasive fire-fighting ally than their stereotype stag against a fiery background: The Monarch of the Glen-in-Flames?

Above all there are our horrible habits about litter, for the mess we make is no longer confined to our living areas – we are itinerant polluters of our countryside, shedding litter like loose hairs wherever we go. And since modern packaging is deliberately indestructible the litter is now part of our landscape – tins and tinfoil, glass, waxed paper, plastics of all kinds, as well as the deluge of more perishable paper. In organized recreation areas we can pay for the mess to be cleaned up after us; in other places cunning may work, as on a National Trust common much troubled both by litter and car parking, where licensed ice-cream vans in strategic positions concentrated both the cars and the litter, while their licence fees paid wages to deal with the rest.

But the countryside is too large for such limited cunning, nor are litter-bins as commonly provided much better than the mess they are meant to dispose of; flimsy soon-overflowing containers which often serve chiefly to concentrate the rubbish around them. Something solid and capacious is needed to swallow invisibly whatever we feed it with. Though bins in any form are incongruous in country landscape – especially in the uplands – quite apart from the problem of emptying them. Our litter should go away with us to suitable places: it is the most urgently needed reform of all in the countryside, for compared with the sordid trail we leave behind us the other signs of our passage are insignificant.

Up to now we show little signs of improvement despite the threat of (unenforceable) penalties and the efforts of altruistic reformers. The Civic Trust is an active campaigner, as is the Keep Britain Tidy Group which produces delightfully witty posters much cherished on the walls of sophisticated offices. But too often the impact is on the already converted, and what we need is a huge popular campaign at the level of television commercials, and using all the specifically aimed techniques of modern advertising. And why not a national figure like Smokey Bear of America, born of the Advertising Council and so successful in the campaign against forest fires that despite three times the number of visitors the number of fires has halved? Smokey, say his creators, 'slipped into the hearts and homes of millions of Americans'. And no wonder, for he is an irresistible father-figure who quickly becomes a dear family friend. Children copy him, film-stars smile on him, national societies support him, a thousand fans daily write to him, four million Junior Forest Rangers emulate him, and a hundred million television watchers saw him in the Tournament of Roses. (Roses!)

The uplands are one of our national resources, and if developed far-sightedly by comprehensive planning, these generous stretches of empty and beautiful country could be valuable both for our own use and for tourist revenue. Already this has passed £100 million a year for Scotland, and tourism is Britain's fourth largest export and biggest dollar-earner. For if Britain has grown smaller with modern transport so too has the rest of the world. Whatever our Common-Marketing troubles, no one can suppose that our future will be separate from Europe's, and when the Channel is no more than a county boundary between millions of close neighbours, our uplands could be Europe's recreation area as well as ours, for few places are both as remote in character and as potentially accessible. The very qualities which have led to their depopulation — their rugged wildness and loneliness — are attractions to holiday escapists from cramped urban lives. Even the mountain weather — the two, four, ten times more rain than average, the mists and storms, the snow which lies on high ground for months together and turns the hills to mountains — no part of the upland scene is more authentic than the upland weather. And when the sun shines there is nowhere more delicately beautiful than our western uplands.

From our cosseted comfort we relish austerity — like climbing easy mountains by difficult routes and camping on the snow in winter. Christmas on Snowdon may even become as crowded as August on Windermere, for the South Pole itself was so popular in the International Geophysical Year that a patch of snow was only preserved for study by a pleading notice saying PLEASE KEEP OFF THE SNOW. Only a generation ago we went with Scott to the Antarctic to pioneer and die: now we go with Scott's son to enjoy the scenery and avoid the holiday crowds.

Our comfort is now transportable with oil and electricity and insulated living, so that we can now return at will from stormy mountains to hot baths and central heating. And in cars we can take our comfort with us, travelling through the harshest climate enclosed in a bubble of tropical air; we can savour the weather as we please; walk out into winter or close the doors on our private summer. It is this double environment which underlies our pleasure in mountains (it is what gives wilderness its new double meaning) and deliberately created it seems likely to be the future pattern of recreation in the uplands. Various new schemes are already in progress, including holiday chalet villages and modern hotels, and the Scottish Development Corporation has done a study for a £35 million development in the Cairngorms. The Aviemore centre in the Spey valley is already highly successful – a self-contained urban environment in a mountain setting which provides a wide range of recreation. This is a new combined pattern of young and old, Nature-lovers and the Rest, for even the most devoted lovers of mountain solitudes appreciate comfortable company on winter evenings which begin in the afternoon.

In Scotland any large-scale tourist development may well mean friction with owners of deer-forests, which in 1957 were estimated at roughly $2\frac{1}{4}$ million acres (900,000 ha) – a simple guide to their presence is the extra height of forestry fences. It was long believed that the law of trespass did not exist in Scotland, but it now seems it was not the law that was lacking but the trespassers, and if numbers increase owners may resist public access on private land. Equally, however, society may resist the sterilization of huge areas of land for private pleasure, and already the vast estates of the old aristocracy have broken up, and castles are advertised for sale to all and sundry with thousands of acres of land. Privilege only survives in the right social climate, for where are the hunting-forests which once covered much of the lowlands? Official persuasion to grant rights of access could be very forceful in the uplands, so equally could the profit from deer-stalking by a far wider public than at present. In the general upgrading of all our sports the present hunters of rabbits may soon aspire to deer, as anglers have already progressed from coarse fish to salmon, making salmon-fishing a profitable Highland industry. There is also the new interest of local people in urban-style recreation (like the local farm-boys on our Pembrokeshire holidays who always joined us on the beach, though until we arrived they very sensibly had never thought of immersing themselves in their chilly sea).

New centres created by tourism could be nuclei for other new life attracted by the new facilities, and the large-scale developments could stimulate small local projects, such as modernizing old cottages or the wing of a farm to let to visitors. And why not factory-built easily-erected chalets carefully designed to suit both the upland scene and modern demands for comfort, like the holiday chalets in

*Central square with shops at Aviemore. Short days in winter mean long days in summer. Photograph was taken at 9.30 in the evening.*

Sweden? Perhaps a kind of single-unit motel where visitors could do for themselves, or have meals on the farm or in nearby centres. Crofters are encouraged to put up chalets, but unless well-designed structures are cheaply available it is easy to imagine the makeshift shacks which are only too likely.

In every kind of new development the most careful amenity control is essential if the plums are not to be snatched at the cost of despoiling the tree − a depressingly familiar pattern which already threatens in several places. Naturally it is difficult in areas anxious to attract new life to realize the need for restrictions, it means an imaginative leap to a future with values completely different from the past, where hill scenery is far more valuable than hill sheep and far more vulnerable. The landscape itself will be created and maintained

159

by hill farming and forestry, or on land too poor for profitable use, by the more or less natural habitat. It is essential indeed that the upland scene should be as little disturbed as possible, and any landscape design should seem completely natural.

But the intractable problem still remains of how to manage the popular places when the number of lovers of upland solitudes is more than the solitary uplands can hold. It is no use lamenting lost privilege like a chorus of Cobbetts, for solitude takes up too much space to provide it in popular places in popular seasons. Those who value it can choose their time, for even in the popular areas of Wales and the Lakes the high-intensity use is surprisingly limited. Out of season or early and late in the day we can still have the mountains to ourselves, and even on a recent fine week-end in early September there were surprisingly few people in the Snowdon National Park.

But when we are away the mountains should be free of us absolutely – free even of reminders of our urban presence – and here it is essential to recognize a fundamental difference between the view and the landscape. The view is the scene which exists when we are there as viewers, and includes the people on hilltops, cars on roads, picnickers, walkers and all the rest. The landscape, however, is the scenery which exists (with apologies to Bishop Berkeley) whether we are there or not. The landscape not the view is the permanent reality, and it is therefore the uses which alter the landscape which matter: the irreversible changes like new buildings and obtrusive car parks and widened roads. These are inbuilt disturbances of the upland scenery which is the essential basis of every view. The uses which only disturb the view itself are far less important, for our mere brief holiday presence has little effect on most of the uplands. We are there a very short part of the twenty-four hours of only a few of the 365 days of the year, we keep mostly to roads or footpaths, or merely walk over land already dominated by farming and forestry. For it is through our permanent agents, sheep and trees, that we change the upland landscape, not through our holiday presence. Cars and people go home again, with no more lasting effect on the hills than the shadows of passing clouds (so long as we take our litter with us).

The view is therefore fleeting and expendable for a season. The landscape is long-term and must be protected for good.

# Part Two: Landscapes for an Industrial Democracy

# 9. Planning and the Future Landscape

'A great nation', said Engels in 1892, 'never learns better or quicker than by undergoing the consequences of its own mistakes.' It is a pronouncement which planners must find depressing or encouraging depending on when they date the start of the learning process, but if we begin with Engels, then our national éducation has been both swift and effective.

The mistakes of the nineteenth century taught society that *laissez-faire* in an industrial economy is a ruthless process which exploits and destroys on a hugely efficient new scale intolerable to the community. The nineteenth century was therefore a period of sweeping social reform – conditions of employment, public health, a police force, universal education and so on – public control of private action was widely and thoroughly established and has never been seriously questioned since. The Welfare State is accepted as inevitable by even its most disapproving critics, and no one imagines for instance that the National Health Service could now be abolished.

The development of social planning has been swift, not only because conditions were intolerable but also because its time scale is that of the human beings it serves. Land-use planning has been slow in comparison and by the same reasoning: the mistakes do not affect us so immediately and the time scale of change is that of the long-term landscape. The tentative growth of physical planning in the early part of this century was stimulated by the 1939–45 war, and was established as an effective process by the 1947 Town and Country Planning Acts. These gave us what was then the most advanced system in the world, and it worked by two complementary processes: (1) development plans drawn up by local authorities showing the proposed land-use for each area and (2) the requirement of planning permission for all intended development.

Whatever its shortcomings, no one can doubt that the system has worked. It has checked irresponsible development and encouraged appropriate use of land, and the fact that the rate of spread of built-up areas has been halved despite our vast expansion is indisputable proof of its effectiveness. Of all public benefactors, however, planners are the least appreciated; their successes are taken for granted and ignored and their mistakes gleefully publicized. A planner, we feel, is someone who prevents us doing what we ourselves planned, and though other people should certainly be prevented, the rules are for them not for us, and our ideal planner would control other people for our benefit. Which planning does of course – the trouble is that in most situations we are the other people.

As well as our natural resistance to control, planners also inherited vast problems from the uncontrolled past (in landscape for instance the 150,000 acres (60,000 ha) of derelict land). Their powers came late in our industrial development, and all sorts of horses had bolted from all sorts of stables before anyone dreamt of shutting stable doors. Planning too, of course, has made mistakes: of commission, omission and everything else. But how could it be otherwise? It has had to provide for an unknown future which is a whole new development in human living in untried conditions, with nothing in the past for guidance and no way of foreseeing the way ahead except by extrapolating present trends. Planning depends in fact on the correlation of large numbers of facts with large numbers of forecasts (not to say guesses) which may well be disastrously wrong – like the declining birth-rate so confidently predicted before the war. Plenty of us must still remember the gloomy warnings of a shrinking population (in France there still is a lingering aura of virtue in *familles nombreuses*).

In the twenty years since the 1947 Act a great many things have changed, and that Magna Carta of land-use planning now needs re-writing. 'Three major defects have appeared in the present system,' so stated a White Paper in 1967. 'First, it has become overloaded and subject to delays and cumbersome procedures. Second, there has been inadequate participation by the individual citizen in the planning process, and insufficient regard to his interests. Third, the system has been better as a negative control on undesirable development than as a positive stimulus to the creation of a good environment.'

Outsiders see further shortcomings such as lack of clearly defined powers, the need for a central coordinating body, and insufficient staff of the right quality. Which may all be true, but makes the achievements even more impressive.

The White Paper's new proposals are based on the recommendations of the Planning Advisory Group, and suggest first a 'structure plan' as a statement of basic policy which would need the Minister's approval to ensure that it tied in with national planning; and second, the 'local plans' of the local authorities showing the detailed working-out of the policy. This could mean a far more positive approach to future planning than the early restrictive attitude which was the first essential defence against the engulfing flood of new development. But given this breathing-space, and despite one's cowardly misgivings, the best defence, as Napoleon urged, is attack. The rising flood cannot be controlled by resistance but only by providing channels for it to flow through, and planning is increasingly concerned with new development as positive growth instead of as concessions in a holding action. This is clearly so in the brave New Towns, which despite their faults are a bold and creative achievement which all the world comes to see, and which Leslie Lane impressively describes as 'the greatest conscious programme of city-building ever undertaken by any country in history'.

This new conception of planning as 'the exploiting of situations and development for the general good' is of fundamental importance to landscape, and landscape planning could in its turn be defined as the exploiting of situations and development in terms of the physical habitat.

Equally important is the growing concern for the quality of our environment. Amenity is no longer brushed aside at the slightest practical objection, and it is heartening that the higher we go in the planning hierarchy the more seriously amenity is taken, with a positive place in the policy for roads, electricity, water, forestry and so on. It is also the direct motive of much planning legislation, and planning which does not now take amenity seriously is in fact inefficient in a prosperous and therefore selective society.

Tourism and the Development Areas are obvious arguments, but above a reasonable material level we are all increasingly selective about our environment, and just as we choose to enjoy extra leisure rather than take extra part-time work, so we use our increasing prosperity for the pleasant rather than the useful. 'If you have two loaves of bread sell one and buy a lily' – the Chinese are realistic aesthetes and the spare loaf is the first essential, and equally for us the lilies depend upon developing our industrial resources. But with an essential bread-supply ensured it is lilies we are short of and their price is high. The three most important qualities for selling a house, said an experienced house agent, are surroundings, surroundings and surroundings. A prosperous society will pay for amenity, and attractive areas do attract – people and trade and money. Amenity in fact is now a decisive practical factor in land-use, a value with new importance everywhere through the prosperity of an industrial society.

And from private possessions the new concern is spreading to public environment, as in the policy of National Parks and Areas of Outstanding Natural Beauty and the other designations which now cover more than one third of England and Wales. Even though the practical application may still be doubtful the policy is clear – fine scenery is precious because it is beautiful: its beauty has a price we are willing to pay by giving up unsuitable land-uses and by grants of money if needed.

A further policy of essential importance to landscape is the intention of keeping town and country as separate environments. Without deliberate control the difference would soon disappear in a country as small as Britain, and many planning measures are aimed at preserving it – from specific Green Belts, through general discouragement of scattered rural housing, to positive concentration of new development in New Towns. The control has succeeded well enough to preserve genuine country even close to cities, and despite the pressures on land our countryside is the envy of many countries with far lower population densities.

Linked with this concern for the rural landscape is a new recognition of farming as a land-use needing protection. Until recently farmland was simply the unregarded green background which provided an inexhaustible supply of land for more profitable uses,

*The new grass-roots concern for environment. Housewives are guarding a local tree from the developer's axe.*

and we have only been shocked into different ideas by the obvious fact that our farmland is *not* inexhaustible, and that our sprawling cities could easily coalesce. Nonetheless we still take farmland for other uses with what our descendants may well consider criminal extravagance. At present we import half our food and take it for granted that the world will continue to feed us and our livestock in exchange for our manufactured goods. But we are no longer the pioneer industrial nation in an agricultural world, and in the food shortages forecast for the future we may well have to grow our own.

167

The Agricultural Council considers we shall need to double our present food production by the end of the century, and we may even find, as some believe, that future customers are more interested in buying our grain than our cars. Up to now new developments in farming have increased production to compensate for loss of land, but this is a perilously short-sighted reason for lavish land allocation for new development (even given the excuse that concern for dwindling land has so recently replaced concern for dwindling population). Reversible land-uses like Country Parks and recreation areas are much less important. Such land is banked and can be taken back into farming if needed, as it was in the 1939–45 war, but urban development sterilizes the land for good and is an irreversible loss of our food production area. Recently there has been slightly more hesitation in taking top-quality land, and a new survey is being done of agricultural land quality, which may help to save the best. But almost as vital as the area of land taken is its siting and distribution, and the growing importance of large holdings safe from urban disturbance is a value which much modern planning not only ignores but deliberately destroys.

There is hope, however, of somewhat redressing the loss of land by new policies of restoring and using derelict areas. Telford New Town for instance is sited on land ravaged by early industry, and perhaps all derelict land may soon be regarded not as a matter of local cost or profit but as irreplaceable acres of the very small patch of the earth's surface which must provide our millions with homes and food for centuries to come – or so we hope.

Also new is the growing realization that Britain is now a single interrelated environment from the Highlands of Scotland to Piccadilly Circus, and not a collection of separate areas in an insulating matrix where if things went wrong in one place we simply looked the other way. The other way is a very limited view in modern Britain, and different areas are now only different rooms in a single house. Even without division our living-area is inconveniently small, and like society our landscape can only now survive as an organized whole: separate areas are out of scale with both our population and our new mobility, as the coast for instance proves very clearly.

Complementary to this new sense of a single environment is the growth of regional planning. The old divisions of County Councils and County Boroughs are increasingly unrealistic as town and country grow together, and bodies are now needed to plan for regions as a whole in the context of a central policy, as did the Advisory Economic Councils set up in 1964. There are now proposals for reorganizing the present 145 authorities into fewer and larger units corresponding to genuine regions, and this would clearly be an advantage for landscape planning.

Multiple use of our limited land is another inevitable development, though still only warily accepted. But though the traditional attitude of one-patch-one-user-and-a-notice-saying-P R I V A T E is a simple solution where land is plentiful, Britain is too small for a no-trespassers complex whether private or public, and in future we shall need more valid reasons for keeping the world at bay than a mild paranoia. A mixture of incompatible uses, however, is no more the answer than indiscriminate trespass, and multiple use of land can only succeed with selected activities in suitable combinations in areas properly planned.

Another new phrase at present very popular is cost-benefit analysis – an elaborate title for the familiar process of deciding any course of action by asking: is it worth it? In simple situations costs can be weighed directly against benefits (like children exchanging Christmas presents), but if the new title is complicated it is because the weighing process is now equally so. Costs and benefits are no longer simple or even clear, and in the elaborate multi-purpose decisions of modern planning they commonly derive from a wide range of contexts beyond the obvious one. What is essential is that costs and benefits should not be narrowly equated with money: non-amenity is a cost just as amenity is a benefit and both are essential in any valid analysis – as are convenience, future possibilities, social effects, alternative uses of land and resources and so on. The obvious difficulty is how to evaluate such intangibles, but we make scant progress by trying to translate all values into terms of money – an essential but specialized assessment which has little relevance to qualities like social well-being or the beauty of landscape.

A more logical and therefore more realistic approach might be to assess each aspect of any proposal in its own specific terms – amenity, finance, social health and so on – evaluating each separately on its own valid scale then relating these to an overall scale of abstract value which would correlate all the evaluations. Just as currency in fact developed from barter as an abstract intermediary for correlating incompatibles, so we now need this further abstraction for the further complexities of modern society.

The problem is formidable, but unless cost-benefit analysis can progress beyond finance it can never develop its full potential as an instrument of planning (and a method ready-made for computers). Certainly in landscape the most comprehensive and enlightened analysis is needed, since both costs and benefits exist in many contexts and in terms of the whole community. Simple local finances may even be irrelevant, as for instance in creating Green Belts.

An even newer development in planning is a movement to escape from the limitations of traditional drawing-board plans. Planning on paper has little to do with the complexities of the modern world; these cannot be expressed in drawings, and equally any scheme defined and committed to paper is thereby committed to obsolescence. A specific plan is the changing stuff of life made static, and change is now so swift that any fixed definition of the situation is a commitment to be avoided as long as possible. What development ten years old for instance would still be the same today? (It is why the least specific design is commonly the most efficient, since it is still adaptable.)

Definition there clearly must be, however, before action is possible, but ideally as the translation of well-defined needs into physical expression. Here the new Tees plan may be a landmark in planning methods, for a wide-ranging survey has been done and the findings transferred to computer tape so that any new information can be added and run through to find its effect on existing proposals.

No matter how excellent the policy, however, systems still depend on the people who work them, and planning needs more trained planners, wider education, more interaction. It also needs the co-operation of the public; not only, as the White Paper says, must people 'be able to participate fully in the planning process', but they *must* participate if the process is to be efficient, and the new system of Green Papers is intended to sound public opinion at an early stage.

At present, concern with the environment is chiefly expressed through the amenity societies, and these already serve three useful functions. The first is preservation – to preserve intelligently and where what is preserved can still survive. This is not easy, especially in landscape, for whereas buildings are relatively static creations in inert materials, landscape, especially the man-made landscape of Britain, is the actively-alive and changing habitat held in precarious balance by factors which may or may not exist in the new conditions. These are problems the National Trust has to face.

The societies' second function is protest in the cause of amenity – to watch what is happening and make a fuss when they do not approve. Not simply when they do not *like* changes but when they consider them unjustified, and even in an urgent national issue like Stansted airport it was public resistance which persuaded the government to think again about a change of site. When their cause is valid the societies greatly strengthen the planners' No, while the very fact of watch-dogs ready to fight makes the ruthless think twice – they may still get away with murder but the crime-rate is definitely lower because of societies like the Council for the Protection of Rural England.

The third function is constructive, and the Civic Trust is notable here, with positive action like renovating areas of towns and removing eyesores. It is also active in civic education, by publications, campaigns and exhibitions, and it helped draft the new Civic Amenities Bill introduced by its founder. This provides for better protection of our architectural treasures, for planting and preserving trees, and for getting rid of large-scale rubbish.

All of which functions are excellent and essential, but only a beginning. 'Planning is for people and about their activities, and bringing people into planning means a great deal more than the right to inspect plans and object to them.' So said the Ministry of Housing and Local Government, and responsible societies surely have a place in the planning itself. Planners are re-creating our environment to the best of their powers, but being on the White Paper's admission both understaffed and overworked, they are preoccupied with practical day-to-day business and have little time left for the less immediate but equally important business of amenity. And this is exactly where

171

*Landscape with figures. An Irish road-labourer's child ('I'm the odd one out. I'm the twenty-first in the family'). Still some way to go in respecting the environment.*

the societies are specialists who have by their voluntary involvement proved what Americans call their dedication. Among their numbers they can also draw on a detailed range of local knowledge which no planner could hope to rival, and since the societies spring from the leisure of responsible and well-educated people the level of ability is commonly high. These are qualities any employer would eagerly grasp at, and not to use such potential constructively in planning is a serious waste of precious resources. Some, like the Chiltern Society, have already evolved to the stage of Translators and now act on their own initiative – mapping land-use, making traffic surveys, studying

172

social habits and needs, and all the other essential preliminaries to introducing new development into the existing environment with least harm – or even with most benefit. If deliberately integrated into the planning process responsible societies could be invaluable both in getting work done and in winning public support for unpopular but essential measures.

In less than a quarter of a century the changes have been swift, with official planning and official societies appearing and evolving at historically astonishing speed. But this alone is not enough. The actual contact of the community and the environment is through millions of ordinary people living their daily lives, and if our environment is to improve, so must our attitude to it as individual citizens. The old social structure was like various layers of cream floating on a large volume of variously skimmed milk; and though stirring the whole together as we are doing may vastly improve the milk, it does not, whatever early revolutionaries seem to have hoped, change the whole mixture to cream. Stirring in five per cent of Country-Coders for instance has had little effect on the other ninety-five per cent of users of the countryside, and we all have to learn to respect an environment we all now share. This common ownership is the new revolution which neither category has yet come to terms with – the former privileged do not like sharing, the former under-privileged do not share responsibility.

The necessary education for the privileged in sharing proceeds of itself by force of numbers, but persuading the former under-privileged to respect the environment needs conscious effort. One fundamental cause of trouble is that the newly prosperous have not yet left the old unprosperity behind them emotionally. Our social democracy is much newer than our political, and from generations as the have-nots of society it is natural to inherit a Them-and-Us mentality: that the world belongs to Them, the hostile powers always ready to do us down. Vandalism is our defiance of Them (it is surely why it increases as dawning prosperity makes us bolder) and the only way of survival is in our defended private corner of existence. Prosperity has improved this private territory, but is only now bringing the realization that the outside world belongs to Us as well as Them, and that our private fence now defines not the limits of our life's territory but only a changed degree of ownership in the whole environment. This is the liberating consciousness of true privilege, an extra dimension of living more dazzling than those born privileged can ever know.

But what we share we are also responsible for, and this is not yet accepted. At present the contrasting attitudes to private and public are everywhere marked – houses are spotless, public places squalid; private cars immaculate, buses and trains maltreated; and gardeners of pin-neat gardens dump their rubbish over the fence (even over open chestnut palings where it still remains part of the garden scene – vision, it seems, like behaviour, depending on public and private). In this version of Galbraith's private affluence and public squalor only our own is valued, and our landscapes therefore will only prosper when we feel they too are ours to cherish as we do our own gardens.

Children are most readily involved, as on the Sheffield parkway where trees planted by Them (the local authorities) were soon destroyed, but when replanted by Us (local children) survived unharmed; or in South Wales where children guard trees they themselves planted on derelict land, putting out fires before the fire brigade arrive. Public parks are a half-way stage of responsibility, for though there are park-keepers to remind us of virtue, on the whole we respect what we recognize as partly our property, and do not for instance pick the flowers, as we easily could unnoticed.

Even our litter-spreading is somewhat reformed in parks, and virtue perhaps will grow with prosperity (despite the glee of two small boys in Regent's Park rose-garden who emptied a brimming litter-basket onto the lake and covered the water with floating rubbish).

But even universal respect for the environment is still not enough. There must first be an environment worth respecting, and even the most excellent planning policy will not of itself create a good environment. This in fact is our present landscape tragedy: that the old was mostly good, the new is mostly not, and that though planning has limited the spread of the new, it has scarcely at all improved its quality.

Planning is primarily concerned with people, with lives not landscapes, and it therefore sees the environment in human terms. 'Recreation areas', 'solitary places' — this is landscape described as an extension of ourselves. Solitude is nothing to do with scenery but only with how many of us happen to be there, and recreation tells us nothing about the landscape. The actual physical components of the scene existing on the ground, and how this is created from the natural habitat — these are seldom considered. Land-use is planned but not landscape, yet use alone creates no more than the conditions where certain kinds of landscape are possible.

In townscape we realize this perfectly well, and no one supposes for instance that simply providing land for houses will create a good living area. The planning is the site allocation but there must also be a design for the housing. In landscape, however, the site allocation alone is expected to produce the suitable scenery, and in terms of landscape most planning consists of siting land-uses and little else. Town and Country planning in fact has mostly meant planning the towns and letting the country look after itself within planning's protection.

*Community flowers — unprotected and unpicked (just).*

175

One planner, however, who understands very clearly that the translation of planning into landscape is an essential further process is Professor Grieve of the Highlands and Islands Development Board. He talks of the 'physical expression of the plan on the surface of the real earth', and 'the translation into environmental terms' without which plans that are excellent on paper may be disastrous on the ground. In particular instances the need for landscape design is now recognized, as in the New Towns where landscape architects are employed from the start. But for the general landscape we have almost no policy except to protect what exists – an area is beautiful, therefore let us keep it so by preventing unsuitable changes. But since the only way to keep an existing landscape is to continue the land-use which created it – the old use by the old methods – the policy may more or less work in the uplands but not for the future lowlands, where all kinds of positive action will be needed in the new conditions. 'We shall have to pay for the view,' says one realist, and this is tentatively recognized by the grants for seventy-five per cent of the cost of preserving and enhancing natural beauty in National Parks and Areas of Outstanding Natural Beauty. But far more than money is needed – enthusiasm, skill, determination, but above all else a landscape policy for the preserving and enhancing.

And however enlightened, protection is often too late. Much of our landscape has changed already, more is changing while we watch, and it is exactly these troubled areas which most need landscape planning. The whole structure of our landscape now needs reshaping from first principles, for the fossilized setting of an agricultural society cannot be made to accommodate our new land-uses by muddled and piecemeal adaptation of the obsolete, however beautiful. Not only does farmland need reorganizing for the new ways of agriculture, but so does land near towns for industrial development, the countryside for urban–industrial living, scenery along roads for motor travel, and the whole land for urban recreation. And because we are not starting with a clean new sheet but with landscapes already widely disturbed, we need an order which can be flexibly superimposed on existing disorder, linking the incoherent parts together into a large-scale whole. We need in fact a clear and simple landscape policy with equally clear methods for applying it. As in planning we need an adaptable working process of principles and techniques, and the new proposals for planning are well suited to landscape. 'Structure plans' could establish the overall landscape policy, and 'local plans' could then evolve their own local version of the general landscape, while within this coherent framework individual designs would create special settings for specific uses.

But at present the position of planning and landscape is like ordering a meal in a restaurant. We have thought what we would like to eat, considered the raw materials available and worked out what we can afford. The planners have even sent in the order – ten National Parks, eight Forest Parks, Green Belts and Special Areas in season, and rural scenery for all. But someone has still got to do the cooking. More than that, someone has still to work out new recipes for the completely new conditions, and the processes essential between ordering a meal and finding good food on our plate are equally essential between designating land as scenery and finding good scenery when we get there.

Yet it is tempting to admire the unconscious beauties of the landscape we are losing and to give up in despair, or at best to become blind preservationists. How can we hope to replace them with anything to compare? Yet to architects and town-planners the beauties of the old towns and buildings must be equally depressing. They too admire and no doubt despair; but they then get on with doing the best they can for the modern world. And if the results are often depressingly less satisfactory than the old, they are also sometimes admirably successful.

In landscape equally we must now accept the same challenge and if need be the same disappointments; for certainly whatever we do will be better than doing nothing. And why should we fail? The beauty of the old landscape is due to three things – the beauty of the raw materials of land and plants; the effects of our mercurial climate; and our particular British gift for compromise, which adapted rather than subdued the natural habitat. 'The art of *assisting* Nature is all our own', said Marshall (the italics are his). And need we suppose we have lost the art? Certainly the climate is still the same and so is the land and vegetation; the same grass and trees and shrubs and flowers

*The unconscious beauties of the old. Who now could crowd housing round a graveyard and make a place to visit for pleasure?*

are there for the using, and will grow as well for us as they did for our ancestors. The old landscape was created by determined public bodies, and if one lot of men can sit down and think clearly and act decisively so can another in the twentieth century. The eighteenth-century 'Improvers' never for a moment doubted that what they were doing was a vast improvement on anything before. We on the other hand shall certainly doubt, since sad experience has made us wary, but we must act just the same. In the next fifty years our urban development is expected to double, and the very scale of the present changes – the fact that all our landscapes are involved, from crowded cities to empty hills – gives us an unrivalled chance to reshape our environment as a coherent whole. But we must act, and act *now*, for by the time scale of landscape development the twenty-first century is already upon us.

As the birthplace of the Industrial Revolution Britain had a world start in landscape destruction – even though competitors now rival if not surpass us in vandalism. Our impressive change of heart, however, in the last twenty years means that in landscape as everything else we now begin to realize Huxley's third stage of self-conscious evolution – for land-use planning is essentially the controlled evolution of the environment. And since with us the world's new industrial society exists in its most concentrated form – with the highest proportion of industrial workers and urban dwellers, the highest density of cars and tractors and almost of people – why then should we not also make a world start in evolving new landscapes for the new industrial era which Britain gave birth to?

In the conscious creation of environment there are four interacting processes – to formulate land-use policies to suit society's needs – to consider what types of landscape are appropriate for these policies in the given habitat – to work out practical methods for producing the suitable landscapes – to develop an administrative system to apply both policies and methods.

The first stage is the province of planners, though it can no more be isolated from the rest of the process than a meal from its raw materials and cooking. The last stage of administration exists to implement policy; it must therefore be flexible, and in Britain at present is in process of fundamental change. This book is chiefly concerned with the two intermediate stages of direct application to landscape. The rest of this section is an attempt to realize what new types of landscape would suit the planning policies discussed in this chapter. The last section proposes simple practical methods for establishing these suggested landscapes on the ground.

# 10. City Regions

Each period of history, says the Greek planner Doxiadis, has its characteristic type of settlement, and in industrial society this is the big city which is now developing everywhere in the modern world. A metropolis has many advantages – a wide choice of work and equally of workers, variety of goods and markets, expert professional services, good transport and shops, education, training and research facilities, the stimulus of lively people and interchange of ideas. For small enterprises there is a wide range of auxiliary services, for large a wide range of population for recruiting of staff, and 'for the real London lover', said Henry James, 'the mere immensity of the place is a large part of its savour'.

Modern culture also is metropolitan; it is generated in large communities and spread abroad by modern communications, and this is fundamentally different from the old urban culture of comparatively small numbers of people living together in a close-knit society. Urban culture was oligarchical, and the best things went on in private houses. But not any longer. The best concerts are not now at private parties, nor the best pictures in private drawing-rooms, and Margot Fonteyn's dancing is more public as well as more professional than Lady Hamilton's Attitudes. Metropolitan culture is not exclusive: anyone can come to a modern city, spend a day in the shops or parks or museums: can dine (according to means not contacts) and spend the evening at a pub or theatre or concert or whatever version he fancies of the Bright-Lights-For-All. Above all we can share the life of the streets, the endlessly various and fascinating extrovert world of public places which is the essential life of a metropolis.

This is the anonymity of big cities which we may find lonely or liberating according to our mood – we share the life of a large congregation of people but as separate individuals. And increasingly we share the life of all big cities everywhere as cultures intercommunicate and the national differences fade. Big-city dwellers breathe the metropolitan air as their native climate wherever they go, and to a Londoner coming back from western America New York is already home.

Whether we like it or not, and whatever setting we live in, the big city is the unit of modern life and the basis of industrial societies. And it is the nature of large modern cities to grow larger, since their mass has a gravity which attracts further mass. But the modern communications which make this possible have two contrasting effects – they concentrate cities but they also spread them. The concentration is of influence – the increasing dominance of the central city on the surrounding regions; the spread is physical – the widening belts of urban development away from the centre. These two counterbalanced effects from the same cause are producing a new settlement pattern of City Regions, and whatever the local variants this is how most of us are likely to live in the future – in vast amorphous areas dominated by large central cities. In America these concentrations are building up along the coasts and draining the inland rural areas (the Mid West, so one gloomy Mid Westerner complained, is a cultural desert for growing corn) and already the Eastern seaboard is a single urbanized area of more than 37 million people, which Jean Gottman portentously describes as 'a totally new order in the organization of inhabited space'.

This impressive condition we reached in Britain some time ago in our six recognized conurbations, where the average population is over 8,000 people per square mile (3,088 per km²). Conurbations, however, are not static; like galaxies they have their youth and old age and new generations. Tyneside, the West Riding and Manchester are elderly and their urgent need is restoration; Birmingham and the Black Country are mature but still growing, London is the green bay-tree, while the Lower Thames, the Southampton–Portsmouth and the Humber regions are the likely new generation. The growth-pattern inside the conurbations is also changing, with a general outward movement which leaves a static or declining population in the centre, and in America there are old cities like old clumps of Michaelmas daisies – dying in the middle but with vigorous new growth round the edges, draining the old urban centres of life and contributing little in return but husbands in offices. In Britain our planning controls have modified this process, but the trend is the same, and central London for instance has been losing its residential population ever since the 1861 census. Little more than a quarter of a million people now live in the central area though five times this number travel in to work, with an average journey of forty-five minutes. The ring of maximum growth is moving steadily further out, and London has become a City Region containing seventy per cent of the South-East's population in an area of roughly forty-five miles (76 km) radius from Charing Cross, and with the recent spectacular rise in population in the areas beyond the Green Belt.

The aim of Green Belt policy is to control the spread of cities, and London's Green Belt was the prototype with three stated purposes – to enclose the main built-up mass of London and prevent further spread; to keep the country towns beyond the Green Belt as distinct and separate entities; to preserve the fine countryside of the Home Counties. An irregular belt of land was therefore made a special area where development was limited to specific uses aimed at preserving a rural landscape. But the difficulties have proved serious and unexpected; the static population of 10 million for instance which the plan provided for has risen to over 12 million and is still obstinately increasing. Nor was the mass-mobility of the motor-car foreseen, or why has most post-war public authority housing made no provision for cars? Presumably the car, like the coach it replaced, was expected to remain the privilege of the few.

Exposed to such pressures the Green Belt is not the clear-cut start to the general countryside as intended, but has become a ring of protected land, by no means all rural, and increasingly leap-frogged by the irresistible growth of the city within. Cobbett was right for once when he saw no 'easy means of dispersing' London, and housing the city's overspill (couldn't someone invent a more sympathetic word?) in new low-density towns on the edge of the Green Belt has not decreased the region's numbers but only established the city's influence further afield.

The growth of most of our large towns is of roughly concentric rings of development like the layers of an onion round the original old centre. In general the successive layers are compact up to the era of public transport when they suddenly spread, and London for instance increased four times in size with the building of the Underground and the electrification of the Southern Railway. Since the 1947 Planning Acts the development depends on how the controls have operated, but where there are containing belts the built-up area changes to more or less green more or less country (anyway it changes) and beyond the disturbed fringes the landscape becomes gradually rural dotted with other development.

But despite its rural background the life of this outer ring is still based firmly on the central city, for 'Mass mobility', said Artur Glikson, 'makes it possible to belong to a particular place, yet to enter into direct contacts with a world-wide environment.' Modern communications (not only transport but telephones, newspapers, postal services, radio and television and all the rest) mean that life is now little different in city or suburb unless we make it so, and for many people the old ideal of *rus in urbe* has changed to *urbs in rure*.

To call these areas suburbs or dormitories, however, is to describe them unfairly in downgraded terms of something else. These are not would-be urban areas but a new type of urban-based environment, while for only one member of probably a four-member family are they five-night-a-week dormitories. This is the home, not the sleeping-place; it is the base of the family life, and we need a new name for these urban-fringe landscapes of the modern world. We equally need a new pattern of development for such city-based living areas, since the private car which has largely created them does not itself produce a settlement pattern but only an amorphous dilution. The private car, however, with its essentially anti-city nature, is unlikely to be the basis of travel either into or inside future cities, and efficient new development seems likely to be linked to public transport even more closely than at present. The electrification of the London to Bletchley railway for instance produced a forty per cent rise in ticket sales in just over fifteen months. Transport of all kinds – not only railways but motorways, docks, Channel tunnels and especially in future, airports – will affect the pattern of City Regions, local conditions will govern local decisions, and equally in the palimpsest development of a long-lived-in country like Britain, old patterns must always

*Inter-war suburban sprawl on the edge of London.*

influence new. Present proposals for City Regions are various – 'a polynucleated urban system designed on a tight pattern and set in a green background' (this for the Clyde Valley). 'Characterful, relatively independent old and new communities set together in a regional landscape' (no mention of how to create it) and for the South-East 'a series of corridors of residential and industrial development leading from London to new regional city areas'.

Equally various are the proposals for the settlements themselves – new towns, expanded towns, linear or concentric or radial towns – though no one seems to have taken up Le Corbusier's proposal for a huge multi-storey framework with inbuilt services, streets at all levels, and the separate sites sold off privately to build what we like – with Moorish villas and Renaissance palaces next-door neighbours if

*Post-war New Town sprawl in the country. Of the two, the early suburb wastes land slightly less extravagantly, and has certainly come to better terms with its unbuilt areas. Scrub can be seen invading unused land in the New Town.*

we fancy. *Une saisissante apparition* he calls it. It would certainly be that. But Le Corbusier was a fountain of ideas before his time, and as we have been producing them as new ever since, even this astonishing structure may appear as a new suggestion in another generation or so.

The proposed size of settlements also varies from small village-like groupings to large new cities. But the size increases rapidly; most of the new towns are already enlarging, and Sweden's experience has led to larger assemblies even when the separate units are small; for though we may like to live in intimate groups we now need contact with centres of increasing size for services, and Swedish communities of 25,000 for instance still shopped in neighbouring larger centres.

Thus considerable thought is now given to suitable development patterns, but such town and country planning is still mostly *town*

185

planning, and suitable still means almost entirely in terms of the development itself, not of the larger land-use pattern of which it is part. This is considered, when at all, in the most perfunctory way, yet the functioning and character of the countryside will be largely determined by the development pattern of the region. And in terms of the larger landscape many new proposals look alarmingly like the old mistakes all over again but on a vast new scale. What are linear cities for instance but ribbon-building blown up large? Or low-density towns in the countryside but larger housing areas in a larger Green Belt? As for 'dispersed cities integrated with farming' what else can this mean but suburban spread over huge new areas of our small-scale countryside? In terms of landscape and farming such patterns are new large-scale versions of old disasters.

These are proposals in narrowly limited terms of local people, not of the whole environment, and more specifically here of people in motor-cars. For dispersed cities are fundamentally a pattern for cars, and however precious 'the gift of private mobility' we are not yet merely the drivers and providers-for of our vehicles. Need we then capitulate so completely? Certainly it might be interesting to build a city for motor-cars if only to quote as an alternative to poor Los Angeles, but not at the cost of thousands of acres of our dwindling countryside.

The ideal development for the car is diffuse with frequent roads and parking spaces – that is, *car* living-space. The ideal for the countryside is as dense and compact as possible. The ideal for people is somewhere between, for too-compact settlements deprive us of cars and gardens, while diffuse development means unconvincing urban centres, journeys for everything we want, isolation of the car-less (children for instance), loss of vital food-producing farmland and destruction of the true countryside. Yet enjoyment of the country is one of the very reasons urged for thus destroying it – that new development in rural areas will 'simplify access to the countryside for recreation'.

This conception of the country as a self-perpetuating amenity landscape is our typically urban blend of reverence and ignorance before the joys of nature, and is already proving disastrous. Urban access means rural destruction. This is the harsh and unpalatable truth which we have not accepted, but if we continue to ignore it we shall degrade increasing areas of our landscape. How the town can enjoy the country without destroying it is not an insoluble problem, but at present it is certainly unsolved, and as Professor Wibberley warns, planning blight is now as real in rural areas as urban. Plans for urban development in the countryside drive away the younger and more enterprising farmers in the neighbourhood, cause investment to run down and farms to deteriorate. Farmers do not see themselves as a background for urban recreation, and from a farm preserved as amenity landscape for one of the New Towns there are cautionary tales to drive away any farmer – cows were impossible because of worrying by dogs, and of crops only barley successfully discouraged courting couples (too spiky for comfort, too low for concealment). Even so the farmer's combine 'harvested as many old bicycles, bedsteads, tin-cans and other hardware as it did bushels of grain'; one summer the fire brigade was called more than twenty times: and so on through a long tale of woes.

'Time's up – I'm coming.'

To plan urban access therefore without planning rural protection is to plan for trouble, and town and country are *not* integrated simply by drawing them side by side on a map. The new strategy for the South-East is conscious of past misfortunes, and plans to keep large stretches of countryside undisturbed between corridors of growth, deliberately aiming to 'preserve the bulk of the region for recreational and agricultural purposes'. But whether this potentially destructive combination can work will depend on realistic and detailed planning to avoid what one gloomy farmer already foresees – 'the whole of Britain arbitrarily divided into dormitories, factories and recreation areas, with a few remaining farmers allowed to muddle on in a sort of National Park'.

Urban areas disturb the farming landscape in three chief ways. The first is the straightforward loss of land to development; this is the only officially recognized form of urban disturbance, and is a relatively small area which is constantly quoted to prove that the present loss of farmland is insignificant. The second is the visual invasion of rural scenery by non-rural development; this is chiefly an amenity objection, but the disturbance is out of all proportion to the land used, and five acres (2 ha) of development may disturb 5,000 acres (2,000 ha) of scenery. The third is the disturbance of the process of farming, both by urban recreation and by urban-fringe development. Not only for instance do new roads slice up farms into unworkable divisions, but even increased traffic on existing roads can sever farm buildings from fields. Cows have now joined the list of road casualties, and for farms in the motor age roads near urban areas are becoming not routes but boundaries.

Roads, however, are only an obvious example of the disturbance which is now creating a new form of marginal farmland. Land is marginal when the intended uses only marginally survive against the influence of a neighbouring hostile environment. In the uplands it is the mountain habitat which restricts man's farming, while near urban areas it is the hostile urban environment. City-fringe land is equally therefore marginal land: it is urban-marginal land, a new type created by man not nature.

This urban-marginal zone can be clearly seen in London's Green Belt. The original intention was to contain the city's spread by

*A dying farm on urban-marginal land.*

preserving the countryside up to its boundaries, and in a pre-industrial landscape the two were compatible. But in modern conditions they are not; no policy can surround prosperous industrial cities with undisturbed farmland, and in practice the Green Belt consists of two kinds of landscape which roughly correspond to the two incompatible aims. One is the outer belt of rural countryside with urban-rural settlements, and here the policy is largely successful. The other is the containing buffer area between country and city, and this no one could think successful. For whereas neglected upland-marginal land may go back to the beautiful wild, neglected urban-marginal land creates scenery which not even the most determined and disassociated aesthetes have managed to admire. 'London melts by wide ugly zones into the green country,' said Henry James in prose more attractive than the scenery, and a disillusioned planner's description is nearer the nasty truth – 'a landscape of poultry farms

189

and piggeries, of wire-netting and bungalows, of gravel pits and scrapped car-dumps, of airfields and motorways and filling stations. The motorist in particular travels through a landscape of eye-sores.'

This inner belt may be as narrow as a single neglected field or may stretch for depressing miles, its spread may be limited by Green Belt controls (or Grey Belt as a planning friend nastily calls Birmingham's proposals), but to some extent the zone exists round all built-up areas, like the pale fringe round an ink-spot on blotting paper. This is the disturbed landscape of industry and urban-marginal farming, for whatever its incidental use this is essentially urban land; its condition is created by the neighbouring built-up area and it must therefore be planned as part of that area. It thus urgently needs a new land-use policy based not on restrictive protection of old rural uses which cannot prosper, but on positive promotion of new urban-fringe uses which can. The chief cause in fact of its present moribund state is that we have prescribed the wrong treatment for its ills.

PERIPHERAL LAND IS URBAN LAND – it should be printed large across every plan for every new development in the countryside. Green wedges are urban, green spaces are urban, so is the margin of all development. And since urban land needs urban uses, what therefore goes on in the wedges and spaces? Planners (like us) may dream of wheat waving gold to our doorsteps and of mild-eyed cows gazing over our garden fences, but we are all of us urban generations out of touch with any practical knowledge of cows and wheatfields. The farming countryside is not a decorative land-surface which can be used to break up and beautify urban areas for the benefit of urban dwellers, but is a working landscape which can only survive in suitable conditions, and these we need to understand clearly.

In both farming and landscape the size is important since rural countryside needs large undisturbed areas. So too is settlement pattern, and almost as much as its area the shape and layout of new development determines how much land is lost to efficient farming. As a general rule all land in all development plans should belong to one of the following three categories:

1. Built-up areas with their own urban landscapes.
2. Rural land sufficiently undisturbed to be efficiently farmed.
3. Non-farming land with a definite use which provides its own maintenance.

Any land not covered by one of these categories (and in many proposed schemes there is a disastrously large amount) is potentially in trouble. For the green landscape needs a policy of land-use as clearly thought out as the built-up areas, and with equally careful layout and planning. Green open spaces as envisaged by planners are *not* the land left over between areas of development. That is disturbed and potentially derelict land; it is like the topiary peacock a friend once produced in our garden simply by cutting out the shape from an existing yew-tree as if it were a lump of butter. I think he never understood why it died, and the death of topiary-style rural spaces will equally surprise urban planners. For certainly it is not planning policy to create large areas of urban-marginal land, and green wedges are intended as country landscape not as vast empty stretches of grass between houses and town centres – voids whose only function can be to keep the population healthy by enforced walking, and to encourage thrift by the need to buy cars. But it is practice not policy which is at fault, and we could say of such planning what Cobbett said of charity schools: 'It is impossible not to believe that this is done with a good motive, but it is possible not to believe that it is productive of good.'

At present most planning presupposes that from choice most people will live away from city centres, and this is justified both by the movement of population and by preferences shown in surveys. But will this necessarily be so in the future? We can only choose from existing alternatives, and at present to live away from the centre is the simplest way of avoiding both high housing costs and the present shortcomings of city life. But shall we want to avoid our future cities? Industrial cities are too recent a development for us yet to have learnt how to live in them, and our present state is probably no more than the mud-hut stage of big city development. Yet we have already laid the basic foundations of providing food and safeguarding health for large congregations of people; if we can equally solve the

191

new problems of transport and of taming the metropolitan environment, then cities could once more become desirable places to live in as they were in the past (and still are to the many people who would always choose the exhilarating metropolitan climate whatever its drawbacks).

At present there are plenty of factors to drive us out of cities – cramped living-space, high rents and rates, noise and dirt, lack of privacy and quiet, of gardens and garages and all the well-known rest. But these need not be inevitable even in high-density living – space can be better planned, circulation be multi-level, houses can (in time) be sound-proofed, gardens can be room-sized on roofs, cars for leisure can be stored underground, while the future possibilities cannot even be guessed at.

'Sunshine in the rooms, blue sky in the windows, green trees to wake up to – and all in the city.' So Le Corbusier enthused (though his own inhuman Cartesian city of identical towers set equidistant in vague grass spaces would be a radiant nightmare). Our own current solution by tower-blocks is also a very partial success, but that proves nothing, and the first villages were doubtless no more successful. 'Habitat' at Expo 67 is a more recent experiment, but we need floods of new ideas and probably generations of mistakes, and this in no way invalidates the fact that high-density metropolitan living with the city on the doorstep can mean the Good Life at a very high level – despite one nervous citizen's forebodings of 'ant-heap cities on a diet of drugs. You'd look out your window and there you'd see an LSD love-in on your front lawn.' (It is interesting that his ant-heap includes not only spacious front lawns but also by implication back lawns as well.)

Many critics, however, believe that high-density living is bad in itself and that its ills are intrinsic. Arthur Young did in 1771: 'The principal objections to great cities are that health here is not so good, that marriages are not so frequent, that debauchery prevails and that abuses are multiplied.' (Tea-drinking ranked high in his debaucheries.) 'Population depends chiefly on the poor inhabitants of the country, and the debauched, unhealthy lives of cities are terrible scourges to the human species.'

Young's strictures were certainly valid in his day, but what they

*Slum alley –*

# New Lives, New Landscapes

*– or fashionable Mayfair mews? The same city, the same metropolitan stresses, potentially the same kind of area (the wall on the left is a pub in both). But environment, like landscape, is the interaction of habitat and people, and the people in the first picture are in trouble.*

proved was not the demerits of cities but only the need for public health measures and for law and order. Peter Blake is equally gloomy about future American cities 'inhabited solely by the very poor and the very rich, plus a few divisions of police to protect the latter from the former'. But his strictures too prove only that we have not yet solved the (still very recent) problem of big-city living, nor yet learnt to create a good metropolitan environment.

Other opponents of high-density living quote the social ills and the high crime-rate which often go with it; but what of the poverty, bad housing, poor education, frustration, lost social patterns, breakdown of family standards and the whole background of social ill health which often accompanies high densities in our old cities? These may be the cause of trouble but that does not mean they are the result of close living. Such arguments are the illogical reasoning of *post hoc ergo propter hoc* (although now we no longer learn Latin we could call it top-hat logic instead, from the man who argued that since people in top-hats seldom died of starvation the cure for famine was a universal issue of hats).

Similar arguments from prisoner-of-war camps are no more relevant, nor from rats and mice imprisoned at unnatural densities. Mice cease to breed when overcrowded. And men? Such a fundamental biological difference should make anyone wary of simple conclusions. And why mice? Why not bees in hives or starlings in flocks? Man is gregarious; no one makes us live in cities nor keeps us in crowds when we get there. We congregate from choice, and do not even spend our leisure recovering in solitude as we could, but gregariously with friends and at clubs and pubs and parties and meetings and celebrations and demonstrations and every kind of communal gathering. Of course we like crowds or why do we make them? Most of our crowds are for pleasure.

Indeed one of the most important forms of multiple use of land and resources in the future is surely the development of cities as recreation areas. Cities at present are chiefly where we work not play – except of course when we are abroad and cities immediately become holiday magnets. And this could equally happen at home: especially for people who live away from the centre. Here are the same shops and restaurants and gardens and parks and culture and entertainment – all the attractions in fact which we value abroad (and which visitors value here). And as we build new cities and rebuild the old they must lose their recent gloomy image; there are plans already for London's Thames as a playground, and future cities could absorb huge numbers of people for recreation; the essential facilities are already there – roads, transport, public buildings, and all the elaborate services needed for large congregations of people, and which are at present barely used out of working hours. Our cities in fact represent an extremely wasteful part-time use of very expensive facilities.

Meanwhile, however, the problems of high-density living are certainly formidable, though low density does not solve them but merely substitutes a small-town or suburban environment. Nor is it simply a question of which density is preferable, as many critics imply, but of high density concentrated in one place or low spread-out somewhere else. We might well prefer a large ground-level garden to a small roof-top patio, but what is the difference worth in travel time to work and isolation from city shops and services? (Not to mention the loss of farmland and country landscape.) Nor by living outside cities can we escape the stresses of modern life. These are fundamental in a meritocracy, and must increase as the system becomes more efficient and competitive and international. Mere difference of environment cannot save us, but it is always simpler to blame our troubles on extraneous conditions, and many of the arguments against city living are suspiciously emotional. High density is blamed for stress, but low density is equally blamed for loneliness and for 'suburban blues', and the true country equally shunned for its 'intolerable isolation'. Some people even blame Britain as a whole for their difficulties and flee them by emigrating. Many also come back.

But though there are no all-in answers, different people clearly find different environments more sympathetic, and no matter how city living improves they may still prefer to live away from the centre. But our needs and preferences are not static, and a future pattern might be of different settings for different stages of our increasingly transportable lives – a town flat for our young independence and love affairs, a house further out with more space and a garden to bring up our children, then a smaller house or back to the centre perhaps or further out into the country for the second independence of middle age. This is already a pattern for the prosperous, but why not for most people in the future as mobility and transport increase? Both by private and social reckoning it is the most efficient and economical use of the community's housing resources.

What we certainly need is variety – always and everywhere – with different living-patterns and environments to choose from. There can never be single answers; all solutions are partial, and the present condemnation of tower-blocks for instance is as narrowly unrealistic as the earlier hope that they would solve all city housing problems. Families with young children commonly dislike high living, yet penthouse flats are also the most sought after, and in a recent rent list from the Barbican the higher the flat the higher the rent. Like country cottages and suburban houses, tower-blocks are right for some ways of life and wrong for others, and planning's task is to provide the variety we need in the best proportion and pattern for the environment as a whole – *including the countryside.*

A City Region is not a city area but a city orbit. It is a social and economic (and potentially an administrative) entity but it is only incidentally if at all a region with any particular identity as landscape, and will include all types from the built-up urban to the remote and wild. In the North especially there is splendid upland country sweeping in close to the central areas, and my vividest memory from two years in Manchester is of looking down from the Pennines near the Snake Pass one clear winter day and seeing the city below drowned in a solid lake of fog swirling pale in the sunlight like a milky green opal. Even in the less dramatic lowlands there is unexpectedly wild country close to big cities – the New Forest, Cannock Chase in the Midlands, the Surrey Hills and the Chilterns on London's doorstep, and in America's eastern metropolitan area half the land is forest.

A far larger area of City Regions is rural countryside, and even in the densely populated South-East the outer country ring of London's metropolitan area has only two people per acre (five per ha: the average for all Great Britain is only just under one per acre) with 80 to 85 per cent of the land either farming or woods, while even in the London region as a whole only thirty per cent is urban development.

Since planning policy is to preserve this rural matrix, Green Belts and similar controls, whatever their landscape quality, are valuable extra powers in these primarily administrative areas. How long the inner belt can contain the built-up centres nobody knows; certainly Tudor attempts failed to limit London's growth by legislation, and every new road and pylon now spreads the city's influence further abroad. Nonetheless if future spread is against opposition it is more likely to be essential and well-planned development, and containing belts have therefore an important function whether or not they still survive as green open space in a hundred years' time.

But the pressures are alarmingly high and increasingly harder to resist, and in their present half-used state Green Belts are dangerously vulnerable. Nor are the arguments easily refuted – if an area is already disturbed by urban intrusions and farming is marginal then why not develop the land as a completely urban area? Both owners and developers would rejoice, and only policy stands in the way. But policy ultimately depends on public opinion, and the public in general are only mildly enthusiastic about untidy private fields on the edge of towns. If containing belts are to survive they need new and positive land-uses both suited to their buffer state and popular with the public.

To some extent the problems of urban-marginal land are common to the whole of a City Region, and despite the wide diversity of scenery the area therefore has a distinctive though non-visual identity in that all types of environment are exposed to similar pressures. The demand for land and houses, the spread of industrial installations, the presence of large numbers of people with cars and leisure – these are landscape hazards which are here particularly acute (as they also are on the coast, which in this context could be thought of as an extended linear City Region). They are pressures which produce a constant tendency for the area to degenerate either to disturbed or at best to park-style landscapes, and if City Regions are to be saved from this dismal fate it is essential to consider what types of distinctive landscape are valid for our new land-uses.

The following chapters discuss these potential landscapes, beginning with the urban centres and moving out to the wilds.

# 11. The Built-up Urban Landscape

We experience landscape as we do architecture in many ways, and one of the most important is the consciousness of space. Here there are two quite different experiences depending chiefly on size. Large-scale landscapes are stretches of ground patterned with masses and open areas, and except on hilly land are chiefly two-dimensional: they are a composition at a distance which we see as a view – that is, we experience them chiefly from the outside. Small-scale landscapes on the other hand are three-dimensional volumes which enclose us, and our experience of their space is from the inside. The obvious parallel is a building considered from the outside at a distance or from within, and if the building is enlarged to city-size then the rooms become self contained urban landscapes.

To those who live in a big city it is not a vast inhuman whole but an assembly of separate human-scale places. We do not, any more than in large forests, encompass it all at once; we cannot see the wood for the trees and we therefore live in the small-scale intimacy of our own forest clearing. The built-up landscapes of cities are half-indoor half-outdoor environments – their size is intermediate, so is their climate, their surfaced ground is like floors, and their spaces are partly roofed – entrances, awnings, arcades, covered markets, as well as the buildings and transport we move in and out of.

Modern man in fact is typically an indoor animal; we live and work chiefly indoors and go out as a conscious experience, and this is so even in equable climates where on holiday we live out-of-doors. In car-enclosed America the change is even more advanced than here, and a recurrent dream of visionaries, at least since the nineteenth century, is of completely roofed-in cities – a doubtful utopia which Minnesota is now proposing to build for a quarter of a million people under domes two miles across.

But roofed or not, central urban landscapes are chiefly architectural and their essential materials are buildings and surfaced landforms, though water and vegetation may also be important. Vegetation, however, except in parks and gardens, is mostly decorative, providing free organic patterns in the geometric man-made environment. What will grow is also determined by man-made conditions — root-run, depth of soil, water supply, amount of light and air pollution, and except at ground level, the need to grow plants in containers.

Most urban landscape, however, will not be of this highly architectural kind, but rather what we think of as suburban. Until now the pattern of the typical suburb has been dominated by roads, with the houses spaced out in parallel rows and with larger or smaller gardens round each or each pair. When well done this can be delightful, especially in spring and summer when the flowery-bowery gardens half-hide the houses and the area becomes a residential park, though in leafless winter the lack of coherence between separate gardens makes a far less satisfactory scene. Often in any case it is not well done, but is either cramped or depressingly spread out like units in old isolation hospitals; the houses are forlornly scattered with dreary expanses separating could-be neighbours, and making bleak journeys through the wind and rain to schools and shops and buses. Such meaningless voids are not open spaces but merely the areas of plans where nothing happened to be drawn — smaller versions of the unplanned green of larger development plans. The spaces of self-contained landscapes should be positive volumes defined by the landscape material: the voids of prairie planning are not spaces but gaps. Something could at least be done to make them pleasant by earth-modelling and planting, as the Civic Trust has shown.

Best of all, however, would be to build as many houses again in the empty spaces and create enough life to fuse the scattered development into a community. The people complain of loneliness, and no wonder, for we long to push the forlorn units together into a mutual relationship, and even the early New Towns, for all their merits, would feel far better places to live in if one town were superimposed on another and shuffled together to fill up the gaps.

But new planning densities are rising and this will produce more

*The highest-density early New Town, seen from the town centre. Puzzle – find the houses.*
*Active citizens: they have to be.*

urban layouts whatever their quality, and in general design seems to suffer more from too much space than too little. Artur Glikson sees shortage of land as an advantage, 'a chance to intensify land-use and settlement and of enhancing the identification of man with his environment'. Certainly for every design which would benefit from more elbow-room we see a dozen which would be better with half the space. A restricted site seems to act as a discipline which stimulates designers to the hard-won best they are capable of, and is no doubt why the best buildings alas are so seldom on the best sites.

Tight layout also brings buildings into visual relationship with each other and creates new meanings from the juxtapositions, like the New York skyscrapers which are not separate point-blocks as ours are but congregations conversing, like trees in a forest. But the benefits of close relationship are not merely visual or why do we choose to live in villages? The charm of villages is their cramped layout – the cottages snuggle together in friendly groups, or sit companionably side by side with doors opening straight into streets so narrow that neighbours can talk across the road from their doorsteps.

Modern by-laws very efficiently destroy village character, for if we were to slice up even the most charming of village streets into houses set back on the council's building-line very little would survive. Many by-laws are aimed at conditions which no longer exist, and by avoiding them (private roads for instance) some of the best new housing is recovering village character, notably the New Towns and firms like Wates and especially Span, whose housing landscapes are good enough to have won them planning permission for a new village of 2,000 houses at New Ash Green in Kent.

This living-pattern of small closely-grouped communities linked to larger centres could well become the unit of the future as the village was in the past. Such 'villages', however, have little in common with the old self-contained rural communities isolated from the world beyond their fields. Modern villages are strictly urban, and even if built in Kentish fields have no more to do with the country than if they were in Hyde Park. They are metropolitan outliers, green homes beyond the Green Belt for city workers. New Ash Green is planned as a series of self-contained landscapes united as a self-contained community with its own open space and recreation areas, compactly grouped and insulated from surrounding farmland by trees, woodland, playing fields and roads. But however excellent the quality this is still an urban development in the countryside, and apart from the fact that the extra cost for services in small rural settlements compared with towns is £200 per family a year, if many of us lived in such country villages there would soon be no country left. The proper setting for such communities is surely not rural areas. These are satellites of cities: why not therefore bring them in closer and build them on urban–marginal land where their lavish amenity areas would be justified as part of the larger landscape pattern? Tree-circled urban villages on urban–marginal land would vastly improve most city fringes, with very little loss to farming and none to the rural countryside. To the villages too there would be various advantages: like available sites, nearness to the city, and a setting of protected green landscape.

In this new style of living-area which is now developing, the housing is planned not as collections of separate units but as integrated communities, and this is clearly expressed in the design; the buildings are grouped in intimate relationships and the open areas are true spaces not gaps.

As prefabrication develops this type of planning will become inevitable, for design will not be of buildings but of groups where buildings are the units of the design. Equally the old road-based rows are giving way to new circulation and access patterns, and from these new-style layouts is developing a new kind of landscape created by a

*This green space between houses is private enough for children to play in safety, public enough for strangers to walk through and photograph them. Basingstoke.*

combination of architecture, vegetation, land-form and sometimes water.

Such landscape is strongly three-dimensional, for in small areas the height of trees and buildings is as dominant as their extent on the ground, and the design is a fluid geometry of irregular volumes experienced from within. It is spaces flowing between masses whose density varies from architectural solids to the airy framework of leafless trees. The outdoor space of such living-areas is in fact as compartmented as the indoor space of houses, with private gardens and semi-private courts opening into more public spaces and roads – intercommunicating green enclosures with their own distinct identity as places.

This is an organization of the outdoor environment fundamentally different from the separate-unit suburb, and its success as a residential landscape depends on a new type of house and garden unit. The traditional house is a box for living: large or small and variously shaped, but essentially a private space enclosed by walls from the outside world. There may or may not be a garden, but it is in any case an outside addition separately used; it does not affect the house whose territory begins at the house walls. In many modern houses, however, this clear-cut distinction between indoors and out has gone. The walls have dissolved to invisible glass partitions which separate inside from outside weather but not inside from outside space. We are no longer private inside the house, and this new style is only satisfactory if privacy is provided beyond the windows. The outside space in fact must be planned as an extension of the house, otherwise what should be private rooms are public exhibitions, and the inmates restore the necessary barrier by covering the picture windows provided by architects who can never have considered the people behind them. For unless we are either compulsive exhibitionists or aristocratically unconscious of the world at large we need private places to live in, and if privacy does not start at our house walls it must start somewhere else. If the garden space is part of our house as in Japan and Persia then the garden must be private: if our rooms open onto a patio then that must be private as in Spain; for though our home may now be our greenhouse rather than our castle it still needs its earthworks, and picture windows were not intended merely to promote the sale of sun-blinds.

Combined with this new house-style is the fact that our gardens are getting smaller; we have less land and we share both land and leisure with our motor-cars. This smaller area we are therefore now beginning to use as an outdoor room, and in our patchily perfect weather are finding we can live outside far more than we ever imagined – it is only that no one can bother to rummage out deck-chairs and set them up on squelchy grass. We need south-facing sheltered corners with dry paving and seats always ready for the summer days which may bless us even in mid winter, and anyone with this kind of roofless extension of their house never ceases to tell us how much they use it.

Whether at ground-level or in future multi-level cities such out-door spaces need treating as part of the inside space of the house. The pattern is already emerging in well-designed new housing, and it also solves the extremely thorny problem of private versus professional taste. This is a new and very real difficulty of our new non-spontaneous design – how far should the trained taste of professional designers be imposed on a public whose untrained taste is different? Since the only value of taste is to give us pleasure the best private taste is whatever pleases us best – gardens of floral clocks if we fancy, or fishing gnomes by plastic pools. But unless our private taste is of a highly-developed kind it will not necessarily give other people pleasure, and it therefore will not do for public places. Public design must satisfy wider and longer-term standards, and therefore needs designers with special aptitudes and training. As laymen we do not suppose we could create good public buildings: we are equally un-likely to create good public landscapes. But where do we draw the boundary between private and public? In landscape the difficulty is even more intractable than in architecture. Living-areas for instance look better if front gardens are run together without fences and laid-out as a whole. But what if the householders hate communal front gardens – as they mostly do? And are tenants of landscaped New Towns to dig up the verges and plant flowers, or build rockeries on the bank across the road? Whatever the private pleasure from such additions they are disastrous to the landscape. But whose landscape? And whose disaster? And where does it start? Such problems are avoided, however, by the enclosed house-garden – within our fence

*An excellent town landscape of interesting hard surfaces and freely-growing vegetation. Plenty of colour in the kiosks and flower-boxes, the clothes of the girls and the small boys climbing the railing. Minimum maintenance, maximum wear. Stevenage New Town.*

206

our own taste is absolute, beyond it we defer to public opinion; and in the best new housing to trained landscape designers.

'Small gardens secluded from the general scenery become a kind of episode,' said Repton, and an important function of the communal landscape is to combine these episodes into a coherent design. Where the gardens are walled or solidly fenced there is little difficulty – they are an extension of the architecture which defines the open spaces, and when the landscape is designed with the architecture the problems are comparatively simple. But most people do not live in fine new designs, and many existing areas could also be vastly improved by landscaping. 'Areas of asphalt separated by stretches of worn and neglected grass are not the right setting for a modern home' – so says the Ministry of Housing, and who would quarrel with them? Here what Brenda Colvin calls 'Pop gardening' will be far more evident, so will garden sheds and garages and the general do-it-yourselfery which is strictly forbidden in the elegant new housing areas. The design must therefore be strong enough to dominate the incidentals, a bold simple arrangement of masses and spaces which provides a controlling framework – as a framework of shelves in a room controls all the unrelated oddments we stuff in them.

The particular character of any landscape must depend on its use, and even where the use is the same, as in housing areas, it will vary with the users – old people, teenagers with motor bikes, small children at play, 'earnest intellectuals' – all need different outdoor as well as indoor environments. Maintenance will also be a dominant factor in the design – whether for instance the grass will be close-mown or rough-cut – but in most public landscapes it is unrealistic to rely on sympathetic maintenance, since labour is often unskilled and most work unsupervised.

Subtle garden effects will not survive either rough maintenance or rough use, for these are public landscapes and need to be tough and hard-wearing like public transport or restaurants. No one would furnish a coffee-bar with fragile antiques, or upholster bus-seats in damask and expect them to survive – or even to look attractive. Buses and coffee-bars have developed their new appropriate styles and materials and so must our new public-use landscapes: no untrodden lawns or carefully-edged beds or delicate flowers or shrubs.

These belong to gardens, and except in very disciplined communities are too vulnerable for places where boys kick balls and ride bicycles, dogs bury bones and cars overrun verges. Much ground will need hard surfacing and in any design the ground-level is especially liable to suffer, whether from over-wear, misuse, litter, or unwanted additions in general. The new style should therefore rely on indestructible effects – on broad massing and spacing, on clear planting of the right trees and robust shrubs, on ground-modelling, on the use of light and shade, of enclosure, and open space, and vistas. Small-scale effects and intimate details must be provided not by careful maintenance but by hard landscape (patterns of cobbles and setts for instance), and above all by the self-renewing patterns of vegetation safely above harm's way.

Our temperate climate is unsurpassed as a home for beautiful plants from all over the world, and self-contained landscapes are the place to grow them in intimate green settings which enhance their individual beauties – thickets of forsythia, clouds of flowering cherries, lilacs and laburnums, almond blossom floating ravishingly pink in our sooty end-of-winter cities, rhododendrons, magnolias, lavishly fragrant banks of syringa, and roses everywhere – not mutilated stumps spaced out in beds of bare soil but unpruned masses and tumbling mounds and flowery hedges, or cascading over walls, or scrambling through banks of laurustinus.

The new clean-air controls now mean that even in grey industrial areas our natural craving for colour can be satisfied. 'Marvellous the difference,' said a park official in Manchester. 'At one time nothing would grow but those old poplars: now we've got roses and flowering cherries – right here in the centre – and all sorts of bedding-out stuff.' And he beamed with satisfaction at a stunning blaze of geraniums and petunias.

More important than the plants, however, is the style of these new urban landscapes which are neither parks nor gardens, and in some of the best new developments there is already the beginning of a distinctive new manner. Like the buildings it accompanies it is likely to be informal, for we have now little liking (and less space) for the grand manner of avenues and formal layouts. Occasionally a superimposed regular plan can bring order to muddled development (as avenues of the same tree through a messy suburb) but in general such insistent man-made patterns disturb rather than harmonize, and we prefer less obtrusive design.

But though the new style may be a controlled naturalism it will need no less deliberate planning, and here there is a fundamental difference between these modern landscapes and amenity design in the past. The old parks and gardens existed in their own right; they were self-sufficient works of art whose sole function was pleasure. But landscapes we live in have a great many other more workaday functions; their design is no longer a fine art but an applied art, and though the function of design in applied art is still to give pleasure, it does it by making *use* pleasant. Design must therefore start not from abstract aesthetics but from function, from the forms most appropriate for what the landscape will be used for; and the best design will be that which provides the best solution for the given uses – always including amenity. It is the business of landscape design, as it is of architecture, to enhance the life it provides for.

# 12. The Green-Urban Landscape

The landscape of our city fringes, whether Green Belt, Grey Belt or no belt at all, is depressingly similar everywhere — an incoherent limbo which is our particular twentieth-century contribution to the scenery of the world. It is a landscape of mutual destruction by two incompatible environments, and the sickness infects them both: cities invade the countryside with eyesores, while to travellers from city centres the opening landscape reveals mostly ugliness.

In limited areas trees could swathe the wounds in green and heal together the two environments, but round large cities the areas are far too extensive for trees to be more than part of the answer. The explosions of urban concentrations in the countryside are like volcanoes erupting through the local rock: as well as the actual volcano of the built-up area, the heat of its presence causes profound changes in the surrounding land, and the process which transforms limestone to marble in human affairs changes farmland to disturbed landscape. This therefore, in its own troubled right, is a new type of environment which must achieve its own distinctive landscape salvation by providing good settings for its distinctive land-uses; it must be used in fact, as marble is, for its own specific qualities.

Since this is essentially urban land the new style of scenery will be a new type of urban landscape which now needs a new distinguishing name. Urban-fringe or urban-marginal suggest merely downgraded forms of true urban which this is not, nor will all development be near towns, but some unavoidably in country areas. Green-urban landscape would therefore be a more hopeful and less specific title, and if green-urban seems a wildly optimistic name for our thousands of acres of heaps, holes and other eyesores, everyone nowadays knows that praise works better than blame. And if we can transform our present disturbed areas to good green-urban landscape, it will be more effective than any other single reform in upgrading our general outdoor environment.

The future of land round cities is to a large extent inevitable. Industry and its services will multiply – more roads, wireways, electrical installations, reservoirs; vastly more sand and gravel workings and so on, and all this whether or not we control the more biddable uses like housing. Equally inevitable seems the decline of farming, for apart from the city's presence the new developments will in themselves further break up the farming structure and make holdings unworkable, while the choice of other jobs in the near-by city makes farm labour harder to come by.

City fringes, like other marginal land, suffer not from over-use but under-use, and this is so whether the use is urban-marginal farming or land without a ground-use, while where extra controls like Green Belts operate the under-use is often exaggerated. Since it is use which keeps land (like bodies) healthy, a first essential in disturbed areas is therefore to find new land-uses whose vitality can carry the landscape transformation. A motorway over derelict land for instance, like the M 1 in South Yorkshire, will not only clear up the hard-core dereliction in its path but will also bring the incentive to improve the landscape along its route.

Equally in Staffordshire the National Coal Board has recently discovered rich open-cast deposits on 1,800 acres (760 ha) of old derelict deep mine workings, and in developing this 'exciting find' the land will be restored to make a new recreational area for the Midlands. It is essential in fact that derelict land should be *used*, not only because we cannot afford to waste these areas near towns, but also because it is the most practical way of getting rid of dereliction. At present the cost of restoration is high, and though it is still a new process and therefore likely to become cheaper, yet even so restoration simply as an amenity exercise is likely to be slow.

Despite its often neglected state, urban-marginal land is valuable – potentially to the community if not actually to its owners. Certainly society pays a high price for its non-use (by longer journeys to work for instance as well as by suffering its unsightliness) and at present is getting very little in return. New land-uses therefore should benefit the general community (as is implicit in its use for roads, reservoirs and so on) and an obvious further use is amenity. This has long been accepted in the German Ruhr, where all open country between the towns is regarded as amenity landscape, and where pleasure-grounds, lakes, caravan sites and so on are established and popular. Our own Lea Valley Park will be a similar use of 6,000 acres (2,400 ha) of disturbed landscape, much of it derelict by default, and similar new proposals are springing up everywhere for new parks in Green Belts, for reclaiming canals, converting gravel pits to pleasure lakes and so on. The public desire for such facilities is enormous even if mostly mute, for it is only the organized sports (in any case declining) which have organized pressure groups demanding more playing fields, and what we need far more urgently are boating lakes, golf courses, picnic areas and all the other things which far more people would enjoy. Recreational land is especially short in the Midlands (the South has its commons, the North its hills) and here the large areas of industrial under-use could be particularly valuable for recreation, with the two negatives cancelling out to make a new green-urban positive.

First, however, we must accept the presence of industry as an innocuous or even welcome companion of our leisure, and this should become easier both as industry reforms its manners and as the old associations die with the generations. With the shining new palaces of automation there is no difficulty, but these we accept not as industry but as public buildings, and it is industry unmistakable that we need to respect in its own valid right.

At present, however, we are still pathologically schizophrenic about industry and the benefits it brings us. We want the benefits, we do not want the industry – or not where we can see it. (Unlike good social workers we love the sin and hate the sinner.) Yet since despite our escapist fantasies the Good Life as we enjoy it depends directly on industry, we might be thankful for processes which give so much to so many. We might even of course be *proud* of our industrial skills (though I doubt whether I should like pylons any better if they all flew banners saying 'Hot Baths For All'). Pride perhaps must wait, but we could begin by accepting industry as an integral part of our environment, learning to live with it as naturally as we once did with farming, instead of emotionally rejecting the foundation of our lives.

'We are trying to introduce a new set of basic values into the relationship between industry and the public at large', said a spokesman for the Central Electricity Generating Board, and though for those like me who were emotionally conditioned when young, heavy industry may always be the dark satanic mills, it will not be for the coming generations. Already there is growing interest in industrial processes, visits to factories are popular, documentary films are widely watched, and everyone enjoys seeing the new machines at work – as building contractors recognize by putting up public viewing platforms. The new generation may be equally without prejudice about the past, not only sophisticated young architects admiring the intransigent northern cities, but hundreds of local enthusiasts who now study industrial archaeology (and even I was almost persuaded to join a Society for the Preservation of Bottle-kilns).

Nonetheless we have scarcely yet begun to recover from the old schizophrenia either in public planning or private attitudes, and only on the intimate domestic scale have we made the necessary change of heart. For the industrial area of a house is the kitchen, and until very recently this was shunned as undesirable. Kitchen work was menial work to be done out of sight, and kitchens and sculleries were hidden from consciousness behind closed doors. But the kitchen revolution has changed all that. Cooking is now a fashionable hobby, and our new ideal kitchens are the proudest and often the best-designed rooms in hundreds of houses. They are more advertised, in brighter colours, in glossier magazines, than any other room except the equally upgraded bathroom and lavatory.

Schools too have wonderfully risen in status, and since the war their design has produced some of our most admired modern architecture. For we always build best for what we believe in (churches in religious ages, palaces when princes are powerful) and one thing the modern world believes in is education (which probably explains why villains in science fiction so often suppress it – to us the burning of books is sacrilege, as heresy once was to the devout and revolution to the powerful). We believe in education and we also willy-nilly believe in industry. To the Victorians indeed its dawn seemed the promise of a glorious future, and to house it they built what is surely their finest architecture. So equally may we, when we once recover from the early mistakes and the late disenchantments and set about transforming our disturbed industrial areas into proud new model-kitchen landscapes.

The industrial services we already accept – roads, bridges, dams and all the large-scale public structures of our new economy – it is easier to see these without prejudice as the splendid artefacts they often are.

Good bridges need no one's praise, the new motorways sweep superbly across the countryside, the parabolic shapes of cooling-towers are beautiful in all lights and all weathers. Heavy industry too can be visually magnificent if we ignore the ground-level clutter which besets it. As distant vistas framed in the picture windows of new high buildings the old conurbations are astonishingly beautiful, and certainly no subject is more likely to win photographic competitions in smart colour supplements than atmospheric views of heavy industry.

The windows and cameras eliminate the inessentials, composing the scene to reveal its distinctive qualities and enhance its intrinsic merits. They perform in fact the function of landscape design, and create small-scale in two dimensions to look at, the good industrial landscapes we now need large-scale in three dimensions to live in.

This very size is an added advantage in combining industry and recreation, for recreational landscapes are equally large-scale, providing for large numbers of people and mostly in motion. Wide open areas, sheets of water, belts of woodland – all these are the right size as a setting for industry, which in turn has the necessarily dominant character to register in large-scale landscapes. Industry can also give weight and focus to what might otherwise be indeterminate scenery; for unless it is of masterly design park landscape easily degenerates to the characterless genteel, or the vapidly vulgar. From such dangers industry can save it: chimneys and cooling-towers are neither genteel nor vulgar but functional shapes indisputably valid, forms of abstract sculpture large enough to register on the landscape scale.

Surprising numbers of travellers on the M 1 admire the fine chalk quarry near Dunstable (now alas disappearing behind a well-meaning but mistaken row of Lombardy poplars) and others watch out for the spoil-heap near Doncaster as a welcome landmark, while our new industrial cities with their pale tower-blocks catching the light in the silvery haze of polluted air can be more beautiful seen from a distance than any other townscape. Certainly it is industry which makes the London Thames so endlessly more satisfying than the Paris Seine. The Seine is a drawing-room river, reliably beautiful but limited and sometimes genteelly dull. The Thames has swept away drawing-rooms, is often ugly but often unbelievably beautiful, a mysterious river, always changing, with the sea-tides flowing in against the embankments and sliding back to the ocean over levels of shining mud. The very mud and the riverside squalor are beautiful in their own landscape, the fringe of cranes along the docks (the trees of London's industrial river), the ships and commerce and culture, the old and the new all superimposed to make the intense and unconcerned life of a modern working metropolis. The Seine is beautifully preserved pre-industrial; the Thames has said Yes to everything even when it should have said No, but it has gained by accepting industry and so can our greener landscapes.

The distinctive style of the future green-urban scenery can only yet be guessed at, but much of what it must be based on already

*Contrasting styles in sculpture for the modern landscape. Temple Newsam, Leeds –*

*– and Hounslow Heath, London.*

exists in the present condition of disturbed areas, the inevitable
further industrialization of city fringes and the probable further decline of urban-marginal farming. Despite the difficulties, however,
farming is still an excellent land-use here; certainly from society's
point of view if not from the farmers'. By providing a ground-use it
maintains the landscape while producing profitable crops, and also
creates the rural scenery we are anxious to keep near cities.

'The cheapest way, indeed the only way of preserving the countryside in anything like its traditional aspect is to farm it.' So said the
Scott Report, clearly recognizing the farmer as society's landscape
gardener. But the natural crop of land near cities is now neither
wheat nor cows but buildings and people, and farmers therefore need
encouraging in more positive ways than by mere approval. The new
powers for improving farm structure could be particularly valuable
here, where the inevitable rearrangement of land due to new develop-

216

ment could be used to create more compact and insulated holdings. Although motorways for instance slice up farms, they also make excellent boundaries; as do reservoirs, transformer stations and electrified railways. Here too is a chance to create the show farms suggested earlier as part of both landscape and recreation, and indeed it is possible that by careful planning of city fringes as a whole, farming could actually increase instead of steadily declining.

The basis of all our landscape is land-use planning, but this is particularly so in green-urban landscape, and here four types of land-use are possible. The first is farming and the second is amenity, including recreation. These are both desirable uses but both need deliberate provision, and both are also necessarily limited – farming by conditions, amenity by cost. The other two uses are dependent on planning; neither is considered desirable and which occurs in any area is determined by policy. One is industrial land-use and the other is dereliction by default. Of the four the only use which thrives without anyone's help is dereliction, thus when farming and amenity are limited by necessity and industrial use by policy, then neglected land is the unavoidable result. It is this inevitable outcome of landscape-planning in terms of pre-industrial landscape which has produced the limbos surrounding our cities.

Unused space is dead space (it is another adage to pin over desks) and in disturbed landscape dead space is an unattractive corpse to live with, even if abandoned cars are now to be removed from time to time. Christening it Green Belt does not change it, since the only defence against dereliction by default is alternative green-urban uses: farming where it works, amenity where it pays, but otherwise (and this is the new difference) by encouraging uses at present discouraged by the Green Belt classifications of land-use. Industry for instance, instead of being herded into industrial estates, could improve much neglected land and help to carry the cost of shared recreation areas. Recreation and farming alone can never surround our cities with green-urban landscape, but prosperous industries can realize the benefit of an enhancing park setting and of pleasant surroundings to tempt good employees. Why not lunch-hour sun-bathing and after-work golf for the new-style workers of the future? And why not share the same roads and car parks and lavatories? – even the same

# New Lives, New Landscapes

*A main road and a belt of trees successfully insulate green-urban farming from new housing. Leeds.*

canteens and rest rooms? With a five-day week likely to shrink even further, this (like the development of cities for recreation) is surely the logical use of otherwise half-used facilities, especially since by their very nature as work and leisure the uses would automatically alternate. Lavish grounds and elbow-room are now only justified if fully used – as universities for instance already share their sports grounds with local people and their accommodation with summer conferences. All kinds of old-fashioned compartmented ideas about private property are already going: they take up too much space in modern living, like private cars in city streets compared with public buses.

Green-urban areas could equally be the setting for all kinds of public institutions, for there is now no great difference between factories or offices or universities or hospitals or other large public buildings. They could all be combined harmoniously in landscape designed to suit their scale and to provide recreation for their (increasingly similar) users. And as car ownership increases, institutions will be more not less accessible on city fringes than in city centres. It is pre-car thinking which equates distance with isolation, for it is not a swift five-mile drive (8 km) to a waiting car park which isolates car travellers, but road congestion and lack of parking space. Car journeys are reckoned by time not distance.

All large modern buildings are in effect built on derelict land, since whatever the quality of the site to begin with their very creation destroys it. The processes of modern large-scale construction produce their own dereliction which must afterwards be restored, and the logical sites for such violent birth are in landscapes already disturbed; where the heavy machines, the spoil from foundations, new planting and grassing and so on can be used as part of the area's larger restoration. Even more important, the alternative site will be undisturbed, for no matter how good new developments may be in themselves, in terms of landscape they are bad; they are so many extra areas of spreading urbanism. And of all our crimes against posterity this in the end may count as the worst because irreversible – that with thousands of acres of derelict land and thousands more of disturbed, we do not restore and use it but go on invading our dwindling heritage of irreplaceable countryside.

Such multi-use of the green-urban belt would be to make use of its distinctive merits, and the advantages would be many. Recreation for instance would protect the inner Green Belt far more effectively than any legislation, for the public are ready in fierce defence of amenities they value – as various people have found to their cost down the centuries. And recreation would not only contain the cities' spread but could also mean closer planning of the inner urban environment. For though we need open spaces in cities they should be urban spaces contained and created by the architecture – squares, patios, playgrounds, paved areas off streets – spaces woven everywhere into the city's life but taking little land compared with parks for organized recreation. Except in the largest cities large open spaces inside cities disrupt them: developed green-urban belts can contain them. This is the pattern which makes Cumbernauld (like the ill-fated Hook) such a marked advance on earlier New Towns; the closely-grouped town on the hill is ringed by playing fields, a golf course, parks, and industrial areas.

Such belts would also be good-neighbour fences on the landscape scale, separating the incompatible farms and cities; for neither industry nor recreation contained in suitable areas are anything like the same trouble to farmers as free-ranging urban neighbours on the other side of the hedge.

The actual character of the green-urban landscape would to a large extent develop spontaneously from the land-use planning and from the general landscape treatment suggested in the final section of this book. Deliberate design would chiefly be needed for the difficult task of composing the landscape as a whole – linking the city with the countryside beyond, and using the recreation areas and trees and new development of the green-urban belt to fuse the scene to a balanced composition, where the different areas complemented each other as parts of a coherent whole.

This is always the aim of landscape design but is here doubly important, since if a good overall design can be even partly achieved the quality of the materials is far less important. In more familiar contexts we know this is so – well-styled clothes can look excellent in cheap cotton, good interior decoration can turn rough materials to advantage. And it is equally so in landscape; beds of weeds in neglected eighteenth-century parks make attractive undergrowth between trees and grass, or wasteland and willow-herb an excellent foreground screen for industry.

The landscape character will vary with the land-use and the original state of the area, but much recreational land will probably be park-like compositions of open spaces, leafy walks, man-made lakes, golf courses, riding tracks, games pitches, paddling-pools, tot-lots, grassy areas for games and picnics, for week-end camping and caravans. Some of the old parks of aristocratic mansions already function well for public recreation; such as Clumber Park, owned by the National Trust and enjoyed by over 100,000 visitors one recent Whitsuntide. These are arrangements of grass and trees, land-form and water, in a naturalistic style which achieves its effects by ground-shaping, by the masses and spaces of the vegetation, and by the subtle contrasts of colour between dark trees, pale grass, sky and sky-coloured water. We ourselves would now provide the life supplied in the eighteenth century by animals (sometimes by life-size animal cut-outs when the genuine article failed to stay where needed in the view). Some new parks might be similar in style – plebeian latter-day descendants with industry replacing the stately-home life.

By no means all green-urban landscape, however, would be park-like. In derelict areas man-made land-forms would dominate and could be used to create new kinds of scenery, like the cheerful landscape of steep little hills of heather and birch which has developed spontaneously on spoil-heaps from early mining on the site of Dawley New Town. Both knowledge and methods for treating derelict land are rapidly improving, and Germany is even planning a Nature Park on brown-coal mining wasteland. With the huge new machines spoil-heaps can be regraded to gentler slopes, and grass can generally be established on difficult areas by hydromatic seeding (a slurry of suitable seed and fertilizers with a binding mulch sprayed under pressure). On weathered spoil-heaps left undisturbed suitable trees may grow directly in the waste, and Lancashire runs courses on planting spoil-heaps which are partly aimed at children.

Derelict land is not all heaps, however, for holes cover an equal area. Holes are potentially valuable for dumping new waste both from cities and from industry, and the 1970 Conference suggested a

*The kitchen revolution begins to spread. Hospital boilers housed in glass and used like eighteenth-century temples as a decorative feature in the grounds. Young Batman considered them 'smashing' – an ominous but so far unfounded description.*

national system to correlate waste-disposal and land reclamation. Some land can be restored to farming and other uses, but wet holes, including mining flashes, are valuable water areas. Derelict land in fact has great possibilities for recreation, and certainly spoil-heaps should not be indiscriminately flattened whatever our present revulsion. With imaginative shaping and landscaping they can have the same attraction in flat country as islands in water, and they also make excellent playgrounds – not only for genteel games of hide-and-seek but also for more violent joys like sliding down their precipitous slopes on large tin trays (the speed was glorious, the crashes many, the dirt all-pervading; and though we went home in a state of filth no modern mother would put up with, surely suitable heaps could be surfaced for the benefit of a cleaner generation).

Gentler slopes make excellent roller-coaster areas for children on bicycles (though we only had scooters, mine made by my father from

223

two old pram wheels and odd bits of wood – a very fast scooter with very wide handlebars and two very large cycle bells, whose pitch I adjusted by tightening or unscrewing the tops). Regraded tips could also make interestingly rugged golf courses (there are already a million golfers in Britain). And why not adapt some larger areas for motor-cycle scrambling? And in winter for tobogganing? Or even, with our increasingly prosperous leisure, for artificial ski-slopes?

Where they are used functionally the new techniques in land-shaping are already creating a new type of landscape, as in the cut-and-fill of motorways, dam embankments and especially in road crossings and flyovers. This is engineering landscape of confident man-made land-forms, where the controlled slopes, the sweeping parallels and the clear-cut interacting curves make magnificently complicated compositions of great intellectual beauty. Road inter-changes are modern three-dimensional arabesques on a splendid scale, and on city fringes where they commonly occur are often the final triumphant slicing up of an area messily and irretrievably sub-rural. In industrial parks they could be superb decorative structures flowing with coloured cars like giant toys. Roads and traffic can be exhilarating like airports and railway stations, and the number of people who park from choice beside busy main roads proves that silence and solitude are by no means what everyone wants of their day in the open.

This engineering-type landscape could be an excellent setting for the engineering architecture of many modern buildings, and imagina-tive young architects could design experimental prototypes where no one would have to live with the mistakes. Why not competitions for entirely new structures – for a new form of car park for instance? At present we either leave our cars on a patch of ground or house them in human-style buildings. Why not new structures, half-landscape half-engineering, where cars are the natural inhabitants instead of being, as they now are, a large and prosperous form of landscape litter? For cars are litter in the landscape when alive as well as dead, though dumps of old cars are a peculiarly offensive form of rubbish which will vastly increase in the future. But here the new monster car-crushing machines could transform the squalid dumps to self-respecting open-air factories where cars are the raw material. Sited on urban-marginal land in suitably robust landscapes they could even become attractions for the thousands of watchers who would enjoy seeing old cars crunched up like waste-paper. Violence, sadism, our love-hate relationship with cars – all could be satisfied in the practical process of getting rid of them.

As a simple beginning the methods which produce our fine new kitchens by converting the old could equally, if applied with determination, convert our disturbed areas into green-urban landscape: stripping out everything decrepit and unused and obsolete, replanning to suit our new needs, installing the new equipment of new land-uses, and then redecorating the whole. The raw material is there – the valuable wasted land and the site-use ground owned by public bodies – the money is also there potentially, and so are the planning controls of this urban Green Belt land. We could surround our cities with landscapes directly evolved from industry, combining the wide range of new industrial uses into coherent scenery, as urban landscapes combine an equally wide range of urban uses. A new scape in fact for our new industry, to set beside the old townscape and farmscape.

The scenery would be very various, but like the equally various scenery of town and country could still keep its identity, while as an authentic expression of our new society green-urban landscape would probably evolve a similar aesthetic everywhere – perhaps the sophisticated yet simple-seeming elegance which particularly appeals to modern taste. As in the built-up urban landscapes this will be a new style, but far more than that it will also be a new kind of scenery, and here is an unrivalled chance for landscape architects to do large-scale creative work on their own terms. In urban areas they are mostly governed by architecture, while in the wild and often the rural landscape they must be anonymous. Their task there is not to design new scenery but to integrate new development with a landscape already existing, and in so far as we are conscious of their work they have failed: success is invisible. But in the green-urban landscape they could emerge in their own right, and not only design set-pieces but create an entirely new type of man-made scenery as Le Nôtre did and Capability Brown; create in fact a new kind of outdoor environment.

And it is quite possible that future generations will prefer it to the future countryside – for all we know many people would prefer it

*No need to be Capability Brown to see the capabilities of this derelict land for excellent landscape. Durham.*

now, for no one has studied what exactly it is we want when we set off for a day in the open. That we congregate on country commons proves nothing unless there is a choice of something else, for the day out may not be *desire* for the country but only *escape* to the country as the only alternative to the ugly areas where thousands of people live. There is no reason to suppose that rural landscape is what most people would choose – certainly not the rural landscape of the future.

We seek many pleasures in the open air – freedom in green open spaces, trees and grass, flowers and birds, water – certainly water – but these now have little to do with the countryside of farming, and cannot in fact be provided except where farming is marginal. Industrial landscapes on the other hand *could* provide them, and unlikely as it seems in its present state, derelict land has far more potential as a landscape of pleasure than any farmer's fields. Who knows? – in fifty years' time the West Riding of Yorkshire may be a thriving holiday area whose only competitor for popularity will be its ancient rival Lancashire.

226

# 13. The New Farming Landscape

Few of us admire the landscape of new-style farming – protests from amenity societies, letters to newspapers, complaints to local authorities – our twentieth-century objections to the landscape of amalgamation would make an anthology at least as large as the eighteenth-century objections to the landscape of enclosure. And we can only hope that the parallel is promising and that in time our new methods will produce a countryside which future generations will cherish as we do the old.

One thing is certain: farming must either progress or regress: there is no standing still. Either farming develops as part of the industrial economy or it degenerates. Already where old-style farms survive they grow steadily poorer, and their poverty is seldom picturesque – sagging barns, fallen-in roofs, rotting sheds and fences, broken implements in rat-infested rubbish, poor animals on poor pasture, blocked field-drains, dying trees bark-ringed by hungry stock, rusty iron beds across gaps in hedges and all the depressing rest. This only slightly exaggerated picture, and not the old picturesque scene, is the true alternative to modernized farming, as slums are now the alternative to modernized houses, and where dereliction is held at bay it is only by the overwork of the underpaid.

It is the new developments in agriculture which save our countryside from the farming slums which threatened in the inter-war depression, and whether we like them or not the changes are a sign of excellent health. Our new-style farmland is a living and thriving landscape efficiently adapted to the modern world and productive as it never has been before, and though we may regret the old countryside which it is ploughing away we must still admire its vitality. Regret, however, is much easier than admiration, and there are pessimists who feel that efficient food production and good landscape

*Lane through a fertile valley. A pleasure for travellers, but for farmers all the vegetation in the picture is worthless weeds.*

must always cancel out. But so long as we still depend on plants to convert the sun's energy to food we can still be hopeful, for a countryside of crops grown by no matter what method will always have its attractions. What would be truly disastrous would be the knowledge to produce food without benefit of plants, as we already produce fertilizers without animals. Already too it is possible to by-pass animals by growing meat-cells in a nutrient solution, to extract proteins from oil, and to produce milk by chemical digestion of grass. It is not inconceivable that plants too might be by-passed, and the green miles of farming countryside replaced by a new synthetic food industry. Long may the secret of chlorophyll remain undiscovered.

But since the crops which are still safely with us are now the only logical vegetation of farmland (a field of wheat needs no hedge to protect it from a field of hay) and since trees and hedges may be visual treasures yet seldom make farming sense, farmers are understandably unimpressed by arguments which seem to them mostly rationalizations by non-farming preservationists. Our present countryside, however, was not achieved by preserving the old open-field landscape but by the mellowing of the raw new system of enclosure, and our future scenery equally must be based on civilizing the raw new landscape of amalgamation. This is certainly necessary, but there is no reason why good health should mean bad manners.

After the loss of trees and hedges the commonest complaint is of the unsightliness of new farm buildings – the crude structures and brutally ugly makeshifts now increasingly common on farmland. Certainly the National Farmers' Union is not justified in claiming that 'farmers have cooperated very successfully with the planning authorities to ensure that new farm buildings do not spoil rural amenities'. Some have. Some have not. All should. Many buildings available to farmers however are ugly, though the Farm Building Association is actively concerned with reform, and the standard is likely to improve if only to avoid further planning restrictions.

With the present speed of change, however, farm buildings quickly become obsolete, and solidly-built permanent structures are not economic. But why not a well-designed range of standard basic components (walling, roofing, partitions, etc.) which could be taken down and re-assembled to suit changing needs? Remploy have already done it with their Lundia shelving (designed for factories but invaluable for houses) which can be rearranged in endless combinations of shelves, cupboards, working-tops and so on – built-in furniture in fact which in half an hour can be rebuilt somewhere else as something different. Certainly farm buildings need not be ugly even if no longer picturesque; they are simple and functional like the new landscapes they belong to, and some of the large shapes like Dutch barns and the increasingly common silos compose well with the new open landscape.

But farm buildings still need care – with placing and planting (a tree or two, even a few hawthorns will ease them into the country-side) and also with colours and surfaces. Repton recommended an 'invisible green', but unless green is camouflage khaki it is generally a bad colour in the landscape and neutrals are better. (Repton also had a horror of white paint as garish, and would certainly have deplored my own low taste for poppy-red tractors and marigold combines like children's bright toys in the new enormous fields.)

In old farmsteads what we admire is generally a combination of three things – the buildings themselves, their immediate setting and their relationship to the landscape. In a close view the buildings are the most important, but the emphasis changes with distance, and in the general countryside it is the siting which matters most. Often indeed this is an old farm's greatest beauty, for unlike urban country-lovers farmers were not concerned with looking at the landscape but settled in the most comfortable place and became part of it. The farm is an incident in a wide scene, and organically related to the land to which it belongs. Where well-designed new buildings are on the same site as the old they take the same place in the landscape, and some new farm groupings are as attractive as the old.

But not all are on old sites; roads and other services now often dictate new positions, and rows of raw brick and asbestos huts along a laneside field are a very different matter from cow-byres grouped round a cow-yard. Farms have always been factories for producing food, but when they *look* like factories they destroy our idea of the rural countryside. Many new farm buildings are industrial buildings just as new farm houses are urban-style houses, and it makes little difference to the landscape what they are used for or who lives in them.

It is possible, however, that factory-style buildings for housing animals will not be common in the rural scene of the future. A large part of animal husbandry (as of all farming operations) consists of moving things about – feeding-stuffs, water, waste products and so on, and ultimately transporting the output to the consumers. Carry-ing the home-grown portion of their food to the animals may well be only a minor consideration compared with water supply, sewage disposal and distance to markets; and the siting of animal husbandry

*Modern silo and barn – as at home in the landscape as the church they resemble.*

may therefore be determined by local roads rather than local fields. Its logical place may often be on urban-marginal land near the cities it serves, like the new-world dairy-farm outside New York which uses the heat from cooled milk for central heating and hot water. This would take factory farms out of the rural countryside into the green-urban landscape where they appropriately belong.

Many things we dislike in modern farming, as Jane Jacobs says of cities, are due to problems not yet solved. The burning of straw for instance (and often of neighbouring trees and hedges) is a crude and wasteful process, so is the indiscriminate toxicity of sprays which have caused such lamentable destruction of wildlife. Where are the skies full of larks? How much longer shall we hear the vanishing cuckoo? Or owls on winter nights? Buzzards and magpies and jays are rare where they once were a pest. Our butterflies are disappearing with their food-plants. But farmers are scarcely to blame for using the poisons so freely offered and so efficient at increasing production. And what about gardeners who attack them? Have we never used the same poisonous sprays on our roses and fruit-trees?

But the misuse of sprays, like the misuse of factory farming methods, is valid ground for quarrel. Both, however, are potentially controllable, and as landscape the really intractable problem of modern farmland is its visual vulnerability. In the new open country-side everything is mercilessly exposed. With no distraction, no saving barrier of hedges, every incongruous addition in the landscape is revealed like the litter on commons when the screening bushes are destroyed in fires. A single ill-sited filling-station or ill-advised group of houses can become the destructive focus of a whole stretch of countryside. 'It is not the removals but the harsh additions that have been made which are the worst grievance' (there is a certain wry comfort in recognizing our modern complaints in Wordsworth's *Guide to the Lakes*). 'How much the charm of what *was* depended on what was *not*' – it is doubly true of our open farmland, and much of our dismay at losing the hedges is at what is revealed beyond.

For more than four fifths of us now the only material involvement with farmland is that it provides half our food. But since prosperous industrial man does not live by bread alone (nor even by cream and cheap chickens) urban enjoyment is also a vital if invisible crop in the countryside. Therefore even though we may no longer walk on modern farmland with its new intensive methods, yet we ought to be able to look at it with pleasure. Farmers cannot afford to preserve the past at the cost of efficiency, but they can be expected to avoid needless ugliness in a countryside we all have to share; and just as we must avoid material damage, so they should avoid visual damage. We all need better countryside manners. Why not a Country Code for Farmers?

Public concerns like airports and defence installations are at present free to be as intrusive and unsightly as they please, yet all development in the same landscape needs the same visual controls. And though we have little reason to hope that most developers will be conscious of amenity, we have every reason to expect that planners should, and it is here in the new open landscape that results are most visible and controls most effective.

But though farmers, like everyone else, should be enjoined to avoid unnecessary eyesores, they are not, except unconsciously, landscape designers. Farmers are agriculturalists, with British farmers among the world's most efficient professionals, and where their straightforward functional landscapes are satisfactory as scenery there is no one better to manage them.

But if we want something else – design for amenity for instance – then farmers arc not the people to do it. In Holland the State encourages farmers to employ landscape architects by paying their fees, and though this seems an unlikely development with sceptical British farmers, we are certainly ill-advised to ask landscape design of men who have neither the training nor the aptitude for it. Nonetheless there is much hopeful talk of farmers replacing the vanishing trees in our landscape by planting new groups on odd corners of land, and also replanting small woods and windbreaks for shelter and farm timber. Farmers in fact are to do society's amenity planting. But they show no signs of obliging – which is just as well, for we delude ourselves if we imagine that farmers would decorate the countryside with charmingly-composed groups of deciduous trees. If they wanted timber they would naturally plant conifers, as they also would for quick growing windbreaks. Nor would they plant in casual groups but in regular strips and rows between fields. One rural adviser in fact specifically recommends Western red cedar in single rows as a windbreak, also squares of conifers aligned in nines or sixteens, and rectangular game-coverts laid out with rows of laurels and other aliens.

But fortunately farmers show no more interest in planting for pleasure than for profit, for if as professional farmers they would plant conifers, as amateur landscapists they would certainly plant cherries or purple-leaved prunus. Farming itself is surely skill enough for anyone to master, and what we should ask of farmers in the countryside is that they should do their own job well; should create a good functional farmscape, efficiently because profitably cared for, well run, with the land in good heart, the crops and animals thriving, and the landscape clean and uncluttered.

In any case the old countryside pattern will not disappear all at once. Some in fact is permanently inbuilt like the network of lanes, and the old villages with their magical old names; and even the vanishing field-pattern is a gradual dissolution which we gradually accept. There is a huge inertia in the countryside which delays all change needing positive action, and the old land-structure of small farms is still strongly entrenched. Also large areas of the country-side, especially in the most attractive places, still belong to the traditional large landowners who have always been concerned with amenity, and this continues to be an important factor in preserving the traditional beauty of our rural landscape.

Some woods too are likely to survive for generations still, and some hedges as boundaries and as barriers along roads (where human animals will still be loose in the landscape and still need containing). Here we might retain or even replant the old flowery walls of hawthorn with all their hedge-bottom life.

And could not the National Trust preserve some typical old-style farms by old-style methods? Very soon they will be just as much historical monuments as any ancient buildings, and future generations would be fascinated to see our agricultural past still surviving in south-western dairy-farms, and upland sheep-farms and zoo-and-botanical-garden-farms in the Midlands.

The rural landscape, however, is not all farmland. Housing for instance has a valid place in our long-lived-in countryside if suitably sited and grouped like the old villages. These are pearls in their green settings, and though we may be less enthusiastic about our modern productions, some new community developments are a promising advance on the usual spread of square-spotted chicken-pox, especially when planting ties them into the countryside. Tree-planting near towns will also mean more vegetation in the general landscape (more trees now in urban than rural areas) and the new Country Parks and recreation areas will also include trees and woodland.

Far more extensive, however, will be the natural tree-growth of unused rural land. This is already evident on commons and is now beginning to spread to other areas doubtfully profitable for modern farming. For in the new conditions the use of marginal land is fundamentally changing even in the lowlands. There are two million acres of marginal lowland and less than half of this is considered improvable for new farming methods. In the past, when no agriculture was intensive by modern standards, different types of farming were more or less profitable, and all land was therefore more or less usable. Poor land meant poor returns, but as wages were cheap it also meant little outlay. This is no longer true since the wages of non-

*A sole surviving oak from the vanished hedge – a relic of the past like an archaeologist's potsherd. The surviving farmer has certainly gained an impressive amount of good arable land.*

mechanized farming are themselves a major outlay, while mechanized intensive farming is an expensive process which needs good land to cover the cost and produce a profit. The difference therefore between good and poor land which in the past was a gradation of merit is now becoming a difference of kind; and unless land can be improved to support mechanization it is likely to be of little value for farming. Already in the uplands much poor land is abandoned, and the neglect is now swiftly and widely spreading to marginal land in the lowlands.

Whereas therefore the old landscape was a variation of farming intensities from rough grazing to arable, the future countryside is likely to consist of two distinct elements – open land intensively worked, and little-used areas eventually returning to woodland. It is an incipient new pattern already developing over hundreds of thousands of acres.

Our future landscape in fact may be as leafy as the old, but not the profitable farmlands. Here fields as we know them will logically disappear, and 'field' return to its original Anglo-Saxon meaning not

235

of hedged enclosure but of open space. (Cart-track is already an archaic name, for when did most of us last see a horse and cart on a farm?) Fields have no intrinsic relevance to land but are artificial divisions of area as weeks are of time; they are arbitrary units created for farming convenience (clearings in wooded country, enclosures in open landscape) and which therefore change as farming changes. Already many hedges and ditches could count as archaeological relics, and we can imagine future historians studying surviving areas of the old field-patchwork as we now study Celtic lynchets and the open-field system at Axholme.

But the new open farmland, if we cease to look at it nostalgically, has its own distinctive beauties, its very openness being one. 'There are few minds that are not exhilarated by extensive prospects,' said Marshall, and after the claustrophobic bustle of cities the calm expanses can be a liberating relief. There are no barriers, we can travel the landscape visually in great sweeping flights. Open land is large and simple like the sea and flows round us to the horizon:

> To one who has been long in city pent
> 'Tis very sweet to look into the fair
> And open face of heaven.

Keats lived in Hampstead, which is scarcely pent, but the open face of heaven is an unlooked-for new pleasure of the new open landscape, where we are conscious of the sky as we never are in wooded country. The fenland skies are famous, but it is not the skies which are different but the fens beneath them, the wide flat landscape with nothing to distract us from the great arch of sky from horizon to horizon. Constable painted clouds as others paint faces, filling notebooks with studies of their changing moods, and in open landscape we too see the clouds, as various and decorative as trees are in different countryside. The sky, said Le Nôtre, was one of the elements he composed with to create his landscapes, and in the scenery of open country half the view is the various and beautiful and above all the *unspoilable* sky.

In large-scale arable farming we are conscious too of the land, the earth itself. We can see the shape of the ground as we never can in small hedged fields, and in our rolling landscapes the modulations of the surface are in themselves beautiful. It is partly because trees smother the shapes of the hills that we resist the upland forests, but the forces which violently moulded the uplands have more delicately modelled the lowlands, and stripping the ground of all vegetation but level crops can reveal unexpectedly subtle land-forms. 'Less is more,' said Mies van der Rohe of his classically simple architecture, and it can also be true of landscape. Certainly it is true of the chalk – 'huge billowy swells of green,' said Richard Jefferies, 'open and unenclosed for mile after mile', and the naked shapes of the hills under changing weather are more beautiful than anything which grows on them except the close skin of flowery turf.

It is only the much-maligned plough, however, which preserves the open man-made landscape of the chalk-hills, for now sheep have gone it would otherwise be quickly smothered in scrub – as it is already on slopes too steep for ploughing. We may lament the loss of the downland turf, but the choice is not between arable and turf but between open arable and enveloping woodland.

In a large-scale countryside quarries and mineral workings – if well managed, as they can be – though still violent wounds in the land are also a fascinating exploration of the solid substance of the ground below the surface shape; they are sections for amateur geologists newly conscious of the earth beneath our feet. The scale of the landscape is also changed without trees and hedges, for whether or not we realize it trees are our yardstick for size in the country. Without them we have no measure of distance any more than we have at sea, and for scale we unconsciously substitute bushes or other tall vegetation, upgrading all other sizes proportionately. It is why a treeless landscape always seems larger than it is, and why planting so reduces country like the Lake District.

This difference of scale is part of our different experience of open landscape. So too is the new loneliness of the farming countryside, for farmland is now an almost uninhabited landscape; people no longer live isolated in the fields, nor except for brief spells with machines do they work there. In the old man-worked countryside the year was a long succession of labourers – ploughing, harrowing, drilling, rolling, reaping and binding, stooking, carrying, raking and gleaning (as well as the little girls bringing the tea). But the same land now is worked swiftly and impersonally by machines – one day the grain is ripe, the next it is gone, and there must now be thousands of acres of arable where no one has walked for years. It is probably true in fact that fewer people now set *foot* on our farmland than at any time since prehistory. Industry has made our truly rural landscapes more solitary, more remote and countrified; it is a difference we notice travelling the poorer parts of Europe – how small the hand-worked fields are, and how like vegetable gardens covering the land.

And in this landscape empty of trees and people – of everything but crops – we are close to the actual processes of farming. The soil itself has a satisfying good-earth quality, and we need not be farmers to appreciate a well-ploughed expanse of furrowed earth or a well-harrowed field like a garden seed-bed. The crops too are prosperous as never before, thriving and exuberantly healthy: thousands of golden acres of cereals, lavish prairies of untrodden grass grown lush and green with nitrogen.

There are also now more varied crops as breaks for grain or as forage crops for silage, and even the close-cut hedges have their

season, waist-high at midsummer and awash with tall grass and flowers. 'Much as these scenes have been injured by what has been taken from them – buildings, trees, and woods – such is the benignity of Nature that, take away from her beauty after beauty and ornament after ornament, her appearance cannot be marred.' It is Wordsworth consoling himself for the stripped-down hills, but it could be our stripped-down farmland. The land has many ways of beauty besides those we are used to.

And the new ways may suit other new uses than farming – as the landscape of travel for instance. Travelling man is seeing man and our contact with the landscape is almost entirely visual. We see it as a changing view, a panorama unrolling along our route like a Chinese scroll, and from our fast-moving cars we see a completely new countryside. The details have gone; flowers which charm us at a strolling three miles an hour are invisible at sixty, trees in hedges

*New-style road and new-style farming can enhance each other. The ' billowy swells' of the chalk are as distinctive under corn as under grass; the road curves with the land-forms; the hedgeless verge leaves open views of the countryside.*

flash by as distractions, and winding lanes are inconveniences not delights. But in return we experience the landscape in a way we could never imagine at a semi-stationary walking pace. We realize the shape of the land directly – not merely *see* the outline of hills but, as on a roller-coaster, actually *feel* the curve and moulding of the ground as we move across it, and in place of the intimate surface detail of the foot-pace countryside we are conscious of the underlying structure of the earth itself.

The best landscape for fast travel therefore is spacious, a bold and uncluttered composition of wide views and clearly-defined effects, broadly stated like a painting of wide brush-strokes, and nearer in fact to the new open farmland than to the delicately-etched country-side we are losing. Our new farmland and new fast roads can make fine landscape combinations in the same large scale and simple functional style, and in its different way swift motorway travel brings us as vividly close to the countryside as walking. Like air travel it is a valid new twentieth-century experience of landscape.

And sometimes of course it is not. Sometimes the landscape is merely dull. There are people whose favourite scenery is the Fens but I am not one of them. I can imagine they are sea, can admire their skyscapes, but on grey skyless days the flat expanses are for me only depressing. Parts of the Midlands are scarcely better and of Lincolnshire worse. Here there is not enough to compensate for lack of trees in the farmscape of large-scale allotments, and since in drained marshes the old landscape of reed-beds and alder-carr has gone completely, the land lacks natural character.

Yet simply by planting trees along the roads the landscape as travellers see it could be vastly improved. Small groups or single trees planted as frame or foreground to the view would transform the dull levels to the background distances of a picture. We have only to consider paintings or photographs of landscapes to realize how fore-ground trees can create a view from indeterminate expanses simply by framing it, and so could trees along roads through dull or empty country. Without diminishing the *trompe-l'oeil* scale of the treeless levels they would define the line of the road as trees do in Dutch landscape paintings, and telegraph poles on our present roads.

It is not only from roads, however, that views of the farming countryside are important, for even though no longer suitable for recreation the landscape of food production still has an essential secondary use as 'offscape'. 'By the site', said Repton, 'we mean not only the place itself but likewise so much of the surrounding country as may fall immediately within the view,' and farmland, though we never set foot on it, may be the all-important element of a site, as the sea is in coastal scenery even though we never leave land. Yet we have huge areas of countryside which most of us never see. At ground-level we realize little of the country which surrounds us, and crowded in cities or travelling on crowded roads 'the sweet Fields do lie forgot', as Andrew Marvell complained to gardeners. It is only from the air that the land-use figures make sense, and we realize that eighty-five per cent of land undeveloped is not merely a figure on paper but miles of green landscape on the ground.

Yet the country landscape is a precious amenity now protected by planning policies we all have to pay for by various inconveniences, and what use is country preserved if we can neither walk on it nor even look at it? In a survey of public preferences a view came second only to water as an attraction, and many beauty spots are essentially viewpoints. The country here serves as offscape and we could deliberately use it thus, as a visual extension of other areas (Country Parks for instance) by a sense of distance and rural landscape. This is the use of farmland simply as visual open space, and many people in the country want exactly that − staying near their cars from choice, or even admiring through the window if given a suitable vantage point to park. And why not? Certainly there can be few ways of providing so much from so little for so many. Even the most xenophobic of farmers cannot object to such use of his land by urban visitors. It is in fact the only recreational use which can actually combine with intensive farming as distinct from being tolerated or contained within it. And at its best our new-world farmscape can satisfy a new-world aesthetic which admires aeroplanes and Swedish glass and modern architecture − simple, functional, sparse, elegant, bare of incidental decoration, and essentially large-scale even in small units.

At present, however, there is a fundamental reason why we feel our new landscapes unsatisfactory whatever their individual merits.

In the land we live in we need a balance of open and wooded country, and need it not only for the practical business of farming and forestry but also as the experience of different habitats. A satisfactory environment provides both the expansive freedom of open country and the sheltered intimacy of woodland; it is a human need which has little to do with the quality of the scenery, and a good view for instance means a good *range* of view not a view of good landscape. It is the openness and space we enjoy, as we equally enjoy in a different mood the enclosing shelter of woods.

In the old landscape the two environments existed as the bare open spaces of the uplands and the sheltered lowland farmscapes of hedges and trees and local woods, and it is significant that the eighteenth-century liking for bare mountains only developed as the new enclosed landscape developed its wooded character. The open-field landscape had been mostly treeless ('common fields have all the nakedness without any of the smoothness of downs', and John Evelyn complained there was not a bush or a tree within miles of his country house). Since the lowlands were bare no one wanted bare hills as well, and early travellers describe them with unvaried loathing. But as the new farmland and growing towns created a sheltered environment, so the open hills and the sea were appreciated as contrast, and this contrast is still what we half-unconsciously value in our landscape. We don't like 'blanketed' hills and we don't like 'prairie' farming – the very words are revealing – for the landscapes are not attacked as ugly in themselves, but as the wrong environment in the wrong place. Hills should be bare and farmlands leafy.

But the large-scale balance of our landscape is now beginning to alter; in fact a chief reason for the changes everywhere is that the old areas of open and wooded landscape are in the wrong place for modern land-use. The old lowland countryside combined farming and timber-growing as well as being the living area for most of the population. But these three land-uses have now been separated; the population has moved to towns, forestry gone to the uplands, and only farming remains on the good lowland soils now being cleared for intensive action.

Since the changes are recent the new pattern is not yet established, for thousands of acres of future mountain forests are still no higher than grass on the open hills, while the lowland landscapes which lap the uplands are often the leafiest, the small dairy-farms not yet affected by the clean-sweep new methods. But the changes are inevitably coming, and as they develop will reverse the patterns of open and closed areas in our landscape, so that where treeless hills now rise from wooded lowlands the farmlands will clear to an open prairie sea with the forested hills like land on the horizon.

This part of the pattern will inevitably develop from future farming and forestry: what is not inevitable is the necessary third element of a sheltered environment for living. For since our timber-growing no longer provides trees in our living areas we must now deliberately

*Here the balance is already beginning to change. The farmland of the plain was once leafy with hedges and trees: now it flows like a sea to the foot of the hills – formerly open downs but now sprouting scrub like an unshaved chin. Beacon Down, Hampshire. The climax vegetation of this southern chalk could eventually be beechwood, like p. 334.*

provide them by amenity planting, and thus complete a new threefold pattern of open and wooded landscape in areas suited to our new ways of living.

It is partly because the whole balance of our landscape is thus changing that so much now seems crude and unsatisfactory; but when once established and mature we could welcome the prairie farmlands beyond the leafy shelter of our towns, like the hills which Cobbett described near Andover: 'This country, though so open, has its beauties. The homesteads in the sheltered bottoms, with fine lofty trees about the houses and yards, form a beautiful contrast with the large open fields . . . You feel a sort of satisfaction, when you are out upon the bleak hills yourself, at the thought of the shelter which is experienced in the dwellings in the valleys.'

# 14. The Man-Made Wild

'The city alone cannot contain urban man: the country calls him. The country is tomorrow's second city.' So said Le Corbusier in his heroic-prophetic style, and his tomorrow is already our today. The country calls and urban man comes. The country is now our chief pleasure-ground, with an estimated three million acres of land in England and Wales used for recreation, half in upland England and a quarter each in the lowlands and Wales. Most of this is marginal land: either hill-grazing or infertile lowland areas like the New Forest, an ancient royal hunting-ground which escaped enclosure when better land was taken for food production.

Since both rural marginal land and urban recreation are increasing together they are two more problems of our industrial economy which, as in green-urban areas, could cancel each other out by a positive policy of land-use. Marginal land has many virtues for recreation; the loss to food production is minimal, it is often attractive scenery, and the necessary control of vegetation – although essential – is a less urgent problem than on more fertile soils. Where farming or forestry continue these recreational areas are held in a balance more or less satisfactory for both users and landscape, but as marginal land becomes less profitable and visitors more numerous farmers cannot be relied on to serve as keepers of the wild landscape any more than as landscape-gardeners of the rural scene. And that the 'wild' landscape does quite definitely need managing by someone is proved by the state of many commons, particularly in the lowlands.

Commons were originally the common grazing grounds of commoners who shared this and similar rights such as fuel-gathering, and their free-ranging animals controlled the vegetation. Commons therefore were managed by a type of marginal-land farming, and this is still so, if less profitably, on huge areas of upland commons. But in the Home Counties, where lowland commons are most frequent, the new commuting commoners in their expensively-converted cottages no longer keep odd cows or sheep to eke out their city wages. The results are clear, especially since rabbit-grazing has ceased to mask the changes, and thousands of acres are becoming impenetrable thickets of scrub which make the land unusable. The fact that such commons are much used for recreation does not provide the necessary ground-use for their management, even though some have survived relatively well (Chobham) while others suffer from over-use (Frensham Ponds) and on some (Oxshott Heath) deliberate efforts have been made to keep open areas and glades for walking.

But these are exceptions, and in the report to the Royal Commission on Common Lands the descriptions are predictably similar − 'scrub and bushes', 'little used, much scrub', 'much deterioration', 'all unused', 'much scrub'. Since the report was made conditions have greatly worsened, for with scrub as with saints *c'est le premier pas qui coûte*, and once established above grass-height bushes grow at alarming speed. The same process is already advanced in America where 'many regions are getting bushed-up at an astounding rate, and unkempt forests are cluttering up the scenery in dozens of states'.

That scrub is rare in nature is small consolation, since natural open areas for scrub to invade are equally rare in a forest climate, but as soon as the open land of farming is free of control vegetation erupts in revolution. It is as if the peace of our countryside were the peace of a slave state, and the gentle field landscape a ruthless oppression. As it is of course, since most land below 2,000 feet (610 m) in Britain is potentially forest, but when methods of oppression are efficient we see only the battened-down calm. Incipient scrub always lurks, however, only temporarily suppressed: it is the state of original sin in our landscape.

On southern commons revolution is already advanced and is spreading now in the uplands as well, especially where busier roads make grazing perilous (commons may not be fenced or forested). The present registration of common land is therefore the first move towards using it more fully, but there is still the serious landscape problem of how commons and similar marginal land can be managed, and any large areas of land allocated for recreation will face the same difficulties.

The Country Parks as so far proposed seem to be envisaged as relatively small and organized – as parks in the country in fact, not as lowland versions of the National Parks. But these too are likely to develop on marginal land, if only by default, and it is essential to work out suitable ways of managing large areas of country for recreation, otherwise we risk the equally undesirable states of neglected scrub or unsuitably urban-style maintenance.

Much marginal land already has its own distinctive character as landscape – sandy heaths of birch and heather, chalk downs, grassy uplands, heather moors and so on – and we shall want to keep such areas as they are with the least possible sign of man's interference. These, however, are not natural landscapes (except as man is now a force of nature) and a policy of 'leaving nature alone' will certainly not preserve them. Nature left alone is in any case impossible in Britain, and even in the protected wilderness areas of America disturbance is difficult to avoid. Controlling forest fires for instance may change the natural vegetation, water for distant cities may lower the water-table and upset the whole ecology of a region, fertilizers and pesticides carried from distant farms can disturb the delicate balance of plant and animal life. Even therefore in man's absence the changes may be profound, and in Britain he is rarely absent. Nonetheless our heaths and downs and moors seem natural to us, and maintenance should aim to keep them so.

Clearly the simplest solution is to continue the land-use which created them, and in the new conditions this is likely to mean extra encouragement, perhaps by subsidies. This solution already works in the uplands, for whatever the intention of hill-farm subsidies their result is to encourage farmers to stay on as keepers of the hill-farm landscape. But to use the same method in the lowlands new categories of marginal land would have to be recognized; both areas too poor for intensive farming but suitable for recreation, and also the urban-marginal land near towns. As a way of management this has many merits – it extracts what profit there is in the land; it keeps a rural landscape; since farmers are skilled in its methods it is more efficient than any other maintenance; and it puts the cost of recreation areas where it fairly belongs – on general taxes not local authorities.

Forestry is the other obvious form of management; it is already widespread on marginal land in the lowlands as well as the uplands, and like farming might be subsidized as the maintenance of unprofitable recreational land. Farming and forestry, however, even in adapted forms, will only work for relatively large and little-used stretches, and more specific methods will be essential for smaller and more frequented areas as well as for lowland commons. Here we need to create a new type of scenery – the man-made wild – a landscape which seems natural but is deliberately designed and managed for recreation. At present we have almost no idea at all of how to do this.

'However we may admire natural beauties,' said Repton, 'without some degree of art and management it is impossible to prevent the injury which vegetation itself will occasion. There is no medium between the keeping of art and of nature, it must be one or the other, and this practical part of the management forms one of the most difficult points.'

It does indeed, and Repton's own solution is of limited use to us, for his landscape parks were chiefly maintained by grazing – a cheap and simple method which partly accounted for their wide popularity – and a practical solution on land which was little-frequented, privately owned and firmly enclosed. But we clearly shall have to find other ways of managing our natural beauties, and Repton goes on: 'We must endeavour to imitate the causes by which Nature produces her effects, and the effects will be natural.'

To imitate nature, however, we first need to understand her, and especially here the processes which change neglected farmland to forest. Forest is the most complete community of plants, and includes trees both large and small, shrubs, flowers, grasses and mosses. These we group for convenience into different layers like the storeys of a building, and the three chief layers are trees, shrubs and herbs. The tree layer may consist of two levels, the tallest forest trees and the smaller under-storey trees which grow below them, while the herb layer includes both flowers and grasses. Mosses may count as a fourth ground-layer, and in man-made landscape mown grass is often nearer the moss than the herb layer.

All vegetation can be roughly divided into these layers, but commonly they are not all present together in any particular plant-formation. Nor is forest established all at once, but generally develops by growing up from the lower layers. 'In the vegetable, as in the animal world, the stronger subdue the weaker: the herbaceous tribes bow to the shrub, and this to the more robust forest trees; and in an unpeopled country a state of woodiness prevails.'

This process described by Marshall we can watch on railway embankments, neglected gardens, or any other abandoned areas of bare soil. The first noticeable growth is usually herbs (weeds and grasses) which quickly cover the soil and create a closed community of plants with no open spaces between them. This herb layer is sooner or later invaded by shrubs which soon outgrow the herbs and often spread to make continuous scrub. The shrub layer is in turn invaded by trees, either seeding in with the shrubs or appearing in the shrubs' protection, and as the trees grow the lower layers are hindered or suppressed.

These first trees, however, are often not the species ultimately best suited to the area, as birch for instance is commonly a pioneer on land where it does not survive – it has light wind-borne seed and is quick-growing, but since it cannot tolerate shade it is suppressed by denser-leafing trees. For as the first type of woodland is established, that too is invaded by further species, perhaps by trees with shade-tolerating seedlings like beech, or whose heavy seed travels only slowly abroad from the parent tree like oak, and it is those best suited to the particular area which will in time dominate and suppress the others.

This final adjustment of the vegetation to the habitat is not confined to trees, for shrubs and herbs go through similar changes in the changing conditions of developing woodland. The early pioneers are crowded out, shaded out, and must compete for root-room as well as space and light. Only those survive which fit into the complicated jigsaw of the final community, both in growth above ground, roots below, and also in adaptation to conditions such as seasonal light intensity. Most woodland flowers for instance blossom in early

*The progression from grass to woodland in a single area. The short turf on the foreground path is bordered by coarse grass with shrubs and seedling birch. Beyond are trees of all ages up to mature birchwood. Oxshott Heath, Surrey.*

spring before the trees cut off the light, or they spread by runners instead of seed, which needs sun for ripening.

But light is only one obvious factor in plants growing together; there are also changing soil conditions, micro-climates and so on, and the final community is a delicate and complicated balance of a great many interacting factors. By changing what perhaps seems only an unimportant detail we may disturb the whole structure, for a community of plants is like a delicately-adjusted mobile, and by altering a single weight we may destroy the whole balance. It is why

250

the original plant communities are now so rare in Britain, and where they still exist are treasured as classic sites.

This evolution of the vegetation from one group of plants to another is known as the succession, and is the natural process of development everywhere. It may be hindered or reversed by outside factors like forest fires or men with axes, but provided the habitat is otherwise unchanged it will again proceed (as every gardener on holiday knows) towards the original goal when these factors are removed. When once established, however, this final community of plants is likely to persist; it is the most successful vegetation for the particular area and is therefore known as the climax formation – a convincingly scientific term which suggests we have firm control of the unruly facts.

This discovery that there are definite plants natural to every area fascinated the early amateur scientists, who firmly believed in the soil's power of spontaneous generation. 'The Earth of itself doth put forth plants without Seed ... and the Nature of the Plants doth follow the Nature of the Mould itself; as, if the Mould be Soft and Fine it putteth forth Soft Herbs; as Grass Plantine and the like; if the Earth be Harder and Coarser, it putteth forth Herbs more Rough, as Thistles and Firres [pine-trees], and Earth being taken out of Shady and Watry Woods will put forth Herbs of a Fat and Juicy Substance.' So Francis Bacon believed in the early seventeenth century, and the early inquirers carried out the most unlikely experiments to prove their somewhat mystical assertions. (About the results they are – not surprisingly – very guarded.)

Our modern knowledge of the woodland climax of Britain is more sober and more reliable. It is different in different regions, but each type is a distinctive group established by ruthless competition over long periods. It is a community not only of plants but also of animals, since both are interdependent – plant-eating animals, plant-pollinating insects, insect-eating birds, herbivore-eating carnivores and so on – these all influence the vegetation and are factors in the balance of the environment, while the aggressive new creature man now dominates all other life.

To imitate nature in any particular area we therefore need to study its ecology both natural and man-made; to know the potential climax vegetation; what plants make up the stages of the succession in achieving it; how the vegetation has responded to man-made conditions in the past; what factors produced its present state; whether these will continue; if not what will happen when they change – and so on. We need in fact very complicated knowledge of an area to find simple ways of developing the particular quality of its landscape.

Much research is already being done on existing environments by bodies like the Nature Conservancy and the County Naturalists' Trusts, and much is already known in a general way: that the grassy uplands are produced by sheep; that heather moors and lowland commons are controlled not only by grazing but also by periodic firing and so on.

Some areas like the Dorset heaths and the Norfolk Broads have been studied in detail (though the Broads are filling up fast with vegetation encouraged by holiday sewage and no longer discouraged by reed-cutting; and since the Broads are the flooded hollows of old peat-digging they are clearly not being added to by the process which created them). The vast upland grazing areas are also being intensively studied both for control and for their farming potential, while in well-documented areas, like the southern chalk, simple reflection proves that 'natural' downland and 'primaeval' beechwoods are alternating states of the same land and depend directly on man. The pollen analysis shows beech on the chalk in the later post-glacial vegetation, but this was cleared by early farmers who made impressive chalk earthworks on the newly open hill-tops. The lynchet fields of the hill-loving Celts still ridge the slopes, but when the succeeding Anglo-Saxons settled in the valleys the hill farms returned to forest, and in the Domesday Survey the old open areas are listed as woodland with pannage for pigs. The forest retreated again, however, before medieval flocks, and the sheep-walks are described by centuries of writers from Leland to Hudson. This is the downland which is now disappearing again with the sheep who created it, either ploughed-up for arable or invaded by shrubs and trees overgrowing the old earthworks.

The new growth is seldom beech, however, for beech is not a pioneer tree and only becomes dominant at a later stage. Many existing beechwoods were planted in the eighteenth century, often sown as seed with a crop of corn and the seedlings left to grow on through the stubble. Chalk therefore will neither be downland nor beechwoods unless we arrange it, and though we know how to manage beechwood the beautiful downland turf with its distinctive flowers is as highly specialized and unnatural as a garden, and considerable experiment with grazing and mowing routines has not yet produced generally suitable ways of maintaining it in our new conditions.

This knowledge of how each area would develop spontaneously if farming or other controls were removed must always be the essential basis for country maintenance. We then have three alternatives: we can accept this spontaneous state of the landscape (as in upland areas above or near the tree-line); we can speed up the natural changes to produce a more acceptable state (as by encouraging trees in scrub and short-circuiting the succession to woodland); or we can change the area to something different like open grass.

The further our design is from the spontaneous landscape the more effort it will take to achieve it, but all non-natural landscape depends on some degree of management, and just as farmland is designed for farming and woodland for forestry so recreational country must be designed for maintenance.

In landscape maintenance there are two approaches. We can either arrange the methods of control to suit the design – as in gardens; or else arrange the design to suit the methods of control – whether by natural conditions or maintenance. The difference is not in the degree of maintenance of the same design but in the design-maintenance combination, and every design implies its own specific standard and methods of maintenance (an overkept 'natural' landscape being as wrong as an overgrown garden).

The design of these new country landscapes must also clearly be suited to their use for recreation, and we therefore need to know what types of landscape work best for various types of use. Specific research is being done on this (at Dartington for instance) and much could be learnt by studying existing areas like the New Forest, Hampstead Heath, the Forest Parks and so on. Other European countries (Holland, Germany, Sweden) already have considerable experience of recreational landscape, as has America of wild areas in National Parks.

But whatever else they need to provide, in intensively-occupied Britain these amenity areas should above all provide the experience of 'wild' country. However carefully thought out, they should still seem natural, as if we had simply discovered a fortunate stretch of landscape which happened exactly to suit our needs. In general the design most likely to achieve this will be a mosaic of the different stages of the succession, with the herb layer for open areas, high forest for mass and shelter, and shrubs used as screens and barriers and variety (this should also satisfy the naturalists).

The worse the natural conditions the nearer the vegetation must always be to that natural for the area or it will not survive, but in any case local plants should always be used unless there are overriding reasons for others (like the need for a thorny barrier, or a windbreak to nurse up more suitable species). In popular areas, however, the natural vegetation is no longer forest but people and cars, and here it is essential to know how much wear different types of landscape can survive. Rocky sea-coasts for instance are indestructible (though not the life of their rock-pools) while sand-dunes are extremely vulnerable. Most inland country is between these extremes, and both different habitats and different stages of the succession will stand different amounts of wear without harm. In America this limit of use has been worked out for each type of landscape, and entry to areas is controlled at appropriate numbers.

Management of country recreation areas must therefore be two-fold: the control of wear and tear, and the control of changes in vegetation at stages below the climax. This last may be either by holding back the succession to keep the chosen mosaic (mowing grass, cutting back shrubs) or by accepting the changing succession and adapting the mosaic as it develops. In the New Forest for instance there are 18,000 acres (7,200 ha) which by statute may be enclosed against grazing animals, though only 16,000 (6,400 ha) at any one time. Woodland is therefore managed by a system of ' rolling enclosure', by which areas of safely-established trees are thrown open to animals, and corresponding areas enclosed and replanted in rotation. Human use might also make similar methods necessary, as by moving camping grounds or car parks, or diverting footpaths to let an area recover.

*Both forms of management are needed at Chanctonbury Ring, which is suffering from both scrub and erosion.*

In an ideal design use is inbuilt and we should use recreation areas as naturally as we do a well-planned house — be unconsciously channelled by land-form and vegetation, spread out by an open expanse overlooking a view, tucked away in intimate bays between sheltering walls of green and so on.

Equally the ideal maintenance would be provided by use as it is in farming, but this is only doubtfully possible. Grass, however, can to some extent be controlled by trampling, especially if the tramplers are spread out by strategically-placed shrubs or boulders, and over-worn areas discreetly stabilized (by invisible hard-core beneath the surface for instance).

Some form of rough grazing might also be possible in some recreation areas (despite the recreation of dogs), not by high-grade animals bred for profit but by tough customers kept purely as grass-cutters and able to look after themselves. Here again research is already in progress but since some sheep when worried will turn on

255

dogs, couldn't we breed a race of good turners? And has anyone tried the acrobatic sheep of Soay?

In finding man-made controls for man-made wilds the help of ecologists is essential. Particularly useful would be advice on the most easily-managed stage of different types of vegetation, while control of scrub in open areas is already urgent on thousands of acres. Besides the traditional methods of grazing, ploughing and burning, we now have new machines and chemicals, including plant sprays which act through the bark in winter with less risk to neighbouring flowers. Scrub and rough grass might also be cut in winter when flowers are dormant and maintenance staff potentially short of work; though cutting is less efficient than slashing by the new machines with splendid names like Rotary Slashers and Jungle Busters; for whereas cutting will slice off top-growth and leave the root undisturbed to shoot again, slashing with spinning chains tears up and lacerates the whole plant. But such lethal weapons need space to operate, control being anything but delicate.

In all our new landscapes we need to use our new methods more imaginatively, for despite the cutters-and-chemicals revolution we still mentally inhabit the hook-and-scythe era, and are blind to the new possibilities of our powerful new tools. We now have magnificent earth-moving machines for instance, yet we still do very little land-shaping, and our early ancestors with laborious bone shovels were far more ambitious earth-shapers than we are. What have we to compare with Silbury Hill or Maiden Castle? or even, considering our resources, with the man-shovelled land-forms of the eighteenth-century parks?

We have the tools but not the imagination to use them, and have scarcely yet started even the obvious mundane uses – earth-banks as sound baffles for instance, or shaped ground of scooped hollows and piled-up mounds to screen intrusions. And why not large-scale informal ha-has as barriers to straying but not to looking? The new recreation areas, including footpaths through farmland, will need new-style boundaries which contain us without fences or loss of the view, and ha-has do exactly that.

In using our new cutting-machines we are scarcely more enterprising, and instead of rethinking the methods for the machines we merely use them to manage our old-style hedges. But since our new strong-arm long-arm cutters can mow scrub as easily as grass, why not make a virtue of scrub's embarrassing vigour by using it in thickets yards across and mown from the sides like hay? At no more than a foot or two high it would make a barrier impenetrable to even the most persistent wanderers, and being always dense at ground-level would safely shelter a world of wild-life in its impregnable depths. Or why not use hawthorn like water in a moat, by hollowing out a wide shallow trench (what are bulldozers for?) freely flowing to suit the ground-form, filled with hawthorn like water and mown from the banks? With no sense of confinement such a barrier would be an uncrossable surface, like moats round animals in zoos. We could now create scenery in fact to provide its own natural boundaries.

Mechanical saws are another new tool which make new methods possible, for just as hedge-cutters make shrubs cheaply manageable so do saws make trees. Coppicing for instance is once again a practical operation, and might be a simple way of preserving young woodland and holding back the progression to high forest by cutting trees back to the stool in selective rotation. (The wood might even sell for pulping and pay for the maintenance.) Coppice-growth has its own particular attraction, and coppice woods are especially rich in wild flowers, while coppiced beech and hornbeam hold their dead leaves through the winter in warm banks of russet and gold.

A great value of marginal land, even if unintended, is as nature reserves; preserving wild-life in the increasingly hostile conditions of most of the countryside. Many commons for instance date from Anglo-Saxon times on land which has never been ploughed, and many are listed as Sites of Special Scientific Interest. Whether or not we intend it our new recreation areas also will become nature reserves, both for plants and wild animals. Our birds in particular, being eighty per cent forest species, are homeless in open farmland, but both the new man-made country and the green-urban landscape will provide new habitats. There will be more trees and bushes for nests and shelter, more undisturbed ground for burrows, and though there will also be more people wild animals are highly adaptable. The ideal environment for hedgehogs for instance is no longer the countryside but suburban gardens, as it also is for increasing numbers of

birds, and more birds now breed in urban areas than in open farmland. Even areas as unpromising as city centres may provide new
habitats, and not only for the recognized urbanites. Black redstarts
flittered until recently in London's troubled Barbican area, and a pair
of kestrels reared a family in a broken air-brick in Upper Regent
Street. I have seen them hovering over Soho (mice? dustbins?) and
they constantly fly across between my window and the Post Office
tower – as do myriads of starlings, pigeons in quantity, local gulls
and ducks and swans, geese once on migration, occasional herons
and hundreds of birds too small to distinguish.

Man's activities create special habitats which wild-life is quick to
find. City reservoirs are well-known bird sanctuaries, sand-martins
nest in sand-pits, jackdaws in quarries, pheasants call from the derelict iron workings at Scunthorpe, the dirty mud of Teesmouth is
famous for its wading birds, jackdaws and Welsh poppies flourish in
Lakeland car parks, as do carpets of wild flowers on any waste land –
one area near central London is blue with wild larkspur. Whether or
not we encourage the process by nature reserves our intentions are
unimportant to wild-life ready to help itself. Nor is it our presence
which drives away other creatures but our behaviour, and it is possible we may now be starting a third phase in the relationship between men and other animals. The first idyllic Garden of Eden state
of mutual trust was long ago over (except between penguins and
explorers on polar ice). Elsewhere arrows, guns and the rest taught
animals to flee man the killer; or if they were slow learners then they
disappeared – like the Right Whale, so called because it made no
attempt to escape and was therefore the right one to find (it also had
the added merit of floating when dead). Wild-life still suffers man's
atavistic hunting instinct – for fun if not for food – but there is also
the mothering urge to tame and feed, and in communal areas the
taming predominates (a rare case of crowds being more civilized than
individuals).

Wild-life is now learning to cultivate urban man for urban luxuries
like bread-crumbs, and already in this third stage there are new
species which deliberately seek man's company; like the National
Park bears in America who have learnt to open car doors and insist
on being fed (a disturbing thought when we slept in the car one night

lost in the forests of northern California). If there were bears they never found us, but the tameness of local animals is a new index of an area's popularity. It may be mid winter remote in the hills, but if birds hop out of bushes when we stop the car it means plenty of picnickers in summer.

For us too these new recreation areas could seem nature reserves of wild landscape in the farming countryside, and just as in the eighteenth century we used our gift for *assisting* nature to create natural landscape parks, so we could use it now to create natural country for twentieth-century recreation.

And in the uplands the wildness may indeed be genuine if hill-sheep farming declines. Sheep are round-the-clock round-the-year millions-strong lawn-mowers with a particular liking for young trees, and what some observers describe as the 'dying hills and glens' of sheep-farming decline we can equally see as the liberated hills and glens of the natural landscape. Bracken has already found new freedom and is now a bad weed of hill-farms. In the past it was cut for litter and trampled by cattle, but as cutters and cattle have gone so bracken has spread, and once established is hard to get rid of, being replenished by underground rhizomes which may weigh up to forty tons an acre (100 tonnes/ha). Bracken grows up to 1,920 feet (586 m) above sea-level but is generally lower, and the bracken-line is below the tree-line.

The natural trees of the uplands are various – birch, oak, ash, wych-elm, rowan, aspen, alder, hazel, holly, bird-cherry, and in Scotland pine. Their possible return would depend on local conditions and neighbouring seed-parents, and especially on intensity of grazing. Where grazing is light enough for woodland to survive it lowers the tree-line by worsening the already poor conditions, and in the same way heather-moorland heavily grazed changes to grass, but returns to heather if grazing is lightened. As in the lowlands the most suitable landscape for recreation would probably be a mosaic – bare mountain-tops, open areas of bilberry moors, grass and heather, with varying densities of woodland on lower ground. The previous vegetation of many areas is known, not only from pollen-analysis and remains in peat, but also by more recent evidence like the pine-stumps on Rannoch Moor and woodland flowers still surviving on

*The man-preserved wild at Beinn Eighe in the Highlands which could serve as a model for the man-made. The trees are the northern variety of Scots pine.*

deforested Welsh hills; while nature reserves may be relatively un-disturbed landscape. Whether or not ecologists would favour deliberate reintroduction of local plants, new vegetation would probably reappear spontaneously in time, as it does so dramatically swiftly where land is fenced off for forestry, and careful control would then be needed to hold the landscape in the desired balance; perhaps by limited grazing by deer as the natural mountain denizens, and the deer controlled in turn by permits for shooting (a method well established in America and already a profitable Forestry Commission side-line).

Natural conditions everywhere must now include man, but that need not mean only man the destroyer as it has in the past. In the beauty of nature reserves like Beinn Eighe near Loch Maree we can see how much we have lost by man's destruction, and Dudley Stamp quotes J. W. Watson on the vanished scenery of the Highlands. 'The primeval landscape has through time been almost obliterated. Still we can glimpse its general outlines, the forests of oak that carpeted the lowlands, broken here and there by heathy crags and cliffs, or by gleaming marshes; the forests of pine and birch that swathed the hillside . . . and moor and heath contending on the mountain.'

He deplores the present desolation of the uplands as 'a true and terrible mirror' of man's exploitation, but it is now possible to hope that the worst is over, since at any level of reckoning the future will find most profit in preserving the natural beauty of the uplands. And if we choose we can use our increasing knowledge and control to reduce our human impact on the natural habitat and to limit the man-made factors which now govern the upland landscape. Geneticists, by controlled crossing of domestic animals, have bred back a primitive type of cattle indistinguishable from the cave paintings; and in the same way ecologists, by controlled conditions, might re-create a primitive type of landscape.

Already it is an unlikely concomitant of the population explosion that just as farmland is emptier so the wilderness is wilder than it has been for centuries. The farming of the past was ubiquitous, but since industry (including now agriculture) by using land intensively needs far less area, it is therefore not industry but agriculture which most extensively alters the natural habitat. The large areas of land with no future ground-use may well return to a state approximating the natural habitat, and our new industrial economy may in fact answer Gerard Manley Hopkins' plea for the Highlands (in what so far as I know are the only four simple lines he ever wrote):

> What would the world be, once bereft
> Of wet and of wildness? Let them be left,
> O let them be left, wildness and wet;
> Long live the weeds and the wilderness yet.

# 15. Roads as a New Environment

A motor-car is a way of life not a way of travel. We travel because we have cars rather than have cars because we need to travel. Without them we arrange journeys in terms of public transport; with them of individual mobility.

This is the obvious first advantage of a car – that it takes us where we like when we like. It is not, like public transport, an external system which we use, but an extension of our personal range like acquiring seven-league boots. But a car is more than extra mobility: it is also an extra living place, a small room packed with everything we need while away from home (back shelves can be intimately revealing). It is also warm and sheltered, a mobile extension of the indoor environment which transports us through the inclement outside world. With a car as our porter and outer layer we need never equip ourselves as independent open-air creatures, but are shell-living animals making only limited sorties from our shelter, and habitual car-dwellers away from their cars have an indefinable air of exposure, as if they had merely stepped out-of-doors. With a car we can sit in private easy-chairs in the public road, and when we park we establish our temporary private territory, so that picnicking by our car is like eating a meal in our garden and is why picnickers seldom spread.

Like the American Indian on his horse we are becoming a new hybrid – Motor-man – who not only travels in cars but lives in them. They are the containers of a portable new way of life and are fundamentally changing the way we use our environment. It is possible of course that cars and the roads which are their territory could be superseded in the future, as canals were by railways and boats by aeroplanes; but there is no sign yet of any alternative for private travel, especially in a small and highly-populated country like Britain

New Lives, New Landscapes

with an intensive system of roads already developed. And as the basis of travel roads are also the basis of land-use and therefore of landscape; even the Roman road-system is still relevant to modern development, and settlement patterns down the centuries have been founded on roads. It is why the car was so swiftly established – it was simply a new source of horse-power in a country already organized for horsepower transport, and with an existing network of roads ready to use.

Physical planning, from the intimate layout of housing to the siting of towns and the opening up of inaccessible areas, is based on road access. Even a new minor road alters the potential of an area, and a new motorway can change a whole region's development. Cars

*Home from home with the kitchen sink and the budgerigar. ' We always bring him along. He enjoys the outing – talks all the way.'*

and their roads are both creators and consolidators of the land-use pattern, and as well as already giving us the world's busiest roads, every new car streaming out of our factories makes change less likely. Which is just as well, for we have only to imagine the horrors of something else like ubiquitous helicopters to realize the virtue of road-bound transport. From air traffic nowhere is undisturbed, neither private garden nor remote mountain-top, but cars have the inescapable if frustrating virtue of channelling disturbance into narrow ribbons of road and leaving us large uninvaded areas to live in. We should suffer our traffic-jams philosophically.

As well, however, as causing congestion the new numbers are altering the actual nature of road-use. When cars were few and road-space ample we travelled or stopped as we felt inclined, taking it for granted that roads were not only for travel but also for public parking and private garaging outside our door. Some people still consider this happy state of affairs as normal, but as a town family now long adapted to parking-meters at both back and front doors our household remembers such carefree road-use as part of a lost Eden (so do our car-borne visitors who must get up in the mornings much earlier than they like).

Garaging (the storing of a large piece of portable furniture) and parking (the temporary disposal of our shell while we go about our separate business) are problems already acute in towns and will soon become so everywhere. Our future road-space will scarcely be adequate for *moving* cars, certainly not for storing them. Moving cars and standing cars are separate categories of object which need separate areas for their alternating states; and not only need them in towns but also in the country, where cars now drive onto commons and into woods, block the gateways of fields and tear up verges – are beginning in fact to destroy the country scene as they already do the urban.

Another landscape problem of increased traffic is the increasing incompatibility of different types of road-use. The car has replaced three former methods of transport – walking, horse-drawn traffic and trains – and when combined on the same road the combination is murderous. Traffic policy therefore is to sort out the categories; motorways for instance are essentially railways with branch-lines to stations, and motorway travel is much like trains – a swift and

*Bus-route and train-route run together. A41 and M1 approaching London, motorway not yet open.*

uninterrupted (with luck) progress through the countryside as a unit in a non-stop belt of traffic making communal long-distance journeys. On these new roads traffic is limited to railway-type users – no local or access traffic, no walkers or cyclists or other hazards – and we can suitably drive our cars like trains.

Most roads, however, are neither motorways nor trunk roads, but the old network of minor routes and local lanes shared by all users, with long-distance traffic roaring through village high-streets. By-passes and similar improvements are a partial sorting-out of users, but whatever is done to segregate types of traffic the private car still combines them all from cross-country journeys to door-to-door visits – it is in fact its great merit that the same vehicle is train and bus and legs, and we can thus make the most complicated journeys without changing our container. It is because motorways convert our cars to trains that they make so profound a difference to travel and land-use.

The difference therefore between cars as legs and cars as trains will always have to be in our driving, and at present many problems are due to the wrong sort of driving on the wrong sort of roads. For though fewer motorists now seem to dawdle like walkers on long-distance highways, certainly far more rush like trains along lanes and city streets, and parts of London's one-way system are now as bad as Paris, where all cars are driven like expresses and crossing la Place de la Concorde on foot is a test of strong nerves.

From unsuitable traffic the environment suffers as well as its inhabitants; buildings are torn down to widen streets, hedges and trees to widen lanes – and often to little purpose since such *ad hoc* responses to local congestion barely affect the traffic problem. There is always an inexhaustible reservoir of additional cars, and whether we accommodate one per cent or two per cent, though it makes a vast difference to the environment, makes little difference to the demand. The starting point can no longer be traffic, allowed to increase without limit and still expecting to be supplied with unlimited access. The starting point must now be access, which increased traffic must share by efficient limitations. This unwelcome reversal of our original ideas has already been forced on us in towns, where access is already controlled by parking and road-use seems likely to follow.

But what we are far from accepting is that regulation of future traffic will be equally essential in the country, and that the only way the gathering flood of cars will find road-room is by channelling on suitable routes. Future numbers will certainly force the conclusion upon us eventually, but if we are to save any country worth having it is crucial to learn now from experience in towns, otherwise we shall destroy our landscape by relearning from experience in the country.

A local lane for instance is too narrow for increased week-end traffic. There are accidents. It is therefore widened and straightened. The new road brings new traffic – it attracts in fact, as the lane did, all it can carry of the inexhaustible supply. The speed is now faster, the accidents more serious, the lane is destroyed. Only the problem is still the same – the traffic is more than the road can carry.

Our lanes were never meant for traffic as we mean it; they are the old ways between villages and scattered farms and they developed as walking routes for men and horses. As access ways they still work even for cars, but only as local streams not as general rivers, and the relentless current of traffic now beginning to pour through them is washing them away like a river in flood through a narrow valley. For to widen and straighten a lane quite simply destroys it. A lane *is* its boundaries – its containing banks and walls and trees and hedges, its windings and unexpected corners: 'improvement' merely substitutes a new route in the old position, like pulling down an old building to put up a new one. And for many country-lovers old lanes are far greater treasures than old buildings. They are our closest experience of the country, an intricate net of ways through the very substance of the countryside, more intimately delightful than anything now left in our landscape, and for birds and animals green ribbons of refuge in the open farmland.

Lanes were made by walkers and for walkers they are ideal: sheltered and close, with endless variety and hedge-bottom interest; the walkers are happily contained by the boundary hedges and the countryside is displayed as a view beyond. On such routes (as on city streets) cars should surely exist on sufferance – in discouraged numbers and at limited speeds, and certainly they should not be helped in their depredations on the countryside by road 'improvements'. Cars have their own roads with walkers either excluded or existing on

*Successful compromise – a path for walkers beyond the bank. The roadscape is undisturbed and the walkers are safe from traffic, with a view of surrounding country.*

perilous sufferance, but cars are such universal aggressors that they need to be controlled elsewhere. (Either that or walkers might somehow be made as destructive to cars as cars are to walkers – a wonderful prospect of nervous cars scuttling away from enraged pedestrians.)

In the Lake District where in holiday seasons the traffic of the future is already with us, it is already more than the roads can carry by their present free-for-all and therefore inefficient methods. Instead of further destructive road-widening to pour still more unmanageable numbers through the vulnerable heart of the area, there are now proposals for classifying roads as main travel routes (but with a speed limit of 45 mph (72 km/h)), feeder roads from these to recreation areas, and all other roads kept for walkers and local access, with restrictions as necessary.

The partial taming of cars in towns, or at least the exclusion of all but a fraction of potential traffic, has already caused various changes in their use. The average British family spends more on transport than housing (nearly twelve per cent of income) but of private cars only thirty-eight per cent are used for work (so an A.A. survey found), the rest are for pleasure. Already therefore the private car chiefly provides transport for recreation (which means that future city-dwellers will still want cars even if they use public transport inside cities).

The same survey found that more than two thirds of car-owners went away in them for holidays – up to three times a year, and seven eighths of them in Britain, and this apart from the thousands of day-travellers streaming out from cities each week-end. Roads therefore are now as integral a part of recreation as the areas they serve, and in any case the chief use of cars for leisure is not transport to specific areas but transport as such.

This is the car as a way of life, and millions of car-owners seem to agree that travelling hopefully is better than arriving. Motoring is now the most popular sport both here and in America, and 'Let's go for a run' is the new-style invitation to old-style touring – it has only lost its snob-appeal with numbers, as boating also is going down in the world in just the same way. And motoring is much like boating, especially to first-car owners; it is a way of joining the life of the roads as boat-lovers join the life of the water. We pack ourselves in and take off on similar journeys along roads or waterways, pulling up at the banks to transfer to the different element of land, and it is because 'terra firma' is where we disembark from cars as well as boats that it needs equally definite landing places. And if to regular drivers such pleasures seem a busman's holiday, so equally does boating to serious sailors and gardening to farmers.

Pleasure motoring produces its own type of driving, a kind of scenic progression which infuriates travellers in a hurry from A to B. Some drivers' pleasure, however, is in driving fast (or fairly fast with a 70 mph (112 km/h) limit) and their ideal day out includes 'a nice run on the motorway'. Which means we need Country Parks at a nice-run distance as well as near home; the Elan Valley for instance would be an excellent diversion from Snowdonia, and the Lake District will need a park in the Lakeland area of the M6 as well as near the population centres it serves.

But pleasure motoring is chiefly concerned with the route and the landscape it runs through, and its most urgent need at present is for stopping places of every kind — from somewhere to draw up briefly and study the map, to small Country Parks where children can let off energy on long journeys. Present lay-bys are merely unsavoury lengths of widened road where children are let out at their peril with lethal traffic thundering past a few yards away. Both for users and landscape we need thousands of stopping places to attract people to suitable areas and gather cars together behind screens of trees instead of invading and destroying the countryside. But if we are to use the places provided instead of the road-verge they must be a pleasure; not the squalid penance they now mostly are, but inviting retreats from the traffic, properly planned and maintained and with adequate litter-bins adequately emptied. Many authorities are now planning such amenities, and Surrey for instance has some excellent stops on the Portsmouth Road, with paths leading off to the neighbouring commons, and cars and lavatories screened in local trees. For what four fifths of road-users most want, so the survey found, is more lavatories.

The deliberate use of views of the countryside as the offscape of roads is scarcely yet provided for, though wherever a road over hills gives a prospect of surrounding country we are likely to find cars on the verge, since driving on busy roads is too much like navigating a swift river to give us much chance of admiring the banks.

But we need proper places to stop — what the Americans call overlooks — to invite us out of the traffic for ten minutes or an hour and show us what we are missing.

But even if all available views are developed, even so in another car-crowded decade we shall probably be waiting in queues with tickets to admire the scenery between 2.00 and 2.30 p.m. on the second Sunday in May. If we are to enjoy our future countryside we shall need more roads to do it from, preferably scenic roads carefully routed and specifically laid out for the landscape. In our present

271

economic bad weather and inadequate routes for serious business the thought of expensive new pleasure roads seems unrealistic. But the future is not halted by passing austerities, neither are the sixty-two per cent of cars run for pleasure. Recreation and tourism are now very serious business, and what of the factories making the sixty-two per cent? Do we consider this an equally frivolous waste of resources and close the factories? If not then roads for the cars to run on are equally essential.

The cost in money of special roads is logically part of the cost of the recreation of those who use them, and since there is plenty of private money for private pleasure why not toll-roads as in other countries? Not tolls on existing roads, but for new roads which otherwise would not exist. Car-drivers are not poor, only poorly provided for, and scenic roads would provide for a large group of people now too little considered. For most plans for recreation imply that everyone belongs to one of three categories – the active young, the serious nature-studiers, or the three-generation families with grannies and children. Yet we have only to spend five minutes watching holiday traffic to realize that many holiday-makers are none of these things but are quiet middle-aged couples. With our planned small families most people most of the time are childless, and do not want paddling-pools or boating lakes or grass to play ball on; nor even long-distance footpaths or nature reserves – they want to enjoy the country quietly and in comfort.

But no one speaks up for them. They are not news as the young are, nor beloved of sociologists like family groups, nor articulate like nature-lovers. They are nonetheless a large part of the population, and though independent of children they are not of cars, being past their prime as walkers. They are also well behaved and mildly well-off, with money for themselves after years of children – excellent customers in fact for scenic roads with good facilities – viewpoints, picnic places, restaurants, and why not information centres with simple displays of the history and wild-life and archaeology of the area? Education in digestible doses is popular, as the National Parks have proved in America; it is the seven-course-meal make-a-day-of-it museums which daunt us. The American Parkways also have much we could copy, and since vandalism would be slight on toll-roads

*Some not only prefer the road but seem to need it, even when asleep, as an umbilical life-line with the world.*

they are a chance to experiment in the use of roads for leisure (as depressing service areas on motorways have so signally failed to do, being an old-fashioned generation behind the fine modern highways they serve).

Another often-heard objection to more roads is that they would carry more people into the country and disturb it more thoroughly. Which apart from its merits as an attitude is unrealistic. The more people will in any case come, and the question is not *whether* but *how*? Is the flood to spread indiscriminately through lanes and landscape, or is the main current to flow peacefully along roads designed for recreation, with four times the numbers causing a quarter the disturbance? For roads are not only channels which carry traffic abroad, they are also lifelines which bind the traffic to their near vicinity, and even in the populous lowlands any country away from roads is astonishingly empty. By providing facilities we can zone recreation, and by providing roads can invite the users. Roads can be drainage channels for undisturbed countryside.

The last and unavoidable cost is to the landscape. Scenic roads in beautiful country would not improve it, but that does not answer the

273

question of how best to use our fine scenery. Should roads be routed to leave it undisturbed for the few, or for the many to admire it as a view? Certainly many more people enjoy landscape from roads than ever set foot on it; but about enjoying the country from a car instead of on foot we are absurd intellectual snobs. By some mystic virtue of foot-travel, walkers are nature-lovers, motorists are not. Yet the difference is not between walkers and wheelers but between enjoying the country for itself or as background for something else. For even a Wordsworth's legs grow old, and the wind on the heath becomes a searching enemy. Certainly I have never felt so close to the country as one crippled summer when all views were framed in car windows. Many car-travellers are impeccable nature-lovers; many walkers are the jolly young taking jolly exercise.

Which is not a reason for bulldozing roads through choice landscape, but only for thinking twice. In themselves our new roads can be beautiful, and modern road-designers are increasingly skilled at suiting them to the surrounding country. Like the development of pleasure-grounds from the intellectual dominance of formal gardens to the natural style of the landscape park, so roads have changed from dominant routes slashing ruthlessly through the countryside to curving alignments fitted tactfully into the local scene.

How much roads harm the landscape depends on each area, but the Cheviot Hills for instance seem designed to be views, and seen from the train to Scotland are wildly romantic. Yet to walk in they are unexpectedly dull – the scale is wrong perhaps, or they lack subtlety or variety. But as views they are superb, and large enough to absorb a scenic road and lose it. Already in Inverness the new Moidart road winds superbly between mountains and water, making visible splendid but otherwise mostly invisible scenery.

In Scotland and the large-scale North there is plenty of space for roads, and how else but from comfortable cars are comfortable southerners to find how empty half our land is, and how beautiful despite the northern weather? And not only southerners – northerners too – for there is a drift to the South for leisure as well as living, and the proportion of holiday-makers is falling in all the northern National Parks except the Lakes.

The new concern with the effect of roads on the landscape is not limited to good scenery, however, and in areas already developed the problems are even more formidable. Noise is a major nuisance which, since the only effective insulation is space, may seriously degrade neighbouring living areas. A typical noise-level at a motorway fence is 85 decibels, and to reduce this to the 45–50 decibels considered reasonable in suburban and urban areas means a separation of 600 feet (183 m) on level ground. Another problem in our highly-developed country is the number of existing roads and other structures which must be crossed; the average on motorways is five crossings per two miles (3·2 km), and the constant bridging and banking involved makes the earthworks half the cost of the road. These are also a major landscape disturbance, and mean difficulties of fitting the road to the scenery unknown to ground-level road-builders whose only land-shaping is to keep the gradient down to a maximum of one in twenty-five. Also since cut and fill must balance over reasonable lengths of road, embankments often consist of soil alien to the area and therefore unsuitable for local plants.

Despite the difficulties, however, the standard of road design is now encouragingly high, with new routes planned to harmonize with the ground in their curves and levels and land-forms (a computer will draw perspectives of proposed alignments) and to disturb good countryside as little as possible. Roads for instance may cross valleys not on solid embankments but on viaducts with the landscape flowing beneath, while the M1 swerves to avoid Charnwood Forest ('and *that* costs more than chicken-feed', said Barbara Castle). The Ministry of Transport now plants 600,000 trees a year (an important benefit to the countryside): new service areas are larger to give room for landscaping, and so on. This new high standard is partly due to the excellent work of the Landscape Advisory Committee which advises on motorways and trunk roads, and motorways in fact are a unique opportunity to establish better landscape design, which if begun on these much-admired new roads might soon spread to surrounding areas.

Travel by motorway is at present a curiously remote experience, cut off from the life of the areas we pass through as we never are on ordinary roads – it is why some lorry-drivers still prefer the old roads despite the traffic. With towns merely names on notices (and half of them are the wrong side of the road) we can no longer feel where we are in the human landscape. But we ought to know where we are in the natural landscape. Instead of driving along much the same sort of road through much the same sort of farmland we should feel the varying character of the natural regions of the countryside. We should be conscious of the difference between the Midland clays, or the chalk, or the farming loams, or the sand and gravel country, or the sterner rocks of the uplands. Not only could the vegetation change with the different regions, but so could the style of design and maintenance for different types of landscape, so could the land-forms of different soils, and in cuttings the rock itself be left exposed (as it is for instance in Charnwood Forest and on the M6 and surely will be on the new Pennine Way). On motorways the necessary conditions are there – the countryside lies uninterrupted up to the boundary, and the verges within are highway land with controlled highway planting and maintenance. If developed as local landscapes and

*A roadscape depends on all four elements. To widen or straighten this carriageway – to level and close-mow the verges – to fell the trees – to let the boundary hedge grow up and hide the view – any one would destroy the road's character.*

as the nature reserves they are already becoming, motorways could be a fascinating cross-section of the countryside they traverse.

Motorways, however, are only a fraction of our roads, and between the two extremes of long-distance travel-routes and local access lanes (both excellent roadscapes) is a whole range of mostly much less satisfactory roads. Yet this is where most travellers spend most time, and much could be done to improve this new environment of living. The essential preliminary of clearing-up has already started. Major roadside advertising has long been removed, a reform we gratefully appreciate after touring America. Road furniture also is now considered more critically, and recent legislation plus more vigorous action should remove the assorted rubbish which collects along roadsides like flotsam along river-banks. But this is mere tidying-up and most roads need more positive help to become good roadscapes.

A road is a self-contained linear landscape consisting of four

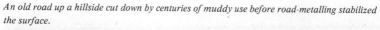

*An old road up a hillside cut down by centuries of muddy use before road-metalling stabilized the surface.*

elements – the carriageway, the bordering verges, a barrier which is the boundary of the roadscape, and the offscape beyond.

In this linear landscape the carriageway is the channel which fixes our viewpoint as we travel, and in existing roads the boundary and the verges are the manageable elements of the roadscape. Boundary hedges belong to the adjoining landowner and are therefore at risk, but trees in road-hedges are treasure to be preserved, and since the pleasure to travellers here outweighs the harm to farmers extensive Tree Preservation Orders are justified, especially in unattractive areas where such trees may be the only virtue in the landscape. Here the public could help by acting as guardians, for if protected trees were clearly marked with a blaze or something similar, road-users could be relied on to watch them and report any harm.

Verges, unlike hedges, belong to the highway authority, being in effect fossilized roads, for the road widths specified at the time of enclosure were for unmetalled surfaces and therefore provided space for the track to avoid winter mud and ruts. A general minimum width was forty feet (12 m). When these roads were metalled only a central carriageway was surfaced, leaving strips of grass between the boundary hedges. Earlier roads are often without verges (some were so narrow, according to Young, that a mouse could not squeeze past a carriage) and these, especially on slopes, are often below the level of the surrounding land, due to erosion before they were surfaced.

Modern roads are still laid-out with verges to ensure land for future road-widening, to carry services like water and gas and telephones, to give space for sight-lines and footpaths and unintended benefits like parking.

The incidental but most important use of verges, however, is now amenity: they are thousands of acres of unused land publicly owned and maintained and bordering the roads where we travel in millions. Like commons verges are excellent informal nature reserves, and since in England and Wales they cover 170,000 acres (68,000 ha), are far more extensive than all the official reserves put together. Many verges have existed for centuries relatively undisturbed, certainly by ploughing, and motorway verges make excellently insulated reserves, like the beautiful Ross Spur and its much-photographed wild daffodils. Verges provide very varied environments in a small space – the open road-edge, long and short grass, ditches and sheltered hedge-bottoms. They are also continuous and therefore vital routes for the spread of wild-life about the country. Birds, insects and many small mammals find congenial conditions in road-verges, and they are also valuable sites for the wild flowers which are disappearing on farmland. Fifty species of flowers are commoner on verges than anywhere else, especially the blue meadow-cranesbill and my favourite cow-parsley – the only flower tall enough and common enough actually to alter the landscape. Other flowers decorate the country scene, but cow-parsley changes the actual masses and spaces by rising as a feathery shrub layer along miles of country lanes.

This magical transformation of the early-summer countryside is rarer with modern verge-control which deliberately massacres the wayside flowers, though the more enlightened authorities have now given up indiscriminate mowing and spraying. Some will time cutting to suit local natural history societies (after the end of May for spring-flowering verges in Buckinghamshire, before early June for summer-flowering, nothing till July in Oxfordshire, after the hatching of partridges in Lincolnshire) and will omit all spraying on verges of special interest. Perhaps the best general treatment might be a yearly cutting in late summer when the flowers have seeded, and with the hay raked off not to smother the choicer species. This is said to cost more than frequent close-mowing with the cuttings left to rot, but if so why not make amenity grants in areas where they apply? It would be a cheap and simple way of turning our country roadsides into miles of bordering wild flowers.

Verges could also be used far more than they are for planting trees and shrubs on public land. Already there are various bodies concerned with roadside planting, but their excellent work could be even more valuable if used in a wider context, and if the planting which is now chiefly decoration of the existing scene were used both to create a better roadscape and also to make the road part of the general landscape. At present most planting consists of popular trees in rows along verges – that is as self-sufficient ornament; but if used to establish a design for the road, planting could screen eyesores, tie-in new development, make a satisfactory balance of masses and spaces, of shade and sun, open and closed vistas and so on. Trees as decoration are only needed where planting for the design is not enough, and in disturbed areas the need for screening is more likely to turn the road to a claustrophobic green tunnel through the landscape. It would therefore be important to open up views with any merit, if need be by removing existing trees. Though this is seldom necessary; views are surprisingly small-scale in terms of foreground, and simply removing the lowest branches of trees will often reveal miles of countryside. It is only the narrow eye-level plane which needs opening (or alternatively screening).

Except where insulated, as in built-up areas, road-planting should also be considered as part of the surrounding scenery. In green-urban areas for instance the trees might be part of the design of neighbouring recreation areas, and in the country could establish the local landscape character; for even though modern traffic-roads must always mean urban disturbance of the countryside they need not mean urban landscape.

Planting on verges is complicated by the need to avoid underground services, but it is not a danger to traffic. Research both in Europe and America has found that roads with trees and without have the same accident records, and that at two-metre distances for ordinary roads and four for motorways trees are perfectly safe. Safety is a specious excuse which only deters us when we choose. All motoring for instance is dangerous yet is largely for pleasure. To be safe we have only to stay at home.

As well as the general methods valid for all road landscape the new fast roads need a new style of design for speed. The landscapes of fast roads are always moving, but our design experience is of static conditions and the difference is fundamental. There is no fixed point from which to organize the view, but a fluid progression from one composition to another; the landscape flows round us, the shapes of the hills change and interrelate, the masses and open spaces of the countryside move into new patterns as we approach and pass them. The effect of parallax therefore becomes extremely important, also the relative distances of objects, and also above all the scale of the design. For the speed which keeps the landscape in motion also reduces all effects, and at sixty miles an hour (96 km/h) we travel in a minute nearly 1,800 yards (1,646 m), in a second nearly thirty (28 m). We therefore need to design in terms of time – if it takes ten seconds to appreciate a feature then it must extend for 300 yards (274 m); a minute of trees means a mile (1·6 km) of planting; and unless a view is open for a fifteen-second quarter mile (0·4 km) we shall miss it while overtaking. The plan of a well-designed fast road will look like the trick drawings of childhood which only make sense when held at eye-level and foreshortened.

All landscape design should be done on the ground not on drawing boards, but travel landscapes should be planned from a fast-moving car – if there is no time to record the desired effects then there will be no time to register them either. Most of our man-made landscapes, and not only roads, are in any case too small. Too sudden and too busy. Nature's effects are large-scale and mostly gradual changes from one condition to another.

But how swiftly road designers are learning we can see by comparing the first length of the M1 with the new stretch into London. The early planting was walking-scale with trees singly or in small groups, spaced out and often aligned, while the choice and mixture of non-local species is best not examined. There is little sense of masses and spaces, little feeling for speed and changing views or for the surrounding landscape. But the planting of the new length, though still barely grass-high, is very different – not separate dots of trees but trees in hundreds to grow into leafy masses whose flowing outlines will compose with the curves of the road and the land-forms and with the landscape beyond, and whose bordering height will mould the road-space. The trees are still too small to recognize without stopping, but some must surely be oaks whatever nurse trees are used in the first difficult conditions. For this was once famous oak country; the dense Aldenham woods which covered the area were renowned for their timber, and oak trees still flourish in hundreds in neighbouring hedges.

The improved design, however, is by no means limited to planting (nor to the elegant new bridges after the notorious brutality of the early ones). The road too is of a new high standard, for though the first alignment and the land-shaping were good, on this new stretch through a difficult disturbed area they are masterly. Only if we watched it being built do we realize the heroic scale of the changed land-

*The green-urban landscape of the M1 near Watford. In the trees on the right –*

forms which now seem natural, and the sensitive skill of their merging into the surrounding contours. The land between carriageway and boundary has been excellently used in fact to fit the road into its surroundings, with varying slopes of banks and widths of verges and the flowing lines of the fences. Even the close-mown border of grass along the road is not mown in parallel but in long sweeping curves.

The first sight of London where the road sweeps out of a shallow cutting to a sudden panorama of the city ahead will be even more dramatic when the trees grow up on the banks. It is a brilliant combination of land-form, offscape and speed, and in this green-urban landscape the new motorway is an industrial structure as appropriate and beautiful as the old villages in the old countryside.

Even more impressive, however, than the road itself is the transformation of the landscape we see from it. The new M1 and the old A41 run through the same area, crossing and recrossing as they approach the city, yet from the two roads the same landscape is

*— the A41 with its slatternly roadscape runs through a disturbed landscape (even with no convenient bridge to reveal the messy industrial land on the left and the old scrap dump on the right). The same pylon is visible on both horizons.*

completely different. Much of the A41 is bordered by ugly development and land derelict by default, and Green Belt or no we travel through the depressing landscape of a disturbed area. But from the new M1 the disturbance which dominates the old road is reduced to incidents in the stretches of Green Belt farmland and wooded landscape. It is not rural countryside — there are factories, a reservoir, urban housing, a transformer station with converging pylons, bridges, flyovers, and an overhead roundabout as well as eyesores in plenty — but seen in terms of the fine new road it is now a potentially good green-urban landscape. For as travellers we experience landscape as part of the road we see it from: the road is our environment and colours our consciousness, and the landscape exists as its extension. For us it is the road's offscape and therefore shares its character, and the same view is changed completely if seen for instance with a foreground of flowery verge or of derelict land dumped with rubbish.

283

Nor is it only the character of the area which is determined by a road but so is what we actually see of it. Whether the road lies high or low on the contours means country displayed or invisible, a row of buildings or a length of woodland may blot out a stretch of country we shall never otherwise see. To realize that our experience of most of the landscape is what we see from roads and railways we have only to imagine making all journeys blindfold. Our knowledge of the land we live in would be limited to isolated patches in miles of unknown territory – as London is for strangers who travel by the underground and never know what lies between stations.

This new condition – that we only see most of our landscape as presented by roads – makes them of crucial importance. Roads are now our witnesses of the landscape; they present us with a particular version of the facts by revealing some or ignoring others; and can equally well blacken a good character by unfair evidence or show us a doubtful one in a favourable light. Roads in fact are a way of lying by half-truths, and can be deliberately used so like photography. From mediocre country they can create for us a landscape we remember with pleasure simply by opening up and framing attractive views and distracting us with wayside planting through duller stretches. 'South Lancashire isn't at all the mess I thought it was' is the commonest comment of travellers on the new M 6, for in disturbed landscape the evidence of roads is particularly telling. They can compose and organize what they show us, can eliminate whole stretches of derelict land with a hedge, or remove particular eyesores by blocking the view at strategic points, or show us a fine industrial landscape beyond a foreground screen which hides the ground-level clutter.

These are powers inherent to some extent in all roads, but especially in motorways where no roadside development cuts us off from the country beyond, and where easy driving lets us look at the landscape. The use of the road as a controlled display of the area it crosses is therefore deliberately planned for the new Durham motorway. 'In a county which is making enormous efforts to transform its old depressed image the problem is that apart from being a healthy vigorous working landscape, it should be *seen* to be so by the travelling public.' With this uninhibited approach a county planning landscape team has worked out a method for analysing the visual corridor of the road, which they take as the area up to three miles distance. They have plotted derelict land, classified settlements, farming, woodland and so on, and made a series of maps showing the landscape quality of different areas, how often each stretch is seen (the 'visual frequency'), the position and nature of eyesores and so on. They divided the corridor into eight identity areas, each with distinctive landscape character, and these they studied as separate zones. From these findings they make proposals – for reclaiming derelict land, restoring neglected woodland, removing eyesores, planting for screening, framing and improving views, persuading farmers to tidy up their land and so on.

The value of the survey, however, is less in its (mostly predictable) proposals than in working out a method which could be applied not only to fine new motorways but also in a make-do-and-mend fashion to existing roads. Every road runs through a visual corridor, and here surely, where most seen by most people, is where to start in the regeneration of our landscape. We need better roadscapes and we need better offscapes, and the two go together. A 'pretty road' after all means a road through pretty country, and 'pretty country' in turn means chiefly what we see from the road.

# Part Three: A Four-point Plan for a New Landscape Framework

# 16. Point One: Landscape Organization

*Four types of environment for an industrial society*

'Proper land-use planning is applied human ecology.' This is a new enlightened conception of planning as the conscious control of environment, and even though present knowledge of human ecology is primitive and sketchy, in theory at least we are now moving towards this all-embracing concept of the relationship between man and habitat. Total environment (a current phrase so far avoided) is also a different expression of the same approach, recognizing the need for a complex but unified setting where we live in balance with all the different factors which make up our lives.

The types of landscape already discussed in the last section are also in effect an attempt to consider human ecology in terms of its setting, and in practice landscape is the most comprehensive expression we have of the total environment. Since landscape equals habitat plus man this not surprising, and in nature it is obvious that the total of ecological relationships is most clearly realized as different types of scenery. When for instance we talk of woodland animals, moorland birds and so on, we are describing the different environments as different types of landscape – not as different climates, or geological formations, or food sources, or any other of the factors which determine their ecology – but as the different landscapes which are the result of all these factors combined.

For man equally landscape is a direct expression of the way we live. Town and Country for instance are primarily descriptions of different types of landscape – not different types of economy, or opportunities for work and leisure, or shops or services or transport or housing or social patterns. All this and much more is implied in our conception of the different environments, but nonetheless town and country mean primarily built-up or green-field scenery.

Nor is the landscape only the direct physical expression of land-

*A landscape where housing, industry, transport, recreation, arable farming and rough hill-grazing are coming to terms with each other and the habitat. Early stage of Cumbernauld New Town.*

use, it is also the actual battleground where land-use works out its own salvation (or else comes to grief as in derelict areas). Economic, social, transport and other problems cannot be solved in isolation, but must first be combined and related in a single situation, and landscape is the melting-pot where all uses – each self-intent and often conflicting – meet and mould each other and reach a realistic balance. It is why total environment is most usefully approached as landscape, which translates this wide range of abstracts (land-use, population densities, settlement patterns, traffic flow, local site conditions and so on) into physical reality. (It is also, for human beings who are naturally visual, a visual statement of a complicated situation.)

In the Tees-side study this emerged very clearly. The computer's solutions were landscape solutions, and landscape proved an invaluable monitor for assessing separate factors as part of the whole environment. Physical planning in fact could be defined as the creation of suitable land-use patterns in suitable landscapes, and whatever the theory, in practice much planning legislation is exactly that: allocating industrial areas, protecting the National Park scenery for recreation, limiting new building in the farming countryside to infilling and rounding-off existing settlements, controlling densities in towns and so on, as well as the general zoning of areas for specified uses. This is essentially land-use planning as applied human ecology, the recognition that man in his different capacities needs specific environments deliberately created, and in so far as it has failed (the disturbed industrial landscape is certainly a failure, and many housing estates and urban areas are very partial successes) it is often because the conception of the environments is inadequate. They fail in range and they fail in complexity.

The pre-industrial landscape types were town and country – two distinct environments evolved through the centuries – and since agricultural man was a relatively simple ecological entity, his limited variety was contained in these two harmonious landscapes. Both, however, were harmed by the addition of new industrial uses, for houses cowering in the gloom and pollution of heavy industry are no more a good urban environment than disturbed landscape is a good countryside. Industrial man is far more diverse than his farming ancestors, and in his varied roles – farming-man and forestry-man, but also factory-man, metropolitan-man, urban-rural man, holiday-man, motoring-man and so on – he combines many quite different creatures, with different and often incompatible effects on his environment. And since his new land-uses added to the two existing landscapes destroy their old harmony, planning has attempted to create better conditions by isolating incompatible activities through a policy of zoning.

Early zoning therefore simply separated-out different land-uses into different areas – housing in residential estates, shops and offices in town centres, industry beyond the pale and so on. But despite man's alternating roles it is still the same human being who lives and works and plays and shops, with the result that such crude segregation-zoning merely dissects the whole body of life into separate organs which in isolation are only partly alive. City centres left dead when workers and shoppers go home are a town-planner's bug-bear, factories herded into industrial ghettos are social outcasts, housing estates are notoriously unlively, and even as a child I always avoided streets of houses without shops or other diversions. Equally in the country it is this same segregation of a single land-use which we dislike in large areas of intensive farming or commercial forestry.

The currently fashionable pedestrian precincts are a similar and potentially sterile form of segregation-zoning which should surely be watched with suspicion except on the limited scale of small traffic-free areas worked into the transport network. Precinct-users are also traffic users: a bus-stop at the door is a universal recommendation, and traffic-free precincts sound much less desirable if described as transportless precincts. Like so much else in life, town traffic needs sorting and civilizing rather than segregating. Public transport is essentially walkers on wheels, and could easily be made to behave as such on walkers' territory by rigorous speed controls, limited lanes and general deference to the rightful occupants of the area. This would be traffic taught to behave according to its function (here legs) and walkers who have learnt to cope with the present murderous free-for-all would certainly not be troubled by tame and docile buses sharing their streets and offering to carry both them and their shopping.

Single land-uses seldom create an environment any more than separate piles of butter and sugar and flour constitute a cake; for like a cake an environment is a complicated whole created by skilful blending and fusing of suitable raw materials. Thus instead of the old-style segregation we now need a new style of integration-zoning, not by land-use but by environment, to create specific areas where suitable groups of uses coexist in a suitable setting. This would be zoning as a constructive process – the integration of separate land-uses to form interacting combinations in planned environments.

But unlike cooking, and this what we have not yet accepted, we cannot ignore the ingredients which do not suit our plans. Out of sight can no longer be out of mind as it has been in the past (and still often is, for how many of us cared about Welsh spoil-heaps before Aberfan?). Our present task is more like fitting goods into suitable containers: everything must be carried – derelict land, industry, car parks, caravan sites and all the rest. The function of environmental zoning in fact is exactly that: to provide appropriate settings for *all* our activities, and most especially for the least attractive since these can only be saved by their setting – as they now are not.

'Amenity can be judged only in a balanced use of all land,' says John Weller in his book on rural planning, and it equally depends on a balanced combination of all land-uses. The problem still remains, however, of how to establish this balance as actual physical land-scape, and this involves three main stages: to define the suitable landscape types and combinations of land-use; to plot these out on the ground; to specify the methods for developing these environments as distinctive landscapes each good in its own right.

Types of landscape for an industrial society have already been discussed – the built-up urban, the green-urban, the rural and the man-made wild. Appropriate land-use combinations, however, will certainly not be easy, since some uses are inherently incompatible (housing and motorways), others we resist from preconceived ideas based on the past (industry and recreation), or simply from the long-established habit of peace by isolation (any KEEP OUT notice).

In the spacious uplands the non-intensive uses can be more or less harmoniously combined, but in the lowlands the mounting pressures of population and land-use make all combinations explosively

293

*Pages 294–7: existing multiple use of different environments in the congested London area.*
*The town centre is shopping precinct, through-route for walkers, open space for sitting, urban*
*park and play area for children. Why not also use the water as a paddling-pool and serve tea to*
*the sitters from the near-by kiosk? Stevenage.*

difficult. Nonetheless we have now got to learn to use our habitat as
plants do: when there is no more room to spread, then trees, shrubs
and flowers go through what in human terms would be called an
agonizing reappraisal and fit themselves onto the same area of
ground in suitable multi-use combinations. We equally, if all our
land-uses are to survive on our limited land-area, must now work
out, however painfully, our suitable human associations for sharing.

Such categories and combinations, however, still have to be sited
on the ground, and here we face 'the constant dilemma of getting the
desired quart into the available pint pot'. Britain is small and gets
constantly smaller with every extra head of population and every new
car and mile of road. Our living-space is cramped, and living in
cramped spaces has its own strict rules, as anyone knows who has

*The green-urban landscape in London's inner Green Belt serves as buffer between town and country, to contain the city's spread, and for recreation (there is sailing as well as fishing). The water is a metropolitan reservoir, the building a bus-repair depot, the landscape a pleasure to commuters. Aldenham.*

295

*The rural countryside as farmland, travel route and offscape for urban recreation. Vale of Aylesbury.*

holidayed in a boat or caravan. We have only to stop and unload to marvel at the astonishing amount which was packed into so little space, and at the compactness and efficiency imposed on our house-keeping by the discipline of fitting into a single small mobile container.

Countries with plenty of land can spread and still function (though the result is neither attractive nor convenient, as America is finding). But in England and Wales we already have sixteen times less space per person than America, and by the twenty-first century we shall be living on our island as tightly as on a boat – not only in towns but also in the country which till now has provided the land for other uses.

*Peaceful coexistence in the man-made wild: bird-watchers, sailors, anglers and wild-life. Sailors and anglers share out time and territory, local naturalists have rented the shooting-rights and have forbidden shooting, wild-life accepts the intensive recreation and the water is well known for its birds. (The man is watching a family of great crested grebes.) Halton.*

The only way to live comfortably in small spaces is for everything to have its place in an efficiently worked-out order — here appropriate landscape zones exactly plotted and land-uses specifically sited. The most realistic start for creating such potential order is clearly what exists already, and the developments of the last quarter century — economic and social as well as in planning — are already creating the four divisions we need, muddled and often ill-assorted but still recognizably distinct — the old town and country landscapes, and the two new subdivisions of town and country created by an industrial economy.

At one extreme is the wild country, often of indeterminate owner-

297

ship, chiefly in the uplands but now increasingly in the lowlands, whose past status as a type of rural landscape industry is now changing, both by making non-mechanized farming unprofitable and by employing its population elsewhere.

The next category is the rural landscape as in the past, lowland farming on enclosed land privately owned. This has changed its appearance but not its function, and though it is eroded and invaded by other uses it is still the landscape of food production.

The urban concentrations equally are direct developments of the old towns, but are surrounded now by the penumbra of disturbed landscape which is the new industrial subdivision of urban.

These four categories are not simply different local scenery but are essentially different types of landscape as the expression of different types of land-use. That is to say they are true environments, and this is proved by the fact that though each may vary widely as scenery, yet we still clearly recognize it as the same landscape category. Farmland for instance may be small hedged pasture-fields or open prairie landscapes of wheat, but both are rural countryside; disturbed landscape may be spoil-heaps or neat rows of urban housing among fields; the Highlands or the New Forest or overgrown Surrey commons are each wild in their different way. All landscape can be roughly classified as one of these categories, the essential type depending on land-use, and the individual variety on local conditions.

These are environments, whether good or bad, which have developed spontaneously, and which present planning policy is likely to make more distinct in the future; and because they are created by the interaction of habitat and industrial man, they are therefore a valid basis for planning. If each category were clearly defined and developed we should have four distinctive types of environment where our land-uses could be combined in suitable landscapes.

In plotting them on the ground (the second stage of the process) large-scale Ordnance Survey maps would be useful, as would land-use surveys (Alice Coleman's team at London University is doing a new one). Air photography is also a valuable new planning tool, but since landscape for those who live in it is essentially three-dimensional ground-level views, it can only be properly assessed by going and looking at it. A number of landscape surveys already exist (there is one by the Council for the Protection of Rural England and others by counties like Hampshire and Sussex) but these are of only limited help here since they judge landscape by quality not type – not how we *use* it but whether we *like* it. They are divided into categories like 'impressive scenic value', 'outstanding merit' and so on, with a bottom-of-the-list-lumping-together-in-disgrace of 'urbanized, suburbanized and spoilt by development'. Such surveys are based on a policy of preserving the best and leaving the rest to get worse, and they completely ignore the fact that the 'spoilt-by-development' areas are exactly the places where most of us spend most of our lives – are our homes in short.

Equally unrealistic as a basis for planning is the fact that what such surveys are chiefly assessing is often in effect the survival of the past. New gravel-working for instance, or even a new farmer – simply by stripping his land of trees and hedges and adding a range of new farm buildings – could change a stretch of country overnight from one class of scenery to another. Such surveys, like much present landscape planning, are using the past as a mirror of the way ahead: it is why their policies so often prove unworkable.

The four categories needed for action are not of landscape quality but type, with each area assessed and plotted as one of the four categories of environment. Such judgements are inevitably personal, but a consensus of personal reactions is the most relevant assessment of landscape (there is in fact no other, whatever abstract techniques we may use to map the findings as measurable quantities). Certainly such categories would give us a far more accurate picture than any existing information about what is actually happening to our landscape; we should have a map of the present, and to this should be added everything we can possibly find out about the intended future. Local development plans are here an obvious start; as also are all proposals for new housing, new industries, new reservoirs, forestry, roads, Green Belts and special areas – every kind of development planned for the future and added to the map of existing conditions. At present we have very little coordinated information about our landscape, and special scenic areas for instance are designated purely in terms of existing conditions, even when their already foreseeable future development must completely change their character.

Development is piecemeal but scenery is a long-term whole, and what we need above all is a bird's-eye view both in space and time.

Long-term landscape planning needs even more than this, since if it is to be valid for the future it must consider not only present proposals but also inherent possibilities. We therefore need maps on the principle of America's 'land capability classes', which ignore existing use of land and assess the potential inherent in its soils, relief, climate, drainage and so on. In an industrial society we urgently need similar maps for other uses than farming, showing for instance areas made newly accessible by motorways and airfields; gravel and other deposits which must ultimately be worked; flat land on estuaries with water for cooling; shores with deep harbours for tankers; obvious routes for future roads; areas with good water supply and drainage; districts with pleasant climate likely to attract population; potentially marginal land for recreation – every quality in fact which is likely to influence future development assessed and combined in a map of industrial capability.

With such information (limited, incomplete, inexact, but still a huge advance on our present uncoordination) all areas could be classified as roughly belonging, either now or in the predictable future, to one of the four landscape categories; and when plotted out these would produce an irregular mosaic covering the whole of the country and representing our four modern environments. In many areas the new categories would differ from existing conditions. They would for instance recognize the green-urban landscape and the man-made wild as valid new landscape types and not, as at present, merely down-graded urban and rural. Green Belts would commonly be divided into green-urban and rural landscape – a realistic assessment of what at present are merely administrative areas with no meaning on the ground. Also potential man-made wild would replace much marginal farmland and would cover some present areas of lowland rural, especially near cities.

Since the new categories would include future development, some land would change its character completely. Proposed New Town areas for instance would show as urban not rural, with all the associated green-urban changes in the surrounding countryside. Likewise some areas, even in Areas of Outstanding Natural Beauty, would change to green-urban, for though the inevitable roads, pylons, new housing and so on may to some extent be screened in the rural landscape, there nonetheless comes a stage where the intrusions are no longer absorbed, and the landscape is better as genuine green-urban than as much-disturbed rural. The existing character of landscape in the wrong potential category can seldom be preserved.

With the four categories plotted on the ground their appropriate scenery could then be deliberately established (the third stage), and new development sited in the landscape where it belongs to produce a coherent environment. Clearly this is not always possible (motorways must go from here to there whatever lies between, while gravel, like gold, is where you find it, even in top-merit countryside). Nonetheless a surprising amount of modern life is relatively unconcerned with exact location; it is why much planning control already consists of guiding, both by stick and carrot, all kinds of development into suitable areas.

In every landscape some alien intrusions will be unavoidable, but these can be played down or screened, and if the future potential of the area has been wisely foreseen the disturbance should not be serious. The future will also produce new land-uses not yet imagined (who dreamt of airports or motorways a century ago?) and these are most likely to belong to the green-urban environment — it is a further reason why the development of a good green-urban landscape is both essential and urgent.

That the rational sorting out here proposed would produce a too-tidy Britain we need never fear. The amount of muddled development irretrievably inbuilt is more than enough to save us from neatness (quite apart from the hazardous future) and the new zones would bristle with old incongruities. Indeed one fundamental reason why most new landscapes are unsatisfactory is that for much new development there *is* no appropriate setting. It is wrong wherever we put it. Like weeds which are plants in the wrong place, much that we now find ugly is not intrinsically so but is in the wrong landscape. Incongruity is in itself a form of ugliness, and whether a particular development pleases or offends us often depends on its siting as much as its design. Even the ideal housing scheme would be an eyesore on the top of Snowdon, and a beautiful technical structure like the Jodrell

Bank radio-telescope becomes a monstrous and sinister growth in a countryside of doll's-house fields threaded with little lanes. However excellent in themselves our new industrial achievements are at present outcasts, both in the small-scale scenery of living-areas where their size if nothing worse is often brutally wrong, and also in the rural countryside as surly and alien presences from a different world. Both they and their setting may be equally good but in combination both are equally degraded.

Gas-holders are an obvious example of outcasts with no proper setting, and whether in town or country we equally dislike them. Yet in themselves they are excellent functional structures, and the designs where the frame makes a decorative coronet are often the most attractive buildings in the area. To see them afresh and admire we have only to imagine them in a different setting – in a World Fair perhaps, as gleaming pavilions with adjustable domes. In the green-urban landscape they could be splendid decorative elements, as also could pylons – no longer apologetic grey, but painted proud scarlet like cranes to display their airy elegance.

To a limited extent planning already accepts the policy of distinctive landscapes developed on their own terms and with unsuitable development camouflaged, like the hydro-electric schemes introduced with such tact into the existing wild scenery of the uplands. But again the concern is only for the 'good' areas; we have a best-parlour mentality about our landscapes, and so long as we keep a little-used area tidy for visiting, we ignore the squalor in the rest of the house. But we live in the *whole* of our country and *all* the landscape matters. It is not a question of good patches in a background we ignore like the curate's egg. And why should we tolerate ugly working conditions and spend our leisure escaping? Whether working or playing we still have the same sensibilities, and do not cease to see our surroundings simply because we are travelling to work instead of pleasure. We not only see them but see them daily, and the most important view in anyone's life is from their own doorstep.

'We do not mean to enter into any argument about whether a state of rusticity or a state of refinement, whether the forest or the city be the state for which the Author of Nature intended the human species:

*Diffident industry –*

*– unconcerned housing. Yet it is the messy housing area which needs screening, not industry's elegant chimneys and interesting roof-pattern in a well-kept setting. Both pictures are from the same point, facing in opposite directions.*

mankind are now found in every state of savageness, rusticity, civilization and refinement.'

Here, with a difference of sympathy and the eighteenth century's superb self-assurance, are our four modern categories described by Marshall, and arguments about better or worse are now as irrelevant as the original intentions of the Author of Nature. We need to extend the concern for amenity now limited to chosen areas so that it covers the whole of our scenery, and creates good landscape for every kind of land-use (or at least *better* landscape, since we must walk before we run).

But better must always mean landscape developed in terms of its own distinct identity. Indiscriminate prettifying and decoration are *not* improvements, and amenity, alas, can be as disastrous to landscape as the usual unconcern. Rockeries on roundabouts and flowerbeds round factories are incongruities which nullify any potential merit the scene might have. We do not dress up a large gaunt figure in frills and ribbons, but we do choose well-cut clothes which make the most of its bone-structure. Good industrial landscapes are *not* would-be gardens, but scenery which develops not disguises its industrial character.

'To improve the scenery of a country', said Repton, 'is to display its native beauties with advantage.' It is equally true of all types of landscape, even though 'qualities' would at present be more realistic than 'beauties'. Good design is not added from outside like sprinkling with sugar − it is a truism which needs no repeating in general design but in landscape it does, for the conscious design of landscape is a new conception and almost everything is still to be said.

Amenity matters − that is now accepted. It matters everywhere − that is not. And potentially all landscape is good landscape − that is barely even thought of. We shall only be making real progress, in fact, when A.O.I.B. means Area of Outstanding Industrial Beauty.

# 17. Point Two: Landscape Pattern

*Tree belts framing self-contained urban landscapes in an open countryside*

Most people have a clear conception of their ideal house and mine is simple: the front door would open onto a busy London street, the back onto farming countryside. As our two doors now do, but in separate houses: to combine them would mean a distance of 35 miles (56 km) of no-man's-land between back and front.

This blurring of the truly rural and the convincingly urban is inevitably happening in the population, but in landscape we are anxious to keep the distinction for the sake of both amenity and farming. The last chapter suggested four categories which would redefine town and country with their necessary new subdivisions, and here surely is the first essential aim in landscape design; to be able to say with conviction: This is town. This is country.

Valid design in landscape as anything else is based on two fundamentals: what the design is meant to achieve, and the nature of the material to work with. If these are clearly realized the design may emerge of itself as the obvious solution, especially when the function is as dominant and the material as intractable as in landscape. The aim here is simple – to create for a large industrial population in a small area authentic urban and rural environments. The material to work with is far more complicated, and includes not only the natural habitat and its existing man-made adaptations but also the forces of change which are everywhere working on it; for no landscape planning can hope to succeed unless it accepts and uses the momentum of its period.

First the existing landscape. The basic material of our countryside is working farmland, and since both for farmers and the community it is essential that agriculture should be efficient, the farming landscape cannot be seriously interfered with. Any modifications of farmland for the sake of amenity can therefore only be minor, and though the character of farm landscape may vary, this will depend on farming exigencies not landscape design. Farmland therefore must mostly be taken as given, and landscape planned in terms of its uncompromisingly functional scenery. The basis of our future lowland scenery will therefore be an approximation more or less complete to the simple stripped-down surface of the land, patterned with various crops; but patterned also, alas, especially near towns, by all kinds of incongruities now mercilessly exposed. In fact of all the landscapes possible as a setting for industrial society industrial farmland is probably the worst.

We ourselves, the industrial population, are also important by the way we react to our surroundings, for the fact that eighty-five per cent of us live in urban areas directly affects our attitude to landscape. It means that the two different environments, urban and rural, are experienced by most people in quite different ways, since the towns are where we live and the country is what we see when we travel. Clearly this is an over-simplification with many exceptions, but still it is broadly true, and we chiefly therefore experience the urban environment as a close and intimate setting where we walk about or sit or stand still, for in the places we live our lives are mostly stationary and movement is only an incidental part of what we are doing. The spaces we inhabit in urban areas are therefore small — streets, gardens, squares, the spaces between buildings — these are self-contained landscapes, and even in a large city what we see in any one view will nearly always be closely restricted, and most urban landscapes are small in area whatever the size of the units which compose them.

But where urban views are in hundreds of yards country views are in miles, and our scale of perception is thus completely changed. Of course we may stop on our travels, may get out and walk, or spend week-ends or holidays in country places, but if we marked these areas on a map they would mostly be quite surprisingly small. Most of our experience of most of the country is by moving across it, generally swiftly, and inevitably the scale of a landscape we travel through is larger than one we live in. Even at footpace the scale is enlarged; the landscape becomes a view not an intimate setting, and its scale is that of the open countryside.

A large-scale rural landscape therefore both for farming and travel; small-scale urban landscapes for living: the two contrasting environments kept distinct and unconfused. It is a difference we need to establish by methods which not only seem natural but which also enhance both environments, and that the design will have to be deliberately created is clear, since the changes are already well advanced and no coherent pattern is emerging. But man's creative effect on the general landscape is limited. He can destroy it of course – at that we are expert – he can also urbanize it and create man-made glories like Venice. But townscapes are separate urban worlds, with little effect on the general landscape, and in so far as man's developments change the open scene it is by their placing; that is, they can be zoned on the large scale or sited on the small.

In neither case, however, do they *create* the rural landscape, and the two elements which chiefly determine the character of our countryside are geology and vegetation. In the uplands and to a less extent in lowland hill-country geology is dominant, but in most lowland areas the landscape character depends chiefly on vegetation – on the difference between woodland and open country, or between large unfenced fields and small enclosures with thick high hedges. If all lowland England were reduced to uniform grass then for non-geologists it would all look much alike. There would still be the hills – the Pennines as our northern backbone, the bosomy swells of the southern chalk, the scarps of the Cotswolds and Chilterns like oblique corrugations across the country, and the land between variously flat or rolling – but all very similar and all very dull. As Willa Cather said of the plains of Nebraska: 'There was nothing but land . . . slightly undulating . . . Not a country at all but the material out of which countries are made.'

Certainly our own unemphatic lowland scenery depends on vegetation – for its scale, for the masses and spaces, for light and shade, for colour, for height and enclosure and vistas, and above all for variety. The land is the site but the vegetation is the architecture, and when a site is built on, it is the architecture we notice.

Man's effect on the country landscape is in any case almost entirely through vegetation, and apart from special cases like reservoirs and spoil-heaps his control of rural scenery is by altering the plant-cover.

307

*Magnificent tree architecture creates a dramatic landscape from the mud-flats of a sluggish river. The Thames at Brentford.*

Nothing else he does is large enough to register, for land-modelling is insignificant in the open landscape where the smallest natural hill is enormous compared with the largest man-made (though I once met an American geophysicist who proposed a half-serious plan for using hydrogen bombs to cover all flat land with hills). Through harmless vegetation alone, however, we can alter the landscape profoundly, changing whole regions from dense woodland to the completely different landscape of open grass, or restoring the forests by planting, or creating intermediate patterns to suit our needs like the landscape of enclosure. The pattern to suit our present needs must also therefore be created by vegetation, by what and where we plant and the way we control its growth.

We have no choice then about the material, and given the facts the new pattern seems equally inevitable.

We need a clear distinction between town and country.

The urban (including the green-urban) environment is small in area and is small-scale landscape set in large-scale farmland. Therefore in the overall pattern the rural landscape must contain the urban.

The basis of our country scenery is farmland which cannot be seriously interfered with.

Modern farming creates an open landscape. This is unnatural in a country naturally wooded, and as a setting for urban development is disastrous.

Landscape is a composition of masses and spaces, and since farming will increasingly supply the spaces, landscape design must supply the masses.

Man's effect on the landscape is through vegetation, chiefly trees.

The suitable new pattern therefore seems inevitable – we should surround our towns and cities with trees. Thousands upon thousands of trees to frame our urban areas in belts of woodland and insulate their urban landscapes in the rural countryside.

This is a conception completely different from present plans for planting trees to improve the urban scene. Such planting is excellent and essential, but the trees are added to existing landscapes and are there on urban terms. Tree Belts as here suggested would be much more than urban decoration – continuous woodland screens planned and planted as a whole, flowing round our urban areas in irregular masses, sensitive to the land-use and the contours of the ground, and their outlines defined to harmonize with the open landscape. This would be vegetation used as mass in a composition – trees as landscape material as grasses are lawn material – and this can never be achieved by uncoordinated planting at the discretion of separate planters.

Tree Belts would have their own identity as sylvan areas, small but definite stretches of woodland, boundaries belonging equally to the rural and urban landscape, separating but also reconciling the town and the country. From the open farmland they would be part of the large simple pattern of our new countryside, woods replacing the lost trees of farmland and completing the new landscape balance of open spaces and enclosing mass.

Within the Tree Belts would be contained the different urban environment, and here the trees would provide not mass but the organization of space; thinning out to enclose open areas of urban scenery, and framing in a leafy background the individual settings of human living – small-scale, intimate, the private landscapes of people or groups of people – houses and gardens, streets and towns, schools, parks, shops and all the rest – all the detail and variety which no matter how delightful in close-up yet in the large-scale open landscape are merely clutter. These need their own self-centred small-scale setting, to be seen on their own terms not as interruptions of a larger pattern – a juxtaposition which harms both sides equally. And of all environments to live in this type of lightly-wooded landscape is the most sympathetic, so that living areas leafy with trees could be a haven equally from our concrete cities and our treeless farmland.

Bowery cities in an open countryside – to such utopian visions there are serious practical difficulties. Where, to begin with, is the land to come from for planting trees by the thousand? But one of the few advantages of our extravagant pre-planning land-use is the amount of land not used at all but wasted. If we take a large-scale map of the edge of almost any built-up area and go over the actual ground, colouring red on the map every patch of land not being positively used, we finish up with a surprisingly red-spotted sheet. Such land may be more or less cared for, but more often it is simply neglected and derelict by default – unusable fragments left over in the carving-out of sites for development. But no land is unusable for tree-planting – awkward shapes and sizes, odd strips or patches of uneven ground – trees will flourish as well as in regular plots. Rounding-off and in-filling with trees – in many places this alone would frame our towns in green, for though the ideal is a belt of woodland this need not be wide to be effective; since we view from the ground and since trees are well above eye-level they need only be dense enough to shut out the view beyond.

This unrivalled power to create a convincing environment in a very small area is one of the many virtues of wooded scenery. In a

*High-density housing creates a self-contained urban environment in a Tree Belt setting in a farming countryside. Siedlung Halen, Switzerland.*

five-acre (2 ha) spinney we could be in the heart of a forest, and this is true of no other landscape. Five acres of farmland or downs or moorland are nothing; they are merely the unnoticed ground where we stand and look at the view beyond. To create a convincing environment in open landscape we need not five but 500 or even 5,000 acres. It is a further reason why open farmland is an unsuitable landscape for town fringes: it can only create rural scenery in large and undisturbed stretches, and needs at least a hundred times more area than woodland to produce as convincing an environment.

Even small areas of trees are therefore valuable, but where land allows, strips of woodland on the edge of cities would have many virtues, and what better use for the many areas of inner Green Belts (proposed or existing) which are now little better than derelict land? With all the inevitable urban intrusions they can never be rural

311

*Even a narrow belt of trees is effective. In winter the houses are just visible but in summer the illusion of woodland is complete. Further along the road the same verge is the usual grass-carpeted void between traffic and houses.*

scenery, but they could be woodland. If planted with trees the intrusions would be lost, for woodland is not only the most concentrated but also the most dominant of all environments, and can absorb an astonishing amount of development without losing its identity. By planting areas of otherwise unused land we could travel into our cities through wooded landscape, and unless there are definite reasons against it, tree-planting could be the accepted and universal practice on all such land, with permission for new development made

312

provisional on planting a suitable share of the local Tree Belt. All land not covered by buildings or hard surfaces will in any case be covered by vegetation, and in our climate trees are the natural answer. It is well known that woodland gardens are the easiest of any to maintain, for a further virtue of woodland is its stability. On our fertile soils all other vegetation is a temporary stage in the succession to something else and therefore needs constant control, but since woodland is the climax there is no further growth towards a different state.

Trees are cheap both to plant and maintain (cheaper than grass if planted by forestry methods), but some care is needed even of semi-natural woodland, and since efficient maintenance is linked with purpose this brings the question of what the Tree Belts could be used for. It is not enough to exist as decoration or a form of large-scale hedge, the countryside is a working landscape and the Tree Belts need a practical use. By far the most satisfactory would be a modified form of forestry, growing hardwoods in natural conditions and managing them by selective felling. But such woodlands would be very difficult to manage – small and irregular plantations, hard to get at, the trees few and scattered and expensive to transport, mostly hardwoods not at present in much demand, and likely to be poor-quality timber exposed to injury during growth. Forestry so inefficient by commercial standards would scarcely be more than a way of maintaining woodland landscape by methods which would avoid a park-like character and might possibly produce enough timber to pay for themselves. The Forestry Commission already does most of the planting for the Ministry of Transport. Why not also Tree Belts? The Commission is proving to be an excellent amenity body in its handling both of scenery and recreation; it also has powers to buy land to improve the landscape, and nowhere would its operations mean more improvement than here.

It is even possible that a stock of hardwoods subsidized by amenity might be a valuable long-term investment for unpredictable future needs, especially since our present supply is mostly from hedges and therefore disappearing. Pulping and processed boards are recent new uses of timber (with factories already in the lowlands), and technical change is now so rapid that no one can foretell our needs by the end of the century. Pendulums have a habit of swinging, and Cobbett considered that conifers 'can never be of any more use to the nation than the sprigs of heath which cover the rest of the land'.

Another possibility might be woodland owned by the urban areas concerned, as in France and Switzerland where towns and communes manage their own local forests. Could not local authorities with the Commission's help develop woodlands for their local needs, including amenity and recreation? By definition the land enclosed by Tree Belts is where most of us live, and their encircling woodland landscapes would therefore be within easy reach of people in towns. As setting for informal recreation light woodland on the doorstep is excellent – for walking, sitting, tree-climbing, love-making, dog-exercising and all the other woodland joys according to age.

There already exists considerable experience in the management of woodland for recreation, both in urban areas and in the Forestry Commission's Open Forests. The Americans with their wide experience of National Forests consider that a new type of maintenance worker is needed and suggest the title of Landscape Forester, and we too should need similar control of the woodlands for amenity, if possible by natural methods, if not by discreet interference – thinning out unwanted undergrowth, arranging felling and replanting, channelling walkers by layout into suitable footpaths, providing suitable vistas and open glades and sitting-places and so on.

In areas of changing land-use, as city fringes must necessarily be, woodland has a further virtue in being easily adapted. 'Over this element of the rural art' (so said an eighteenth-century landscape gardener in pompous eighteenth-century prose), 'the power of the artist is absolute: he can increase or diminish at pleasure; if the place be over-crowded he can lighten it; if too naked he can supply the deficiency by Planting', or if we need sites for new development (so we could continue) we can make clearings in the inner fringes and extend the outer boundary by further planting to keep the screen unbroken. In terms of the general landscape our urban life would be an indoor life, with the urban areas like the rooms of a house separated by walls of trees from the different landscape of the street outside.

Urban areas framed in woodland which in turn is part of the larger rural landscape. Of course it could never be so simple. The country is not uncluttered farmland, nor are the edges of cities neatly defined like the edge of a lake. Whatever we may plan for the future, the fragmented urban development scattered over the countryside cannot be gathered together and framed in trees. And on the credit side there are towns which no one would want to screen − old settlements mostly, which for some reason (a flood-plain? an unbridged river? common land? a static population?) have not eroded their country setting. Far from screening, their presence should be emphasized, if need be, by views opened up from suitable vantage points. But for every town we want to see more of there are ten we do not − certainly not more of their 'base and brickish' outskirts. 'Towery city and branchy between towers' − it is not only Gerard Manley Hopkins' description of Oxford but the Tree Belt ideal of a city.

Towns and cities will always be presences in the countryside, either lying in valleys as stretches of urban landscape like Bath, or on high sites like Durham swelling above any foothill trees, or with new high buildings soaring above the green on level ground.

Certainly Tree Belts are not intended to disguise the urban areas we live in, but rather to enhance their distinctive identity, to establish them as a different urban experience. 'A town is a special sort of park in the countryside.' It is an excellent new concept, and puts the park landscape firmly where it belongs, as town not country.

Such a landscape framework of open farmland and tree-circled urban areas would produce a large-scale countryside with two clear elements − the open spaces of farming crops and the solid masses of trees. As a pattern it would be fluid and adaptable, growing denser with increased need for screening, or thinning to open country in undisturbed farmland; a flowing landscape, well suited to our rolling countryside. It would be simpler scenery than we are used to in the lowlands, more spacious, larger-scale, more peaceful − more 'natural' than the enclosed rectangular field landscape which the eighteenth century so disliked, while the Tree Belts would combine with the wooded areas of commons and marginal land in the same free rhythms.

This, however, is certainly no plan to change the old farming landscape. On the contrary, wherever that still survives our modern methods as a working countryside it should be treasured as irreplace-

*Land-form and massed trees create the flowing rhythms of the landscape park. Shardeloes Park, by Humphry Repton.*

able and protected from all unnecessary disturbance. The new landscape proposed here would only develop in sympathy with farming changes, for as a pattern it would only emerge as the old one disappeared, not only because trees take time to grow, but because it would be visible only in wide-scale open stretches, and while the old hedged landscape remained there would merely be more young trees on urban fringes. Approaching towns from the open country the trees would thicken, scattered groups at first, screening development alien to the rural landscape, then gathering into belts and narrow stretches of woodland on the edge of the built-up areas. It would be as if all urban development attracted trees to itself as a magnet attracts iron filings, or as if some huge and benign amoeba of green woodland had absorbed our base and brickish city fringes in a leafy flow of trees. It would be a gradual transition from open to wooded country, with bays curving in between promontories of trees, sometimes open farmland, sometimes green-urban landscape, but always between the open country and the built-up areas would be an insulating fringe of trees like a wooded moat or a leafy city wall round the different urban world.

*Modern farming can create similar landscape by large sweeps of arable unbroken by hedges.*

Such a reorganization of our disintegrating lowland scenery could solve many of our landscape problems – urban containment, provision of recreation areas near towns, a buffer between farmland and the urban population, improvement of both urban and rural landscapes, coordination of present muddle into large-scale order, and above all the establishment of distinct town and country environments. Equally important it would be landscape developed in terms of the well-known, using no new or untried elements, since farming and forestry are the two forms of ground-use we traditionally know how to manage. It also makes a virtue of the new openness of farmland, for in the combinations of landscape mass and space it is space which is the difficult long-term element, not only to maintain in a fertile climate but also to provide. Space needs far more area to register than does mass (as is clear for instance in small-field landscapes of high hedges and trees, which give the effect of woodland

317

even though most of the actual area is open grass). But modern farming both creates and maintains large open spaces, and the contrasting vegetational mass is much simpler to provide by planting, often on otherwise wasted land.

And unless we do thus deliberately replant our native trees we shall lose them over large areas of the countryside. In Britain we have less woodland than any other European country – seven to eight per cent compared with the average twenty-six per cent – and of this fraction only four per cent is deciduous (chiefly beech), the rest is conifer forests. And this is not what we mean by trees. Trees are separate entities growing along roadsides and in odd field corners, or in small copses and spinneys scattered about the countryside; and the loss of such trees is in no way made good by huge forests remote in the rainy hills. But since the chief value of countryside trees is now for pleasure not timber, and since neither commercial forestry nor farming will therefore provide them in the future, the community will have to plant for itself the trees it wants for the community's enjoyment.

But we could restore our vanishing heritage of native trees in the landscapes we live in, for 'the tree', said Le Corbusier, 'is man's natural companion', and for centuries we have lived with trees around us in the farms and villages of the old leafy countryside. Since in the move from country to town we have left the familiar trees behind, it would surely be natural to bring them with us by planting afresh round our too-often treeless towns.

The benefits of Tree Belts would be enormous: the chief cost would be for land and this is clearly a major difficulty. Yet in many areas tree-planting would be a practical application of the Green Belt policy, by protecting vulnerable land on the edge of cities. For trees commit the land to nothing: they save it from casual development without sterilizing it for further use. With modern machines a cover of trees is scarcely more hindrance than a cover of grass – it is why we cannot hope to keep enough trees by preservation but only by constant new planting.

Nor, alas, can we have quantities of 'Instant Trees' as is now popularly supposed. Semi-mature trees properly prepared and transplanted are far too expensive for any but special sites, while the

'*A town is a special sort of park in the country.*' *Leafy Cambridge with the open Fens beyond.*

much-publicized new tree-moving machines like huge trowels are a very limited success. Certainly they move trees quickly and cheaply, but equally certainly the trees have a habit of dying.

Young trees, however, like young children, grow very much faster than we expect. If the right trees are planted small and close they grow at surprising speed, quickly creating the feel of young woodland. 'The only long-term (but oh, so long-term) hope is to stuff the draughty spaces with trees.' So sighed Lionel Brett — but he is wrong. We could stuff our draughty (and ugly and derelict and wasted) spaces with trees in plenty of time to enjoy them ourselves, quite apart from our grateful successors.

'Planting ranks among the first of public virtues,' said Marshall, and it is a virtue far more necessary now than in the eighteenth century. If we do nothing our landscape will steadily degenerate: if we plant boldly enough it could grow to an orderly green environment for our urban living. Well-grown forest trees are treasure we can have in abundance simply by putting in saplings now and leaving the rest to time, for though 'the works of a person that builds begin immediately to decay, those of him who plants begin directly to improve'.

# 18. Point Three: Landscape Material

*Local variety established in landscape regions*

Tree Belts, if planted lavishly, would establish the difference between town and country, but this is only the necessary first stage in developing each landscape. The country — as a definition it tells us we are not in the town but little else, and the character of rural landscape is difficult to define and establish.

The countryside of Britain has unrivalled variety in a very small space; it is praise all travellers repeat, and is due to our small-scale and extremely varied geology. An area which in larger-scale countries is the same unvarying scene is with us a changing succession of local landscapes. In the past different regions had their own unmistakable character — of farming type, vegetation, building styles and materials; down to the smallest details of laying stones in walls, thatching roofs and corn-ricks, making gates and stiles, and twisting heathering bands along hand-laid hedges, each district had its own particular landscape quality. Even the local girls were distinctive according to Cobbett, 'remarkably pretty', he says, 'in most parts of Sussex — round faces, features small, little hands and wrists, plump arms and bright eyes'. (Though Cobbett's ideal is perhaps too wholesome for modern taste, and we might prefer the wild spirits he met on the windy downs above Marlborough — 'very pretty, but ragged as colts and as pale as ashes'.)

Neither country girls nor country landscapes, however, are what they were. Landscape variety like landscape itself is produced by the interaction of habitat and man, and as man is less or more dominant so the local habitat will create more or less local variety. Preindustrial man moreover was himself, as various kinds of farmer, to a considerable extent the product of his habitat, and local conditions therefore produced local landscapes, certainly in the uplands, though even in the unemphatic lowlands the habitat had sufficient weight to create distinctive regions.

But the balance between modern man and his habitat is very different. Not only is man now dominant in the combination, but industrial man is not a product of a local environment. Only therefore where the habitat is extreme as in the uplands does it still create local landscapes. Here farming and forestry may fluctuate but the upland areas are distinctive scenery, largely controlled by natural conditions (geology, climate, soils) and therefore stable. The lowland landscapes, however, have no such stability in the modern world; they are created by society's use of a mild and more or less homogeneous habitat, and therefore depend not on permanent conditions but on a restless rootless creature in a state of constant change. A different land-use – even changed methods in an old use like farming – creates an entirely different scenery.

Modern farming in fact is most commonly blamed for the loss of landscape variety, with everywhere the same tractor-worked fields, machine-cut hedges, factory-style buildings and all the rest. But regional character is also destroyed in many other ways. Modern transport for instance is not only responsible for *what* it transports, like people and buildings, but also for their alien character. Pre-transport buildings were local both in style and material, but this is clearly not true of our modern factory products, which though not in themselves either good or bad, are irrelevant to the local landscapes.

The ill-judged use of materials has long been a grief to architects. 'Samples of everything,' laments Lionel Brett of an Oxfordshire village, ' red brick, yellow brick, buff brick, white brick, stone, rough-cast, half-timber, concrete tiles in black, grey, brown and red, asbestos, corrugated iron.' And then in sad condemnation the simple statement: 'This was a stone village.'

In buildings the chaos is evident to everyone, but what is less clearly recognized is the equally ill-judged use of plant-material. Yet the same chaos in the vegetable world is even more unfortunate, for whereas all buildings are artefacts added to the natural scene, planting replaces natural growth, and alien plants are therefore even more fundamentally wrong than alien buildings. In the transportless past, trees and shrubs, like materials for building, were collected from the surrounding countryside, but already by the nineteenth century Wordsworth was complaining of Lakeland gardens which contained 'the whole contents of the nurseryman's catalogue jumbled together'. With wider transport we now have a far wider choice to jumble, and our plants are aliens collected from all over the world.

In the private landscapes of gardens our own taste is supreme arbiter, and to plant an alien tree because we like it is excellent. But to plant the same tree in the countryside is not, for here it is part of the general landscape material. And it is wrong material: it is an incongruous intrusion in the rural scene, destroying the local character and creating its own disturbed vegetable landscape in what should be rural countryside. If weeds are plants in the wrong place, then in a country landscape alien plants are weeds, indeed purple-leaved prunus in country lanes are far worse weeds than ground-elder in country gardens, and just as much suburbia invading the countryside as any urban housing. Planting needs as careful control as building, yet we can walk down the country lane of alien houses and list the equally alien trees – silver birch, flowering cherry, horse chestnut, laburnum, weeping willow. And then the same condemnation: 'This was oak country.'

Such an ill-conceived hotchpotch is sad for all sorts of reasons – that as aliens in oak country all the trees are out of place, that they each need different conditions and cannot all thrive, that they do not compose together but are simply an incompatible collection, and that since the same characterless nurseryman's assortment is now planted everywhere, this local lane is indistinguishable from anonymous miles of roads all over the country.

It is not only aliens, however, which erode local character, for even native trees are often chosen with little concern for the region. Even enlightened planters are apt to specify only 'local' trees and leave it at that, but in much of Britain there *are* no local trees any longer. What do we mean by local? Is it what happens to be growing on neighbouring land? But most of the trees in our countryside were planted for reasons which had nothing to do with local vegetation, and even native trees used out of context can destroy an area's inherent character less obviously but no less thoroughly than aliens. Willows and silver birches for instance, however attractive in themselves, when planted where they would never grow naturally, reduce what could be genuine local countryside to an unidentifiable park

*The birch-pine heath on common land.*

landscape. Indeed there is a very real danger of transforming every-thing we touch in the country to indeterminate parkland. We could easily do it by planting enough wrong trees in enough wrong places, even well-meaning native trees; and that we do it with the best of intentions only makes it doubly sad.

In our temperate lowlands almost anything we plant will grow, it is only harsh conditions acting by natural selection which destroy unsuitable introductions and select the vegetation appropriate to the region. This is one reason why the uplands preserve their natural character; they would quickly lose it if their hill roads were lined with flowering cherries and their valleys filled with weeping willows. Equally some poor lowland soils may discourage both farming and alien vegetation, and regions like the New Forest and the Surrey heaths still keep their local character despite heavy use for urban recreation.

It is a chief attraction of such landscapes; we feel we are in the 'real' country, are nearer 'nature', and though we may not analyse our reaction it is this we miss in much of the lowlands. Here the habitat has little restraint on our lack of discrimination, though it is exactly these troubled landscapes surrounding our urban living which most need the coherence of a definite local character.

In many lowland areas we now no longer even recognize the possibility of a distinctive countryside, yet our future landscapes will only have local character if we deliberately foster and re-create it — not simply, as at present, designate special areas whose regional quality still persists and trust they will keep their character (though such designations, by attracting visitors, are as likely to destroy as preserve). Yet exactly because our landscapes are now dominated by man we could re-create the lost variety by deliberate action. We could plot out our countryside in areas decided by their potential local character, and deliberately develop this everywhere to establish Landscape Regions. These would be stretches of country with their own recognizable personality, and though near towns they would include much urban development, the Regions could still establish a local rural landscape as a background to integrate the intrusions.

Landscape Regions would be divisions of the countryside based on local ecology. Not, however, on the academic study of natural communities, for the ecology we need for modern planning must start with modern man, and the Scampi Belt for instance is not defined in terms of the birch-pine heaths or the Bagshot Sands but of human strata. The ecology of most areas is now altered more profoundly by the category of man who inhabits them than by any difference in habitat, and the bleakest hill-grazing looks much like the lush fields of Kent if we compare them both with a city centre.

The suggested map of the four different categories of environment would therefore be an essential start for plotting Landscape Regions, for in effect it would be a map of different types of man as four different factors in the landscape. In the urban environment man would dominate habitat almost completely, but in the green-urban, rural, and wild landscape, habitat would become increasingly important and would therefore need to be classified. Relief is here an obvious beginning, and produces not only the general division between uplands and lowlands but also lesser changes in the lowland hills and plains. Rainfall and general climate are also varied and are partly dependent on relief, while linked to both are the various soils, important in landscape through natural vegetation, type of farming, and the use of the underlying rock for building. Soil maps, where they exist, are extremely complicated, for British soils are so diversified (by weathering and farming processes as well as by geology) that they vary over very small areas. In Kent for instance, where the complexity of the underlying rocks is not covered by glacial drift, the varied soils produce the wide variety of farming so noticeable compared with more homogeneous areas like the often drift-covered Midlands. Definite large changes of soil, however, would be important boundaries, as for instance the heavy clay of the Sussex Weald and the barren greensands which surround it, or the 'chalk and cheese' country of Wiltshire, or the Mountain Limestone and Millstone Grit areas in the Pennines, so closely associated in the Peak that their black and white rocks are used together to build the oddest piebald walls.

These interacting features could be correlated (rainfall for instance has a different value on porous sand and impervious clays; poor soil is aggravated by poor climate) and worked into a map of general habitat. Britain can be considered as three main types of habitat. The

*The 'chalk and cheese' in Wiltshire. The high ground on the left is corallian limestone – good arable land in large rectangular fields. The low ground on the right is Oxford clay with small irregular pasture fields of permanent grass. The scarp between arable and pasture is wooded marginal land.*

327

first is the South-East including the Midland plain, where the climate is most like the Continent, with least rain and longest warmest summers. Deciduous woodland here reaches its finest development and regenerates most readily. The second region is the West including Ireland, where the rainfall is high and the winds severe. Trees only grow in sheltered places, the rest of the land is heath and scrub if well drained, peat and blanket-bog if not. The North is the third region and includes the Scottish Highlands, where the climate is cold as well as wet, and the world belt of deciduous trees merges with conifers. It is here that the famous Arctic-Alpine plants survive as remnants of the vegetation which covered Britain when the ice receded.

As well as these maps of local man and local habitat would also be needed a map of the potential local vegetation of each area, for the once well-established natural differences in our forest cover are no longer clear in our much-altered countryside. Man has not only replaced the original vegetation with plants of his choice (the hedge-row elm, though the commonest tree in many enclosure areas, is nowhere found wild as part of a natural plant community) but has also changed the habitat itself. Felling the woodland for instance in delicately-balanced upland areas has encouraged the spread of bog, while land-draining has changed areas like the Fens to dry land, so that even if all human beings disappeared overnight it would still be centuries before Britain recovered its original plant-cover.

Nonetheless the potential vegetation of each area would be a valid basis to start from and is now reasonably well understood. Our British flora consists chiefly of Angiosperms or flowering plants, the third great flora to occupy the land surfaces of the world. It replaced the previous vegetation in Cretaceous times, a little before the widespread development of the mammals, appearing suddenly in the fossil record, so that in museum show-cases we suddenly recognize a familiar heart-shaped poplar leaf among the alien shapes of long-vanished plants.

Even at its first appearance our flora is already highly developed, with little suggestion of its origins or early stages, and this Athene-like emergence not unnaturally mystifies the fossil botanists. ('The origin of the flowering plants is an abominable mystery,' complained

Charles Darwin.) Early fossils of the new plants are found in Greenland and North America, but they quickly became dominant and formed a single widespread flora over the whole northern hemisphere and perhaps the world. The climate at this period was mild and settled, with a gentle gradation of temperature from the Equator to the Poles, and with no high mountains to disturb the air-flow and create rain-shadow deserts, and in these idyllic conditions palms and magnolias flourished in the Thames Valley (with crocodiles in the marshy river).

But this long prosperity of the early flowering plants was disturbed in the Miocene period, when the climate became cooler and earth convulsions forced up the great mountain ranges of the present world. The climate continued to worsen, and the fossil plants change from subtropical to cool temperate, until immediately before the ice they are much like ours today. The Ice Age which followed was catastrophic, and between plants and their environment there was violent disharmony. As the ice moved south during the successive glaciations so did the surviving vegetation, spreading north again as the ice retreated; but north-to-south movement is limited in Western Europe which is hemmed in by mountains and sea, and the southward retreat of plants was blocked by the Mediterranean and the ice-capped Alps and Pyrenees. In this death-trap many species perished from our European flora.

The extreme conditions also produced changes in the surviving vegetation, and different forms evolved adapted to cold and drought. In general the better the environment the taller the vegetation, and trees and shrubs thus predominate in good conditions. In the luscious pre-glacial flora our modern flowers and grasses scarcely appear; they developed as better able to survive the new hostile environment, either as perennials wintering underground, or as annuals surviving the winter as seeds. Our great modern herbaceous families therefore evolved as an adaptation to disaster, and spread widely on the open ground laid bare by the fluctuating ice.

The flowering plants have proved to be an extremely efficient and resistant flora, and our vegetation has recovered from the ice at impressive speed. Even so the poverty of the European flora is clear if we compare it with that of East Asia or North America. In one small area of North Carolina alone for instance there are more species of native trees than in the whole of Europe; for though North America also suffered the ice, its mountain ranges run north and south and are therefore no barrier to the movement of plants, which migrated to suitable habitats either further south or at lower altitudes.

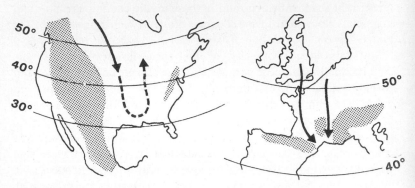

*Survival of vegetation in the Ice Age. In Europe the southward retreat was blocked by sea and mountains, in America warm temperate plants survived in the south and spread to the north again as the climate improved.*

Thus in Asia and America the pre-glacial flora survived to spread north again when the ice receded, and in these areas plants now occur which are lacking in similar climates in Europe. It is why plants brought into Britain as exotics from these regions are likely to thrive in our modern gardens and may even spread in the wild.

Of the limited European flora our British vegetation is an even more limited range, which as the ice receded has mostly spread to us across the land-bridge which joined Britain to Europe until roughly 5,000 years ago. Tundra vegetation appeared first in the arctic conditions, followed by temperate plants as the climate improved; but like the climate the vegetation fluctuated, with birch and pine and hazel common in warmer periods, damp oakwood and sphagnum bog in wet. *The Natural Vegetation of the British Isles* by Tansley is an ecological study of our present plants, and from this and more recent work could be mapped the potential natural vegetation. That all the necessary maps still need making proves our ignorance of the necessary background of landscape planning, but ecologists could certainly plot the probable broad distribution of plant communities (even though scholarly study is temptingly safer than practical commitment).

By correlating these three maps – of man-made environments, of natural habitat, and of potential vegetation – could be worked out a possible pattern of Landscape Regions for the whole country. Some would be small and clearly defined, others large and merging imperceptibly into neighbouring regions, but each with its own distinct character clearly recognizable as the local variant of the country landscape. In general the regions should be spacious, not a fidgety jigsaw of separate small patches but landscapes widely-enough established to compose the discordant elements within them and to register as distinctive countryside. An obvious beginning would be regions already distinct like the Yorkshire Wolds, the Mendips, the Forest of Dean, the Somerset Levels and so on, and in his *Agricultural Atlas of England and Wales* Professor Coppock lists twenty-five areas in the uplands and eight in the lowlands as physical regions with a recognizable identity.

When once plotted the regions could then be established as distinctive landscapes in various ways. Some, especially in wild or undisturbed rural areas, would correspond to the old local landscapes, and here the old distinctive qualities could often be preserved. Brick or stone-built cottages, thatched or tiled roofs, old inns and farms and churches – our prosperous new society is beginning to treasure its picturesque past. Even more important, however, would be suitable methods and materials for new development. Here conscious discrimination will have to replace unconscious local colour, but with care and sympathy the old character can be expressed by new methods (as for instance by panels of exposed flint aggregate in areas with old flint walls – the same materials but handled by machines instead of men). The National Trust is reassuringly confident – 'It is perfectly easy to make sure that each locality has its own uniform and appropriate building materials. It's being done with

331

evident success in the National Parks. Where local stone or bricks cannot be used for shortages or high prices materials can be manufactured with similar colours and textures.' And though 'perfectly easy' seems over-optimistic and 'uniform and appropriate' is likely to annoy any architect, there does exist considerable private goodwill and public control if once suitable methods were worked out in suitable regions. Certainly, however, it is not a question of imitating old styles, but rather of local good manners for newcomers joining an established community.

Local structures in the landscape, like old barns or the field-byres in the Yorkshire Dales, may or may not survive, but walls in stony landscape are difficult to get rid of (except along roads near urban areas where they are carried off and sold to misguided rockery-makers). Such walls give the landscape a strong regional character, built by methods developed from the local rock's natural strata – horizontal courses in Cotswold limestone, random rubble in northern villages, and in the Millstone Grit hills where I first went walking, irregular lumps piled together at an angle, making a barrier precarious to climb over, both for the wall's structure and one's own.

Where such local variations of the man-made country scene still exist as working practice they could be encouraged (though not preserved as self-conscious exercises in rusticity). The Peak District already has an enlightened policy towards its building traditions, Westmorland trains masons in the old methods, new walls along some Oxfordshire roads are indistinguishable from old, and so on. Old land divisions may also survive as boundaries along roads or between farms, like the pine hedges of Breckland, or the sunk lanes of Devon, or the turf walls of Pembrokeshire. And though the old farming methods described in such detail by early farm writers have no place in mechanized farming, yet it is possible that local variations of modern methods might develop in Landscape Regions, as in one district in Norfolk where the hedges along the deep narrow lanes are mechanically cut in a single inclined plane with the banked verge, producing a smooth green ramp of grass and leaves from road-surface to hedge top.

Farming too may create new broad differences between regions as transport becomes easier and different areas therefore concentrate on the type of agriculture best suited to local conditions – more cereals in the east, more fodder crops in the rainy west, rows of shining beet or feathery carrots on black fen soils, flowing seas of barley on the chalk, hop-gardens and orchards in Kent and Hereford, and in the West Riding of Yorkshire the strangely exotic fields of rhubarb which fascinated me as a child. (They still do, for the rhubarb never seems to be harvested. Are the plants put out in the fields, I wonder, for a kind of sabbatical year to recover from indoor forcing?)

But as future farmland mostly becomes large arable fields, the chief distinction between Landscape Regions in the lowland country-side will probably be in the non-farming vegetation, especially trees. Certainly this would be the difference most easily controlled, particularly since the areas now most lacking in landscape character also need the most tree-planting, and simply to specify all new trees planted would go a long way towards producing distinct regions. The choice of suitable trees would involve many factors besides the vegetation natural to the area. First clearly is land-use – slag-heaps, for instance, need binding and covering with any green that will grow: they are no place for purist theories. Nor is it useful to decide that the natural growth of London clay is damp oakwood when its natural growth is clearly Londoners; and disturbed landscapes of all kinds need special combinations of plants to suit their particular conditions. Nonetheless the local communities of plants suggested by ecologists would be the general basis; in wild areas all vegetation should be as nearly natural as possible, and wherever distinctive local plants exist like the ash of the Yorkshire Dales and the beeches of the Chilterns, they should clearly be the basic choice.

In our man-dominated ecology, however, the choice should also provide the plants needed for different types of human environment. The first essential would be a full-size forest tree for establishing the character of the region and providing screen-belts of tall woodland: this would be the most important plant, as in nature, and should be widely planted. Next a secondary tree would generally be needed, smaller and less vigorous, for planting where the first was too large or otherwise unsuitable; and probably chosen from the under-storey trees occurring naturally with the main species. Then shrubs: a tall one certainly for screening, a low one for ground cover without

*The Chiltern hills through the Chiltern beeches. Forestry Commission woodland in London's Green Belt.*

blocking the view, and if possible one to keep its foliage in winter – either evergreen like holly and yew, or holding its dead leaves till spring, like young oak and beech and hornbeam.

In our prehistoric forest cover the oak in its two species was the commonest tree (in England it still is in hedges – thirty-one per cent – though in Scotland it falls to twenty-four per cent and is second to beech at twenty-six), and in Landscape Regions on what country people call 'oak-tree clays' it would still often be the most suitable tree (though how many oaks has anyone planted in the last half-century?). Beech in some areas would be dominant (the pollen analysis shows it on the East Anglian chalk), in others perhaps used with oak or ash in varying combinations. The birch is a typical tree of the Highlands, so are the alder and aspen and Scots pine, and the mountain ash on high ground; the wych elm is distinctive in the North-West, the ash on limy hill-soils, silver birch and pines on southern heaths and so on. But these are mere indications of what might be needed, for each region would have to be considered both on its own terms and those of its bordering areas, since boundaries would seldom be sudden changes but rather transitions where the vegetation merged and changed emphasis. Except in areas with clear natural division (between limy and acid soils for instance or porous and impervious ground) some plants would continue from one region to the next, but with a different importance in the new grouping.

It might be objected by garden-scale thinkers that such simplified planting would make a monotonous countryside, but this is certainly not true. On the contrary, the natural vegetation we most admire is often a single repeated plant – heather moors, beechwoods, gorse-covered cliffs, birch-forests, bluebells. This pattern of a single species growing in large numbers is typical of the vegetation of the North as distinct from the great variety of the tropics, and far from being dull the vivid effect depends on the repetition of a single plant. It is an all-over mixture like confetti which is dull, not neighbouring areas of different colours, and Repton has a very pertinent passage on the difference between mixture and variety. 'By the indiscriminate mixture of every kind of trees all variety is destroyed by the excess of variety – for example, if ten clumps be composed of ten different sorts of trees in each, they become so many things exactly similar;

but if each clump consist of the same sort of trees, they become ten different things – a group of oaks, another of elms, another of chestnuts, or of thorns, etc.'

All the masters of landscape have limited the number of species they used to create their effects. Le Nôtre worked chiefly with hornbeam, chestnut and box, and Capability Brown commonly used no more than five species. It is exactly this controlled variety which we now need in our landscape, and far from being dull it will be important to keep the species as few as possible, sometimes to a single forest tree constantly repeated. For the new planting will only be an addition to the 'indiscriminate mixture' already there and which will need a clear and simple framework of new planting to give it any regional character.

In any case there are many areas where the vegetation will naturally vary, as willows or alders near water whatever the general trees of the region. Nor does the same species always create the same effect, but what Repton calls 'continuity without sameness'. It is only equal-age equidistant planting which is monotonous, for when grown naturally there is endless variety in the same tree in different positions and stages of growth. 'Situations are everywhere so various,' said Marshall, 'that there never can be a sameness' (and he added the disapproving maxim: 'The more we exact novelty the sooner our taste will be vitiated' – a pronouncement our own age might take to heart).

In any region there will be conditions where the local trees grow badly, but that is no reason for planting different species except perhaps as nurse trees. Poor growth is the proper adaptation to poor conditions: it is a direct expression of the local habitat, and that the same trees grow tall and spreading in sheltered valleys but crouch together on windy hill-tops makes us more vividly conscious of hills and valleys. To plant the hills with wind-resistant aliens is to lose the character of the habitat as well as the local vegetation. A natural landscape is not a bed of soil to cover with fast-growing plants like a vegetable garden, but an integrated natural system in its own right and expressed through its vegetation. The Eskimos have forty different words for snow in different conditions, and with our forest background we need forty different words for trees in different situations.

With the local groups of plants established for each region there is then the question of who is to plant them and where in country areas gardeners might be persuaded to grow the local shrubs and trees in their boundary hedges, especially if young plants were provided cheaply (or free), and this would tie gardens into the surrounding country. The chief planting, however, would be on land controlled by public bodies, and its possible part in the creation of a new landscape framework is discussed in the next chapter. At present there is no co-ordinated policy for managing such land. The National Trust with 400,000 acres (162,000 ha), is the largest landowner after the Forestry Commission, and County Councils manage many areas of land without a ground-use, so that even on purely practical grounds of easy maintenance the advice of ecologists seems essential. But lamentably few are employed in any kind of country planning, nor is ecology part of planner's training. It is a further and very cogent argument for establishing Landscape Regions for general reference.

That Tree Belts should be planted with regional trees is clearly essential, otherwise they will merely be urban extensions. Except, however, on hilly ground it is only the outer borders which will be part of the country scene, and so long as there is an effective outer screen of regional trees and shrubs the woodland within can be what we choose – perhaps aliens more suitable for forestry, or simply because we like them and bother the landscape issues.

Native and alien have in any case no exact meaning in our vegeta-tion, for as all our trees have reached us since glacial times they are all very recent exotics by the geological time-scale. How long must we live here to qualify as native? The sweet chestnut came with the Romans, the horse chestnut in Tudor times, the southern pines (a different variety from the Scots) are probably self-sown from eight-eenth-century plantings. Are these natives or aliens? And what of the elm of mysterious provenance, which now produces hundreds of healthy young hedgerow trees unconcerned by Dutch elm disease? The sycamore too is now probably our most widespread tree, a troublesome weed in the lowlands and replacing the local trees in the uplands, yet in the seventeenth century it was still described by Gerard as 'a stranger in England'.

This restoration of our flora by new arrivals is a still-continuing process, which is likely to intensify with modern transport. Nor with our limited number of trees can we afford to reject on purist grounds potential natives which may only be absent through the accident of the North Sea. The Norway maple for instance (*Acer platanoides*) is now rapidly spreading from ornamental plantings; a beautiful tree with its early yellow flowers and handsome shining leaves which turn clear butter-yellow before they fall, and merging so naturally into our countryside that we may never notice it until autumn.

But that introductions run wild is certainly not reason enough to use them deliberately in Landscape Regions. *Rhododendron ponticum* for instance always looks an urban intruder in our countryside, though now widespread not only in semi-natural woodland but even on the stormy cliffs of Lundy sprayed by wickedly boiling seas. The Turkey oak (*Quercus cerris*), the Oregon Grape (*Mahonia aquifolium*), the Rose of Sharon (*Hypericum calycinum*), the Duke of Argyll's Tea-Tree (*Lycium halimifolium*) and various cotoneasters have all run wild in many areas, and so in at least one site in Breckland has the Japanese rose (*Rosa rugosa*). But these have no place in wild or rural planting if we are to keep any local character in our countryside.

In urban and green-urban landscape, however, the case is different, and in difficult situation aliens may be invaluable. Corsican pine has shown willing on derelict land, a hybrid willow is spontaneously colonizing the spoil-heaps near Wigan (the 'Wigan Alps') and red oak and acacia do well on spoil in the Ruhr. In such situations all plants are useful which will tolerate the various pollutions, and in green-urban landscapes carefully-chosen aliens can have a place if they compose with our own vegetation. The tall cotoneasters for instance make an informal and quick-growing evergreen screen which we cannot provide from our native shrubs; the American and eastern thorns are useful small-boy-proof small trees with a natural look, and acacia, though never at home in our countryside as it is in Eastern Europe or even France, is a decorative tree for urban areas.

Mutated forms of trees whether alien or native should also be confined to urban landscapes. Fastigiate or weeping trees for instance are not for rural areas, and whenever we see them we know we are not in true country. Like the equally alien spires of cypresses they are an announcement of non-rural development visible for miles around. Where the scale is large, as in France, the scene can absorb the contrast, but not our small-scale precariously-rural countryside. And that Lombardy poplars and weeping willows are superb in the Thames valley only confirms that this is a brilliantly-managed green-urban landscape and no more the country proper than is Hampstead Heath.

Equally destructive of country character are garden trees with coloured foliage, unnatural intrusions of yellow or raw liver-colour (copper beech is suburbanizing Lakeland valleys). Nor is the countryside the place for Japanese cherries or other grafted forms of the genus *Prunus*. Popular they may be but their milieu is urban; if we want flowering trees in the country we have three native cherries which will grow without grafting, also bullace which flowers as early as almond, and the crab-apple introduced by Neolithic farmers and once common in our hedges, and beautiful both in flower and fruit (when the bullfinches leave any buds). All these could be planted in suitable Landscape Regions, as could broom and gorse and guelder-rose and wayfaring tree and spindleberry and our other little-known and lovely flowering shrubs. We have far more native shrubs than trees, many of them grown by gardeners who have never seen them wild, and here is a chance to re-establish them with the trees which are their natural companions. In fact if we chose the main species wisely for their regions they might themselves re-create in time the conditions where other plants natural to the groups we had established would return spontaneously, as weeds so readily do in the proper open-soil conditions of gardens, and dog-daisies on railway banks and cow-parsley in hedges. We might even speed up the process (a bluebell wood is said to take a century to establish) by sowing seed of local flowers in suitable places, especially on land restored after development.

The establishment of the Landscape Regions as suggested here would cost little except in goodwill and cooperation, for since much of the planting will in any case be done it is chiefly a matter of one plant rather than another. Nor would the native species be expensive: on the contrary, they would be far cheaper than aliens, and being naturally suited to local conditions would grow fast and well with fewer losses. Each region could also set up nurseries to grow mass supplies of its own species, and this would in any case be essential since commercial growers could certainly not provide the thousands needed, especially the plants on their own roots essential for any non-garden planting. It could be done, however, at comparatively little cost, and would provide a cheap and ready supply for planting wherever needed.

The chief tasks in fact would be the surveys needed to plot the regions, the research on suitable methods and materials for development, and the working out of suitable groups of plants. And it would be essential to get these foundations right, not only in each region but also as a coordinated whole, for once established the Landscape Regions would be permanent. Of the three variables they are based on – local habitat, potential vegetation and land-use – only the last is unstable because man-made, and even this should be reasonably reliable if the four categories of land-use environment were plotted with foresight. In any case the regions would be an adaptable system which could absorb considerable changes of land-use into the local pattern, so that in time our landscape, even the essentially man-made areas, would recover its lost variety, and as the new regional vegetation gradually brought order to the present hotchpotch, the countryside would become both more various and more natural.

Everywhere in the modern world local identity will tend to disappear unless we reverse the process, and Kevin Lynch in America is particularly concerned with the loss in urban landscape. He lists his own proposals for developing local urban character, and it is significant to see a town-planner so clearly thinking of environment in terms of landscape. In fact we have only to read region for centre in the following passage for it to be an outline of the measures proposed here for the wider landscape. 'It would be my policy to sharpen whatever is unique in the physical character of each centre and to increase the diversity between centres. Studies would be made of their existing differences and their hidden potentialities – studies of each centre's history, land-form, building type, population and mix of activities. A programme for visible character could be set for each focus.'

Equally in Landscape Regions we should be creating a new and conscious version of the old spontaneous order, rescuing our vanishing native vegetation and creating genuine new local landscapes in terms of our new ways of living. It would be a large-scale exercise in applied ecology, based on the new interaction of modern man and his ancient habitat.

# 19. Point Four: Landscape Texture

*Categories of design and maintenance in a code of landscape practice*

The last three chapters have been suggestions for establishing on the ground the types of environment we now need, but there is still the final stage of designing and maintaining the actual landscape, and this is as important as the raw material itself in creating landscape character. On agricultural land the processes of farming provide both design and maintenance, and this chapter is therefore chiefly concerned with the increasing areas with no inherent ground-use – industrial land, the grounds of large buildings and institutions, roadside verges, land for recreation and so on – areas which are often neglected, or managed in ways which have little basis either in land-use or landscape design.

The commonest present method is some form of garden maintenance, not because this is in any way appropriate but because in the past the only land without a ground-use was parks or gardens, and therefore the only style of design and maintenance we inherited was for pleasure-grounds, with mown lawns, specimen trees, shrubs in beds or hedges, and a general air of the vegetation behaving itself on man's territory. This is excellent where it belongs in parks and gardens, but because it is the one style we know, and because new machines and chemicals make its wholesale application possible, it is now widely used regardless of landscape character. Massive industrial structures for instance are sprinkled round with flower-beds and patches of lawn, and country road verges planted like urban parks with spaced-out trees and grass mown to lawn-like neatness (though where there is much cutting or banking, as on motorways, the effect is less of grass than of moulded green plastic). These expensive methods (on one twenty-seven-mile (43 km) stretch of verge stones were gathered by *hand* for machines to mow closer) can reduce a splendid cross-country highway to a suburban by-pass, and instead of

*Georgian London by Adam –*

*– and others. The east and north sides of Fitzroy Square.*

the road being an enhanced experience of the countryside it crosses, we look gratefully over its fences into the farming landscape beyond. Those locally responsible, however, are not to blame: it is the brief which is wrong not the carrying-out, and if given the park-and-garden style almost everywhere aimed at, then regimented trees and homogenized plastic grass mean work well done. What we urgently need are non-garden styles for the growing areas of non-garden land now needing maintenance, otherwise our newly-efficient methods will spread landscape suburbia abroad over all land not used for farming.

The simple solution might seem to be to enlist landscape architects – the professionals specifically trained in the design of outdoor environment – and in time it may well seem as natural to employ landscape architects to design the outdoor environment as architects to design buildings. At present, however, they are far too scarce for such a hopeful utopia, and in any case much routine landscape work needs simple routine methods not specialist attention. To produce good general landscape mass-production methods are essential – not mass-produced *designs* imposed regardless of local conditions, but standard methods of treatment which when applied to the local situation will produce an appropriate landscape. This is how nature works – not to a predetermined pattern but by submitting the variety of life to the general control of the environment: and on the humbler human level it is how the landscape of enclosure was produced, and also the much-admired townscape of Georgian London. This was chiefly created by speculative builders working in the ordinary run of business, but in a widely-accepted style and to specific imposed regulations for elements like windows, reveals, cornices, skylines, roofs, bricks and so on, as well as for the general effect suitable for different classes of houses. Within this framework the buildings were unobtrusively individual, but as a whole they combined to make up the coherent townscape we still admire, and where it is difficult to distinguish between the work of the famous and the anonymous in the harmonious whole.

Something like this method of coordinating the eighteenth-century townscape we now need for our twentieth-century landscape, for however good the separate projects of landscape architects these alone cannot make a whole. Good design goes from the general to the particular, from outline to detail, not the other way round, and their work needs the setting of a coherent landscape background where it takes its place as heightened effects in the general fabric, as do Adam's buildings in the fabric of Georgian townscape.

We therefore need a code of landscape practice to specify methods of design and maintenance for the four categories of wild and rural, green-urban and urban, and such a code should satisfy three conditions:

1. It should be based on ecological principles so that it works with natural processes instead of against them.
2. The methods should be simple enough for casual labour with machines.
3. The directions should be set out clearly for everyone to follow (and for landscape architects to flout if they choose to, since rules are for breaking by those who know why).

Landscape design, like architecture, is a three-dimensional arrangement of masses and voids. There are all kinds of added complications – colour, texture, light, movement, seasonal changes, atmospheric effects, the beauty of the vegetable material and so on – but the basis is a controlled arrangement of mass and space. In landscape the masses consist partly of land-forms which generally cannot be altered except on a comparatively small scale, and partly of vegetation which can. The voids are again of land-form (valleys for instance) and also of volumes of space where trees and shrubs are absent.

Although in our forest climate time alone will supply the vegetation, such spontaneous growth is seldom what we want, and by our planting we substitute our own choice of vegetation in arrangements to suit our land-uses. In natural landscape both the masses of the free-growing vegetation and therefore the spaces which it creates are subtle and indeterminate, but as managed by man vegetation and spaces are generally far more clearly defined. Space may start at ground level with mown grass (or hard surfaces or water) or may be above-ground space defined by shrubs or trees, and a large part of landscape design could in fact be considered as the organization of the layers of the vegetation as masses and spaces.

345

*A country garden created from local vegetation simply by defining the layers – short grass, long grass, shrubs and trees.*

Design and maintenance cannot be considered apart – or rather they can be but never should; it is when they are that half an acre (0·2 ha) needs as much work as ten acres (4 ha) suitably planned. Equally important is that planting and the control of subsequent growth are two stages of the same creation and must therefore be planned in terms of each other. In fact unless this is so and the maintenance clearly specified the design is unlikely to survive.

Maintenance is chiefly the management of vegetation, which in harsh climates means encouraging growth (by irrigation for instance), but in our fertile lowlands is chiefly the control of overgrowth. For once our vegetation is established it is more than self-supporting, and maintenance is thus essentially of space not mass.

A code of landscape practice therefore needs specific methods

346

both for planting and for controlling growth in different categories of landscape, and since the park and-garden style is familiar to everyone it is helpful to realize why it differs from natural landscape no matter what plants are used. In natural growth the layers of the vegetation intermingle, with tall herbs growing through low shrubs and shrubs merging with trees, with no definition and no gaps between them:

*Simply therefore to separate vegetation into grass, shrubs and trees immediately creates an unnatural effect:*

*It is also unnatural if we omit a layer, as with trees in grass:*

*or if we change the order of the layers, as by growing trees and shrubs with grass between them:*

Whatever the actual plants these common modifications of natural growth produce a garden effect.

347

Even the extreme sophistication of Le Nôtre's landscapes was created by his handling of the layers of ordinary vegetation, and equally the eighteenth-century avenue at Stowe, even though of free-growing elms as in neighbouring hedges, is unmistakably an extension of the territory of the (still invisible) mansion. It is the alignment which creates the avenue's non-rural majesty in the rural country-side, and it is significant here that trees equidistant in rows suffer far more vandalism than when planted naturally — they are clearly the work of Them.

The arrangement of vegetation in nature is thus very different from ours, and equally so is the way of establishing it. This is clear from the earlier brief outline of the development of woodland through the invasion of the herb layer by a competing growth of shrubs and trees which gradually suppress all vegetation unsuited to the final community. Where exposed to light, however, the edge of natural woodland is a solid bank of green with all the layers present from tree-tops to ground level, and since most of our planting is in the open we are mostly planting in wood-edge conditions. It is thus easy to see why our methods are unnatural — we space out plants separately, we omit layers, and we eliminate competition. By planting more naturally we should not only produce more suitable landscapes for country areas, but our plants would grow faster and better and need less maintenance.

At present we spend a vast amount of energy interfering with natural processes instead of using them for the mutual advantage of both planters and planted. The survival of the fittest, for instance, is a rigorous law which (as gardeners know) we only reverse by constant effort, yet which used as an ally can save endless labour by producing the life best suited to the given conditions. By choosing local vegetation for Landscape Regions we follow the law in its large-scale terms, but we can also use it on the small scale by planting close and letting the groups work out their own salvation through competition. The growth of twenty square yards (17 sq. metres) of natural wood-land, for instance, might start as 200 seedlings, which as they grow and the weak are progressively crowded out are reduced in the end to a single tree — the fittest of 200. When we on the other hand want a tree on such an area we transplant a single part-grown specimen to grow exposed in unnatural isolation — no question of choice by competition, nor survival of the fittest plant for the situation, nor of the close shelter natural to young trees. For trees are gregarious, they are woodland plants and seldom grow singly in nature — 'They catch cold and die,' a forester said to me of trees spaced out separately, and Repton is scornful of planters who 'dot a few starveling saplings in an open lawn'.

Between our single tree struggling in isolation and nature's 200 struggling in competition a workable compromise might be ten small trees; which will cost no more than one part-grown, will need no staking, will grow much faster, make better trees for their position, and with ten to choose from we can keep the best (almost certainly discarding any original large ones). And why not fill in the shrubs between them as nature would? 'Let there be at least five or six thorns or hollies for every tree that is planted' (Repton again). 'These will grow up with the trees, perhaps choke and destroy some, but they will rear many.' And once established the trees themselves will do any necessary suppression of their nurses (or if not then we have chosen the wrong trees for the area and the shrubs can take their place).

This was how Capability Brown established the superb trees in his landscape parks, by planting a close group of saplings and protective shrubs and thinning them as they grew. It was the origin of his much-maligned clumps, and why he was mistakenly attacked for 'clumping the common'.

In practice we must obviously modify nature's methods, but these two facts of natural growth are still true — trees are best grown in groups and thinned: the best trees are those transplanted young. This is routine practice in forestry (2,720 trees per acre (6,800 per ha) is recommended for hardwoods) and it is a hopeful beginning that the Forestry Commission now does much of the Ministry of Transport's planting; for no matter how a land-use like forestry may have to be modified to serve as a ground-use for maintenance, it is certainly a better start for country areas than the park-and-garden style which Repton scorned. 'The gardener or nurseryman makes his holes at equal distances and generally in straight rows; he then fills them with plants, and carefully avoids putting two of the same sort near each other. Nor is it very easy to make him put two trees in the same hole; he considers them as cabbages or turnips, which will rob each other's growth unless placed at equal distances; yet in forests, we most admire those double trees or thick clusters, whose stems seem to rise from the same root.' This sensitive relationship of trees to each other is completely lost in isolated spacing. 'It is difficult to lay down rules for planting,' Repton goes on. 'Time, neglect, and accident will often produce unexpected beauties.' Yes. But we *can* lay down rules to produce conditions where the unexpected beauties are possible, as they are not by most present methods.

Due doubtless to the difficulty of control in the machineless past, the use of the shrub layer in landscape is surprisingly small. Trees are self-limiting as the climax vegetation, the herb layer was easily mown by men with scythes, but since management of shrubs was limited to the reach and strength of men with bill-hooks or shears, they were planted in manageable narrow strips – 'live fences' as country people call hedges. We still plant them in this man-power arrangement, though with modern machines, as already suggested, we could use them in far more natural-looking ways.

Shrubs could also be used far more than they are in place of trees where an open ground-space is not needed (and often the only result of open ground under trees is grass mown by men who complain that the trees hinder the machines – an interesting variation of the baby and the bath-water). So why not thickets of shrubs covering the ground and simply left to grow? Shrubs are far more effective than trees at screening ground-level clutter or tying awkward foundations into the land-forms; nor do they grow too tall for their site, as many trees now being planted quite certainly will. Shrub-planting could also restore our vanishing natives, while in poor conditions hawthorn is cheap and easy and needs no one's help – a traditional and beautiful shrub, in May blossom or autumn fruit or winter silhouette of well-grown thorn-trees. We could plant it where it can grow free and flowery as it seldom will on our future farmland, and since unlike blackthorn it does not sucker, its spread is easily controlled by occasional mowing or spraying. Hawthorn, being already ubiquitous, is also an excellent coordinator of all types of landscape, and better than anything else blends intrusions into our hawthorny countryside.

On the disturbed and often alien soils of motorway banks and cuttings for instance, hawthorn would coordinate difficult areas, and also tie bridges into the landscape far better than trees which soon grow to clear trunks, with no ground-level mass to screen awkward ramps, or the skyline parapets which cease abruptly at the edge of the road.

Certainly our man-made landscapes will never look natural unless we do plant shrubs, for we are omitting an essential part of the vegetation which in our open planting conditions would always be present in nature.

The vegetation layer which creates most problems, however, is grass, and the misuse of grass produces a vast amount of expensively-kept bad landscape. This is because in our grass-growing climate it is the way of least resistance in landscape design: it is the lowest common denominator, and what every unplanned urban area lapses to by default. Grass therefore exists in thousands of useless patches and dreary expanses without any function, it permits and even encourages bad layout, and if unthought-out areas grew poison ivy instead of harmless grass our designs would swiftly improve. Even if we only lacked mowing-machines we should soon think again about pointless grass areas cut by hand.

The low densities of the first New Towns have resulted in ubiquitous green stretches mown down everywhere to tennis-lawn smoothness. Often in fact the first sign that the town is near is the state of the grass – verges, open spaces, playing-fields, parks: even what seem to be straightforward fields – everything is affected by the same obsession for close-mowing. It is the Fitted-carpet Complex – every area large or small must be neatly covered with the same short green pile – grass-carpeting as an end in itself irrespective of use or appearance.

In the management of grass our experience is in three chief situations. First is as a farm crop either grazed or harvested, and it is because of the prevalence of grass in our farming that we think of grassland as natural to Britain, which it only is in rare conditions. The second situation is as ground-cover maintained by frequent mowing, and an anti-lawn-mowing intellectual complained that the growth of English grass is responsible for the decay of English

*The Fitted-carpet Complex. Grass as unmowable ground-cover on banks and round obstacles, as jig-saw puzzle with concrete.*

intellect. (One thinks of week-ends lawn-mowing instead of book-reading and sees what he means; but he could just as well blame the growth of English beards – smooth lawns, smooth chins – both are artificial simplifications of the natural scene which need constant maintenance.) The third type of grass management is in the maintenance of open space at ground level, but where the grass itself is of no importance.

Considerable research is already being done on control of grass by different methods, different intensities of mowing, different herbicides, growth-retarders and so on, and new ways may emerge which are suited to the different landscape categories. Grass-control, however, should always be strictly related to the different functions of grass in the landscape, and these are very various. But common to them all is its role as the ground-cover of open areas; for where we want landscape space to start at ground level then grass is the natural surface in our fertile climate; though the grass can be of widely different nature, and its purpose should always be clearly thought out.

In urban areas grass should be a positive part of the design – a smooth skin to reveal the shape of the land-modelling beneath; or on level ground a horizontal plane like a green lake flowing round masses. Grass is also the only vegetation we can walk on continually, and in many places (recreation areas for instance) this is its function: it is a hard-wearing and self-renewing ground-cover. On much land in rural and wild areas, however, the function of grass is quite different, and it here represents control of the vegetation at the lowest layer. The surface may never be walked on, it has no reason to be neat, but nonetheless it is kept mown to hold back the natural succession to shrubs and trees. Road-verges are here an obvious example: the space of the road and its sight-lines must be kept open, but the grass itself is incidental.

Such differences of function are the only logical basis for managing grass. Where good walking-surfaces or lawns are wanted for instance, the grass needs positive treatment by good soil, fertilizers, regular mowing and general maintenance for active growth. But it is clearly illogical to treat grass in the same way when its only function is to *suppress* growth. Nonetheless road-verges are routinely spread with topsoil and fertilizers and planted with strong-growing rye-grass, which is then mown and the cuttings left to rot and encourage more growth for more mowing – an expensive exercise in self-perpetuating maintenance, and verge control in England and Wales costs over £4 million a year. But why spread topsoil? Why not leave subsoil for grass areas and concentrate topsoil for trees and shrubs? (design and maintenance planned together, and also using the knowledge that the worse the conditions the more lowly the natural vegetation). And why plant strong-growing rye-grass? Why not low grasses and local flowers? And why mow close and constantly? Why not occasionally when long and rake off the cuttings, thus steadily reducing the ground's fertility?

These methods were tried experimentally on a small scale on a badly-neglected field on chalk, where the grass (mostly onion couch) was waist-high and full of thistles, ragwort and seedling hawthorn. One area was stripped of topsoil by bulldozer and the subsoil left to

*The same bank, left to grow freely –*

regenerate. After two years the surface was covered by low flowers (no thistles or ragwort); this flower-cover was gradually invaded by thin grass, but even after ten years the growth is still sparse and with a yearly cutting grows barely a foot high. Another undisturbed area in the same field has been cut twice yearly with the cuttings raked off and used as a mulch round young trees. This has changed the original waist-high jungle to a meadow-like growth which is now increasingly invaded by the chalkland flowers, the particular communities of flowers depending on the season of cutting. Paths created through this meadow area simply by regular close-mowing have changed to a lawn-like turf with the usual rosette-leaved weeds of lawns and rivers of daisies in spring.

Here very roughly are the types of grass we need for our land-

354

*– and mown to lawn. There is no reason here for grass, and every reason for a leafy screen. A fraction of the labour for mowing this impossible slope would control unwanted growth and weeds and preserve the ground-cover of wild flowers and the habitat for wild-life. (Both pictures were taken on the same day – that even the planted tree is dead is photographer's serendipity.)*

scape categories, all produced from the same neglected field by three types of simple maintenance and nothing else. And though it is by no means always so simple, yet we could nonetheless evolve similar methods for different conditions, as the Scandinavians have already developed a maintenance-free system of hydromatic seeding of suitable grasses directly on to their sandy subsoils.

The farmers' fear that any growth except mown grass means noxious weeds is mostly unfounded. Farmers' weeds are plants of open ground not of the closed plant communities which quickly develop in undisturbed conditions. Couch grass and creeping thistle

355

are the most serious, but if a general growth of open-ground weeds occurs it means that the area has been disturbed (as by trenching or dumping on verges). An established plant cover is like a protective skin over the ground – it is only when the skin is broken that the open wound of soil becomes infected by weeds. But local outbreaks need local treatment, and are no reason either for spraying all grass with herbicides or mowing all growth to lawn as if all flowers were enemies. The labour saved from such indiscriminate over-maintenance could be used for selective control of unwanted plants. And why not now shrub cover instead of grass cover where there is space? – either cut back at suitable intervals or left to grow where the verges are wide, like the much-admired broom on the M 1 embankments through the Woburn sand (the interplanted Spanish broom is an alien which extends the flowering season and proves that good designers may break the rules).

Where a low herb layer is needed ground-elder is an excellent substitute for grass. As ground-cover in shade it is unbeatable – spreading without help, fast-growing and vigorous, cheap certainly, and since it is shallow-rooting is easily contained by layout. Unlike grass it does not hinder the growth of trees and shrubs, and is also much easier than grass to control by cutting (once a summer keeps a tidy green rug). It is also an attractive plant with its fresh lobed leaves, and my own gardening life became immensely simpler when I one day asked myself *why* I was interfering with the survival of the fittest by weeding out willing ground-elder from unwilling periwinkle? As ground-cover between trees and shrubs it has only one fault that I know of – it does not suppress grass except in shade.

By considering existing examples, by the wide research being done on new methods of control, by consulting ecologists, and above all by new thinking from first principles, we could work our four distinct types of design and maintenance for our four environments. The styles we need are fairly clear, though they differ in various ways from existing types. The formal style belongs to the urban landscape, with vegetation used as green architecture, trees in avenues, hedges like green walls, flowers massed in beds, and grass like a drawing-room carpet.

Urban planting need not be formal, however, any more than urban clothes, but though modern styles are casual it is in an urban not a country way. Nor can vegetation in towns be established by natural methods, since tender young plants do not survive the untender environment. Urban maintenance is equally exacting, for whatever the style high use means high maintenance, either by labour or labour-saving materials. Walking areas, for instance, must either be hard surfaces or grass kept in perfect condition, and lawns either neatly edged or bordered with mowing-strips.

High maintenance need not, however, mean elaboration. Trees in a paved surface for instance could scarcely be simpler – or more urban. But paving is an initial high-labour ground-cover, and the trees must be chosen and planted with care, and skilfully trained and looked after to thrive. Urban landscape needs specialized knowledge of growth in unnatural conditions, and especially of plants as all-the-year-round design material.

The green-urban landscape will cover a wide range of types between urban and rural, and in each area will depend on land-use, scale, existing development, amount of wear, and especially on what maintenance will be available. Maintenance is like income and our style of landscape living should always be within our means, for Mr Micawber's advice is as true of landscape economics as any other – annual maintenance income 20 units, annual maintenance needed $19\frac{1}{2}$ units, result happiness. Annual maintenance income 20 units, annual maintenance needed $20\frac{1}{2}$ units, result misery. In short a well-kept rural style looks better than neglected urban and needs far less labour. For maintenance is also like housework – the return from labour decreases sharply as the standard rises, so that though the first thirty per cent of effort produces sixty per cent improvement, the next sixty per cent effort gives only a further thirty per cent result. (The final ten per cent is a pathological state of perfection.) Much landscape is in any case over-urban, and though the scale is important (as a general rule the more natural the effect the more space it needs) many areas would be improved by more casual rural-style maintenance.

In the rural landscape all urban effects should be strictly avoided, but here we need to change our conception to suit the changes both in farming and maintenance. The old farming landscape is fundamentally similar to the old park-and-garden style. The ground – already unnaturally smooth from centuries of cultivation – is covered by herbs in single-plant crops, this lawn-like surface is divided into rectangles by narrow rows of exactly-aligned shrubs cut back to a regular cross-section, and this landscape grid is punctuated by trees growing as single specimens or in rows like avenues. All three layers of the vegetation are kept strictly separate and are clearly defined by a high standard of farming maintenance.

To those who saw this orderly landscape created from the old open fields and rough commons it seemed like a garden; and so it still does to visitors from less worked-on landscapes. It is why the park-and-garden style suits it admirably if mildly neglected – as it necessarily was without machines or chemical controls. It was simply a heightened version of the surrounding countryside, and it still is along miles of lovely lanes too minor for the full modern treatment. There is nothing more quintessentially the country than a lane with verges which are borders of wild flowers with bosky hedges of may-blossom over-arched by old trees. But if the hedges are ruthlessly machine-cut, the flowers weed-killed, the grass mown to lawn and the trees pruned to equidistant standards? This is now a park, not a country scene.

In an increasingly stripped-down farmland there will be little to counteract the urbanizing effect of such methods on the landscape. The new countryside will be simpler and less sophisticated than the old as well as much barer, and often it is the maintained areas which will themselves create the character of the rural landscape. It is therefore essential that their style should be natural and countrified, and a better arrangement now for a rural road would be vegetation (strictly of the Landscape Region) spreading out irregularly from the hedges, the trees grouped at random or thickening to a tiny copse where land allowed, and underplanted with shrubs. The grass bays should be long and shallow for easy mowing, but this should be timed to preserve the wild flowers, and where a close-mown edge is needed for walking or sight-lines then a single cutter-bar width reads as part of the road with the country verge beginning beyond.

In rural areas there will also be maintained land as the setting of development which has a valid place in the countryside provided it is integrated with the landscape. Here free-growing shrubs might be restrained into informal hedges, trees grouped less casually and grass cut more often, but any urban effect should be strictly avoided.

The wild category is less a type of landscape than a range of distinctive areas whose individual character should be completely respected. Here the function of design is essentially for art to conceal art, and any altered land-forms should seem natural and any planting a spontaneous growth. Forestry areas of alien conifers are always difficult, but the answer is certainly not a mixed edging of incongruous trees – horse chestnuts, cherries, coloured sycamores and so on. Where there is space local trees or shrubs bring welcome variety, but often a simple open area of grass and flowers is the best relief, for the trouble with forests is not only conifers but claustrophobia, and 'a plain space near the eye', said Shenstone, 'gives it a kind of liberty it loves'.

Even, however, with a Code of Landscape Practice clearly established, some skilled supervision will still be needed, as for instance to decide the type of maintenance for any area, to check that methods are properly applied, arrange the layout of new planting, mark trees for thinning as groups develop and so on. Landscape Officers would be needed for the countryside to work with local Forestry Officers, highway authorities and so on, and would best be organized by Landscape Regions. They could also assess the planting needs of their areas and supervise the regional nurseries for trees and shrubs.

The real difficulty, however, is the primary problem of how any large-scale plan is to be applied; not only the Code of Practice but also the Landscape Regions and the Tree Belts. (The establishment of the four categories is the task of planners.) With all three there are the same fundamental questions – who is to create the new pattern, and what land can be used to establish it? Most of the land which constitutes our scenery is owned by people who cherish equally their independence and their own individual taste – it is best to accept such facts of life without illusion, for like the better-known Facts of Life they do not change because we ignore them: they only cause trouble. Most land then is owned by farmers and most farmers are unlikely allies. Nor are measures like Tree Preservation Orders the simple solution many people hope, although they may work in special cases (in urban areas a preserved tree is the newest status symbol of modern gardens).

Any farmer, however, knows half a dozen ways of getting rid of unwanted trees by 'natural' methods, but the new stricter controls may help (though enforced replanting cannot enforce regrowth) and also some farmers, especially when their living does not depend entirely on the farm's profit, might well cooperate in a landscape plan which did not seriously interfere with efficient working – might leave trees along roads perhaps, or plant a few new ones round raw farm buildings. Here the amenity societies could be invaluable, and by individual persuasion might achieve far more than coercive orders. They would be excellent agents in fact for establishing the new landscape by voluntary methods, and for the detailed work in each local area needed to translate any pattern into practice. And it would be constructive work; not negative resistance to change, but making maps of landscape categories, seeking out odd sites for tree-planting, discussing problems with farmers, putting over the idea of Landscape Regions to local people and so on. These are labours of love which no outsider can do so well as those who live in and know a particular district.

Added to such control by persuasion is the direct control of large areas of land owned by public bodies, and which in England and Wales alone already amount to over 3 million acres (1,200,000 ha) of our countryside held by responsible authorities who could co-operate to create the new landscape pattern. Nor does this include the $1\frac{1}{2}$ million acres (600,000 ha) of commons which are technically private property. This public ownership of land is a new phenomenon of our new industrial society, and its increase, probably its vast increase, seems inevitable in the future. It would be justly appropriate that it should be used to create a new landscape in place of the old which industry is destroying.

Industrial land-use itself is a further opportunity for establishing the pattern, since land with no ground-use is potentially free to be used in landscape design, thus turning its inherent difficulties to advantage. Such land has been estimated at over a million acres (400,000 ha), and its present maintenance is chiefly the negative control of vegetation to keep the land open. The same maintenance could equally be a positive part of a general landscape plan, and in some green-urban areas the use of industrial and publicly owned land, especially with its future increase, would in itself be enough to create the new pattern.

As well as actual ownership of land there are also powerful planning controls in Green Belts, National Parks, Areas of Outstanding Natural Beauty and so on, and these could be used, with the special grants, to confirm and establish suitable landscapes in these particularly valuable areas. Such special applications of planning, however, only emphasize the controls which now exist over all our land whatever its status, and which enlightened authorities are already beginning to use. If once a general landscape policy were adopted there are in fact plenty of powers where persuasion fails, and the new Civic Amenities Act encourages suitable landscape treatment as a compulsory condition of planning permission.

Insistence on suitable landscaping by private developers would in fact be a valuable way of establishing the new pattern. Whatever its shortcomings private enterprise is undeniably energetic; we are never more active and determined than in pursuit of our own affairs, and it is important to use this powerful private momentum in the cause of public amenity. Certainly when once accepted as inevitable the necessary planting and so on would deter no one, but such measures make a definite landscape policy essential. It is useless to insist on suitable treatment for an area unless suitable can be clearly specified – as it now quite certainly cannot. Arbitrary planting of someone's idea of local trees cannot count as suitable and may even further disrupt our long-suffering landscape, while if suitable is left, as it too often is, to the discretion of the uninterested the cure can be worse than the disease.

But the Four-Point Plan suggested here would mean that suitable could be exactly defined and specified. All land everywhere would already have its exact place in the potential landscape pattern, and the plan's straightforward terms of reference would provide clear and simple specifications for any land in any situation – for the type of landscape to be established, for a planting pattern as part of the landscape framework, for the regional species of trees and shrubs, for the style of design and type of maintenance.

There would in fact be simple routine answers for all kinds of landscape problems which at present are either treated piecemeal or left to people who lack the necessary knowledge, whatever their potential good-will. Indeed most of the suggestions set out here are not for new action, but only for doing constructively as part of a coherent landscape policy what at present we are muddling through by trial-and-error pragmatism. And we have no time to learn by making mistakes, certainly not mistakes on the landscape scale which involve whole areas and which we must live with unhappily ever after.

## Conclusion

The proposals suggested in this book have been an attempt to translate accepted land-use policy into appropriate landscape by simple general principles. Even if incompletely applied these could do nothing but good – so much less incongruous development – so many more trees – better suited to their areas and in landscapes designed for their function.

It is essential, in fact, in all large-scale or general schemes, that partial achievement should produce no harmful side-effects, for in the nature of things large changes are unlikely to be carried through completely. And often a scheme, though excellent as a whole, will produce only muddle or even harm unless completely achieved. Its end in fact must justify its means. But here both ends and means are beneficial. One tenth of the action will produce only one tenth of the benefit, but it is benefit entirely and begins with the first tree planted.

Nor would the cost of these proposals be high (often it would be less than present methods) and certainly in amenity value-for-money it would be minimal. For this is a matter of organization rather than finance, and its chief cost is of energy, concern, enthusiasm and good-will. And the good-will could prove to be enormous if once given a clear means of positive expression. Far more people and at every level care about our landscape than at present have any way of showing, and as well as the thousands who already prove their concern by joining societies, thousands more would take practical action as part of a constructive plan which showed results.

By the good-will of an industrial population, by the public owner-ship of land inevitable in an industrial economy, by the management of the increasing areas for which industry provides no ground-use, by planning controls in the cause of amenity – this would be to solve our landscape problems, as they must be solved, not in terms of a vanishing past but of the new industrial economy which has itself produced them.

# Acknowledgements

Our thanks go to the following for the use of the plates on the pages indicated.

Aerofilms: 26, 32, 114, 185, 218–19, 243, 255, 290, 319
Atelier 5: 311
British Museum: 40 (top and centre)
British Travel & Holidays Association: 46
Cement and Concrete Association: 266
City Museum, Bristol: 15
Civic Trust: 90, 91
Claas Combines: 52
*Daily Telegraph*: 47
Durham County Council: 226
Forestry Commission: 130–31
Howard Rotavator Co. Ltd (John Tarlton): 78
A. F. Kersting: 150
London Library (books photographed): 31, 60, 61
National Farmers' Union: 84
*Punch*: 99, 187
Pye of Cambridge Ltd: 319
Radio Times Hulton Picture Library: 21, 40, 41, 184
*The Times*: 109, 167
The Author: 62, 63, 83, 88, 89, 97, 100, 117, 129, 137, 138, 147, 159, 172, 175, 178, 189, 193, 194, 201, 203, 206, 215, 216, 223, 228, 231, 235, 238–9, 250, 260, 264, 269, 273, 276, 277, 282, 283, 294, 295, 296, 297, 303, 308, 312, 317, 324, 330, 334, 343, 346, 347, 352, 354, 355

# Notes

| page | line | |
|------|------|---|
| 11 | 14 | Bibliography item 102. |
| 14 | 37 | Shelley's *Defence of Poetry* in a pre-war documentary film for the Post Office. |
| 18 | 4 | Bibliography 81. |
| 20 | 11 | The Home Counties are those adjoining London. |
| 21 | 3 ff. | Bibliography 47. |
| 23 | 8 ff. | Bibliography 11. |
| 23 | 30 | Bibliography 53. |
| 38 | 35 ff. | Ricardo quoted by Engels. |
| 44 | 10 | Bibliography 61. |
| 48 | 34 | Bibliography 34. |
| 50 | 13 ff. | Bibliography 34. |
| 50 | 34 | Garden City Bibliography 56. |
| 51 | 37 | Farming press. |
| 53 | 13 | Bibliography 55 and Bibliography 99. |
| 67 | 1 | Nature Conservancy. |
| 67 | 31 | Farming press. |
| 68 | 17 ff. | Bibliography 31. |
| 71 | 10 ff. | Farming press. |
| 72 | 19 | Farming press. |
| 72 | 27 | Farming press. |
| 74 | 13 | Bibliography 39. |
| 74 | 27 | Bibliography 39. |
| 74 | 32 ff. | Bibliography 31. |
| 76 | 1 | Bibliography 51. |
| 76 | 15 | Bibliography 31. |
| 77 | 2 | Farming press. |
| 80 | 12 | Farming press. |
| 80 | 26 | Farming press. |
| 80 | 31 | Bibliography 101. |
| 81 | 19 ff. | Farming press |
| 82 | 1 ff. | Bibliography 79. |

# Notes

PART TWO

| page | line | |
|------|------|---|
| 164 | 32 ff. | Bibliography 81. |
| 165 | 21 | Bibliography 61. |
| 170 | 27 | Teesplan – a survey and plan (since published) for the redevelopment of an old area of declining industry along the River Tees in Durham. |
| 171 | 29 | Bibliography 81. |
| 182 | 13 | Bibliography 76. |
| 183 | 11 | Bibliography 102. |
| 187 | 9 ff. | Bibliography 74. |
| 201 | 2 | Bibliography 102. |
| 216 | 10 | Scott Report. *Report of the Committee on Land Utilization in Rural Areas*, 1942. |
| 221 | 14 | Hook New Town was planned by the London County Council but never built. |
| 222 | 37 | Bibliography 24. |
| 231 | 3 | Bibliography 101. |
| 233 | 4 | Bentham Bibliography 58. |
| 246 | 13 | Bibliography 54. |
| 246 | 18 | Madame du Deffand's comment on the legend that St Denis walked two whole leagues carrying his severed head: 'La distance n'y fait rien; il n'y a que le premier pas qui coûte.' |
| 254 | 28 ff. | Bibliography 7. |
| 259 | 16 ff. | Bibliography 92. |
| 261 | 14 | Bibliography 95. |
| 275 | 4 | Bibliography 12. |
| 278 | 9 | Trees of particular landscape value are protected from felling by Tree Preservation Orders. |
| 279 | 6 | Bibliography 75. |
| 280 | 18 | Bibliography 85. |
| 284 | 33 ff. | Bibliography 2. |
| 289 | 1 | Huxley Bibliography 102. |
| 291 | 13 | Bibliography 73. |
| 313 | 9 | Colvin Bibliography 100. |

PART THREE

| 326 | 2 | An area of prosperous commuting on the South-west fringe of London. |
| 326 | 29 | The 'cheese' is the clay with its texture of soapy cheese when wet. |
| 327 | 37 | Bibliography 97. |
| 335 | 5 | Bibliography 39. |

## Notes

| page | line | |
|------|------|---|
| 337 | 37 | John Gerard in his *Herball of* 1597. |
| 338 | 13 ff. | Bibliography 29. |
| 338 | 24 | R. Ungewitter Bibliography 58. |
| 353 | 25 | Bibliography 57. |
| 356 | 17 | Bibliography 62. |
| 360 | 22 | Bibliography 33. |

# Bibliography

1. Arvill, Robert, *Man and Environment*, Penguin Books 1967.

2. Atkinson J. R., 'The Durham Motorway Landscape Scheme', *Journal of Institute of Landscape Architects*, August 1966.

3. Bacon, Francis, *Sylva Sylvarum: or a Natural History in Ten Centuries*, 1605.

4. Best R. H. and Coppock J. T., *The Changing Use of Land in Britain*, Faber & Faber 1962.

5. Blake, Peter, *God's Own Junkyard – The Planned Deterioration of America's Landscape*, Holt, Rinehart & Winston 1964.

6. Brett, Lionel, *Landscape in Distress*, Architectural Press 1965.

7. British Association for the Advancement of Science, *A survey of Southampton and its Region*, edited F. J. Monkhouse, 1964.

8. British Broadcasting Corporation, Numerous radio and television programmes.

9. British Travel & Holidays Association, *A Survey of Whitsun Holiday Travel* 1963.

10. Burton T. L. and Wibberley G. P., *Outdoor Recreation in the British Countryside*, Wye College 1965.

11. Calder, Ritchie, *Man and his Environment*, B.B.C. pamphlet, 1964.

12. Casson, John, 'Land-use in the Motorway Corridor', paper to 'Roads in the Landscape' Conference, 1967.

Central Office of Information

13. *Town and Country Planning in Britain*, Reference Pamphlet No. 9, HMSO 1965.

14. *Agriculture in Britain*, Reference Pamphlet No. 43, HMSO 1965.

15. Chambers R. W., *England Before the Norman Conquest*, Longmans, Green & Co, 1926.

Civic Trust

16. *The Rhondda Valley – Proposals for the transformation of an environment*, 1965.

17. *Derelict Land*, 1964.

Cobbett, William

18. *Rural Rides During the Years 1821–26*.

19. *The Woodlands – or a Treatise on Planting*, 1825.

20. Colvin, Brenda, *Land and Landscape*, John Murray, 1948.

21. Conservative Political Centre, *A Better Country*, 1966.

Coppock J. T.

22. *An Agricultural Atlas of England and Wales*, Faber & Faber, 1964.

23. *Greater London* (J. T. Coppock and H. C. Prince), Faber & Faber, 1964.

24. Countryside in 1970, *Second Conference 1965 – Reports of Study Groups*, Royal Society of Arts and Nature Conservancy.

371

# Bibliography

Crowe, Sylvia

25. *Tomorrow's Landscape*, Architectural Press, 1956.

26. *Civilisation and Landscape*, Reflection Riding Lecture to the Royal Society of Arts.

27. *Forestry in the Landscape*, Forestry Commission, 1967.

28. Darling, F. Fraser, Opening address to Institute of Landscape Architects Conference on the Sub-Regional Landscape, Durham, 1967.

29. Defoe, Daniel, *Tour Through the Whole Island of Great Britain*, 1724–7.

30. Department of Agriculture and Fisheries for Scotland, *Land Use in the Highlands and Islands*, HMSO, Edinburgh, 1964.

31. Department of Education and Science, *Report of the Land Use Study Group*, HMSO, 1966.

32. Dower, John, *National Parks in England and Wales*, Command Paper 6628, HMSO 1945.

33. Dower, Michael, *Fourth Wave – The Challenge of Leisure*, A Civic Trust Survey (also in *Architects' Journal*), 1965.

34. Engels, Frederick, *The Condition of the Working Class in England in 1844*, German 1845, English edition 1892.

35. Evelyn, John, *Sylva, or a Discourse of Forest Trees*, 1664.

36. Farmer and Stockbreeder, National press.

37. Farmers Weekly, National press.

38. Fiennes, Celia, *The Journeys of Celia Fiennes 1685–1703*, edited C. Morris, Cresset Press, 1949.

Forestry Commission

39. *Hedgerow and Park Timber and Woods Under Five Acres 1951*, Census Report No. 2, HMSO, 1953.

40. *Report of the Committee on Hedgerow & Farm Timber*, HMSO, 1955.

41. *National Forest Parks*. Forestry Commission Booklet No. 6, HMSO, 1961.

42. *Forestry Practice*, Forestry Commission Bulletin No. 14, HMSO, 1964.

43. *Forestry in Great Britain*, H. L. Edlin, 1965.

44. *Britain's New Forests*, 1965.

45. Galbraith J. K., *The Affluent Society*, Houghton Mifflin Co., 1958.

46. Gasson, Ruth, *The Influence of Urbanisation on Farm Ownership and Practice*, Wye College, 1966.

47. Godwin H., *The History of the British Flora*, Cambridge University Press, 1956.

48. Good, Ronald, *The Geography of the Flowering Plants*, Longmans, Green & Co., 1953.

49. Grieve, Robert G., 'The Work of the Highlands and Islands Development Board', *Journal of Institute of Landscape Architects*, May 1967.

50. Hall, Peter, *London 2000*, Faber & Faber, 1963.

51. Hilton, Norman, *An Approach to Agricultural Land Classification*, paper to British Association for the Advancement of Science, 1965.

52. Holmes, Arthur, *Principles of Physical Geology*, Nelson, 1944, revised 1965.

Hoskins W. G.

53. *The Making of the English Landscape*, Hodder & Stoughton, 1955.

54. *The Common Lands of England and Wales* (with L. D. Stamp), Collins, 1963.

55. House J. W., *Northumbrian Tweedside. The Rural Problem,*

Northumberland Rural Community Council, 1956.

56. Howard, Ebenezer, *Tomorrow – A Peaceful Path to Real Reform*, 1898.

Institute of Landscape Architects

57. *Landscape Maintenance*, report of Symposium, 1963.

58. *Industry and Landscape*, report of Symposium, 1964.

59. Jacobs, Jane, *The Death and Life of Great American Cities*, Jonathan Cape, 1962.

60. Kip J., *Nouveau Théatre de la Grande Bretagne*, 1715–17.

61. Lane, Leslie, *Reshaping our Physical Environment*, Danes Memorial Lecture, 1966.

62. Langvad B., *The Establishment of Grass – a New Method*, paper to 'Roads in the Landscape' Conference, 1967.

63. Le Corbusier, *La Ville Radieuse* (*The City of Tomorrow*), Editions de l'Architecture d'Aujourd'hui, 1935.

64. Leland, John, *Itinerary*, journeys, 1534–43.

65. Lynch, Kevin, 'The City as Environment', *Scientific American*, September 1965.

66. Marsh G. P., *Man and Nature: or Physical Geography as Modified by Human Action*, 1864.

Marshall, William

67. *Planting and Rural Ornament*, 1796.

68. *Rural Economy of the Midland Counties*, 1796.

69. *Rural Economy of the Southern Counties*, 1798.

70. *Agriculture in the Southern Counties*, 1799.

71. *A Sketch of the Vale of London*, 1799.

72. *Landed Estates*, 1806.

73. Medhurst, Franklin, *The Value to Planners of Landscape Survey and Analysis*, paper to Conference on the Sub-Regional Landscape, Durham, 1967.

74. Merriott D. G., *The Effect of Modern Development on Agricultural Land*, paper to Public Works and Municipal Services Congress, 1966.

75. Moore N. W., *Nature Conservation*, paper to 'Roads in the Landscape' Conference, 1967.

Ministry of Housing and Local Government

76. *The Green Belts*, HMSO, 1962.

77. *New Life for Dead Lands*, HMSO, 1963.

78. *The South-East Study 1961–81*, HMSO, 1964.

79. *The Development of Agriculture*, Command Paper 2738, 1965.

80. *Leisure in the Countryside – England and Wales*. Command Paper 2928, 1966.

81. *Town and Country Planning*, Command Paper 3333, 1967.

82. Nairn, Ian, *Outrage*, Architectural Press, 1955.

83. National Farmers' Union, *British Agriculture Looks Ahead*, 1964.

84. Nature Conservancy, *Report on Broadland* – R. E. Boote and B. Forman, 1965.

85. Olschowy G., *The Design of Highway Planting*, paper to 'Roads in the Landscape' Conference, 1967.

86. Outdoor Recreation Resources Review Commission, *Outdoor Recreation for America*, U.S. Government Printing Office, 1962.

87. Pahl R. E., *Commuting and Social Change in Rural Areas*, paper to the British Association for the Advancement of Science, 1965.

# Bibliography

88. Power Farming, National press.

Repton, Humphry

89. *Observations on the Theory and Practice of Landscape Gardening*, 1803.

90. *Landscape Gardening and Landscape Architecture*, edited J. C. Loudon, 1840.

91. Research Institute for Consumer Affairs, *Town Planning – the Consumer's Environment*, 1965.

92. Salisbury – Edward, *Weeds and Aliens*, New Naturalist Series, Collins, 1961.

93. *Scientific American*, New York.

Stamp L. D.

94. *Applied Geography*, Penguin Books, 1960.

95. *The Land of Britain, its Use and Misuse*, Longmans, Green & Co., third edition, 1962.

96. Stapleton R. G., *The Land Now and Tomorrow*, Faber & Faber, 1933.

97. Tansley A. G., *The British Isles and Their Vegetation*, Cambridge University Press, 1949.

98. Tusser, Thomas (Gentleman), *A Hundreth Good Pointes of Husbandrie*, 1557.

99. University of Newcastle upon Tyne, Department of Geography, *Rural North-East England 1951–1961*, report of Development Commissioners, 1965.

100. Weddle, Arnold (editor), *Techniques of Landscape Architecture*, Heinemann, 1967.

101. Weller, John, *Modern Agriculture and Rural Planning*, Architectural Press, 1968.

102. Wolstenholme, Gorden (editor), *Man and His Future* – a CIBA Foundation volume, Little, Brown & Company, 1963.

103. Wordsworth, William, *A Description of the Scenery of the Lakes in the North of England*, 1810.

104. Wright, Myles, *Planning of Cities and Regions*, Canton Lectures, the Royal Society of Arts, 1966.

Young, Arthur

105. *A Six Weeks Tour Through the Southern Counties of England and Wales*, 1769.

106. *A Six Month's Tour Through the North of England*, 1770.

107. *The Farmer's Letters, 1771.*

108. *Agriculture of Herts*, 1804.

109. *Agriculture of Sussex*, 1808.

# Index

# Index

# Index

# Index

# Index